W9-DEY-316

PHILOSOPHY AND HISTORY

PHILOSOPHY AND HISTORY

A SYMPOSIUM

Edited by Sidney Hook

New York University Institute of Philosophy, 5th, 1962

New York University Press 1963

Library of Congress Catalog Card Number: 63-11298
Manufactured in the United States of America

0-8147-0200-7 (HARDBOUND)

0-8147-3388-3 (PAPERBACK)

The contents of this volume comprise the proceedings of the fifth annual New York University Institute of Philosophy, held at Washington Square, New York, May 11–12, 1962. Previous volumes in the series, also edited by Sidney Hook, are:

Determinism and Freedom in the Age of Modern Science
Psychoanalysis, Scientific Method, and Philosophy
Dimensions of Mind
Religious Experience and Truth

Contents

Preface

SO FAR as I am aware the Fifth Conference of the New York University Institute of Philosophy was the first occasion at which a group of professional American historians met with professional American philosophers to consider questions of mutual interest in the philosophy of history. The subject was phrased as history *and* philosophy because of the ambiguity in the expression "philosophy of history," whose connotations embrace notions ranging from theology to epistemology.

In the intellectual history of the past, few American philosophers concerned themselves with the problems of historical theory and understanding. Reflections of an optimistic nature about the development of American civilization were tacked on as corollaries to some religious and idealistic interpretations of the "nature of reality." Here and there, illuminating insights in the writings of William James, and of the generation of philosophers he influenced, touched on important problems of historical causation, but they were not explored. To the extent that one can speak of a philosophy of history in the United States, it was found in the writings of American historians and in their reflections on their craft. American historians were more sensitive to the influences of European philosophers than of their philosophical colleagues at home. Only John Dewey in the first decades of the twentieth century seems to have had some impact upon the attitudes of American historians toward the nature of historical thought.

The comparatively short history of the United States itself undoubtedly had something to do with the relative unconcern among intellectuals about theoretical problems of history. The magnitude of the problems of the present, the sense that America was different, the rapidity of technological change, the diversity of the ethnic strands in its population, contributed to a widespread feeling that American history was located, so to speak, in its future rather than in its past. The history of the past did not so much become a source of natural piety or an object of interpretation in popular consciousness as an instrument for present use in strengthening ties of nationalism and, in some parts of the country, of sectional loyalties. In recent years, faced by the challenge of aggressive totalitarianism, efforts have multiplied to read a sense of underlying national purpose out of the American historical experience. As American political ideas and popular culture, as well as American affluence, affect the rest of the world, interest has intensified in "the meaning of American history."

The specific causes for the efflorescence of interest on the part of professional American philosophers in problems of history have little to do with the quest for historical self-consciousness. They are a consequence primarily of interest in the nature of scientific explanation and the challenge posed by the existence of historical knowledge, with its imprecisions and particularity, to the conclusions reached about the nature of scientific method and objectivity won by an analysis of the logic of the natural sciences.

Most philosophers approaching the study of history on the basis of their interest in the philosophy of science have tended to assimilate reliable historical knowledge to patterns of explanation and objectivity found in other scientific disciplines. Most historians who are reflective about the nature of their activity, although flattered by the exalted ideals attributed to their work by philosophers, seem to be a little uncomfortable, particularly in view of the strong relativistic mood about the nature of historical truth which not long ago prevailed among them. Some historians are inclined to regard as excessive and unscientific claims made by philosophers concerning the possibility of scientific history. The philosophers themselves are at odds with each other about whether one common pattern of explanation holds for warranted knowledge in history and other fields. These issues were joined in the papers presented at the conference and in the lively discussion that ensued.

The New York University Institute of Philosophy is indebted to the Deems Memorial Lecture Fund for helping to underwrite some of the costs of the fifth conference.

Sidney Hook

PHILOSOPHY AND HISTORY

PART I

The Logic of Historical Narration

1

The Logic of Historical Narration

MORTON WHITE
Harvard University

1. ONE OF my main tasks in this paper is to construct a framework for the discussion of a number of philosophical problems concerning narrative discourse. After outlining what seem to me to be the chief structural features of a narrative, I shall turn to my second main task, which is to examine some of these features with an eye to clarifying certain philosophical questions concerning truth, objectivity, and relativism in historical investigation, writing, and criticism. Many of my observations about narration will not be new, but even when they are familiar, I hope that my overall analysis will place old as well as new observations in a fresh and illuminating context, and provide a scheme within which a variety of philosophical questions about history may be understood more easily. Before I do so, I ought to warn historians and philosophers of ordinary historical language that I do not plan to present an empirically accurate description of the structure of any actual historical work. My reasons for not doing so are complex and I cannot discuss them here in detail, since I do not wish to leave the question 'What is history?' for an exploration of the even more difficult question 'What is philosophy of history?' While all of my conclusions grow out of reflection on narratives, some features of history, as I shall analyze it, may never have fully entered the mind of any historian while he was writing his own history. For although I shall strive to keep in mind the ordinary use of the word 'history' as well as the remarks of historians about what they

take themselves to be doing, I shall at some points be obliged to introduce distinctions and terminology that might at first sight—though not, I hope, at second or third—seem excessively abstract and remote to professional historians. I assure them, however, that I do have great concern for their interests no matter how much I may sometimes seem to be exclusively the agent of that foreign land, philosophy. That concern will become more apparent after I develop some of my more abstract reflections on the structure of narrative.

2. I shall begin by assuming that every history is a history of some entity which existed for a reasonable period of time, that the historian wishes to state what is literally true of it in a sense which distinguishes the historian from a teller of fictitious or mendacious stories, and that the task of the narrator is to give a connected account of the entity's development in time. In other words, I shall assume that a narrative has a central subject and that the task of the narrator is, at the very least, to tell us what has been true of that central subject at different times in a coherent way. If we assume that a history has a central subject, we simplify our task, for we confine ourselves to analyzing only one kind of historical writing. We focus on historical works that resemble biographies or novels like Defoe's *Moll Flanders* in being primarily concerned with one entity. E. M. Forster remarks that Moll Flanders "fills the book that bears her name, or rather stands alone in it, like a tree in a park, so that we can see her from every aspect and are not bothered by rival growths." [1] Limiting our reflections to this species of history will not, however, make our problems oversimple. In spite of such a self-imposed limitation we shall have to face a number of important philosophical puzzles that defy easy solution. Moreover, the assumption that the historian wishes all his statements to be true will not make our problems excessively easy or trivial, since, as we shall see, we face difficult problems in evaluating a history even after we have established the truth of all its statements.

3. In order to explain what it means, in the barest terms, to say that a work is a history of something like the United

States of America, I shall first define the concept of a chronicle of such a central subject. The word 'chronicle' has often been used in characterizations of historical writing, and I realize that it has been used in many different ways. Therefore I shall not pretend that I am about to analyze or explain the word's commonly accepted meaning. A chronicle of a subject, I shall say, is a conjunction of nonexplanatory empirical statements which expressly mention that subject and which report things that have been true of it at different times. By a nonexplanatory statement I mean one that does not connect two statements of fact with a word like 'because.' The stipulation that the chronicle's conjuncts be nonexplanatory is imposed in order to remain faithful to the idea that a chronicle merely reports "facts" in a narrow sense. Moreover, it should be noticed that the condition that these statements expressly mention the subject, say the United States of America, severely limits the notion of a chronicle, and that the notion of a history will be correspondingly limited when we explain it. This condition is intended to convey the fact that a history in our sense has a central subject without involving us in a detailed discussion of the semantical notion of a statement's being *about* something.[2] In our model every statement in a chronicle of the United States of America, and a history of it, will expressly mention the United States of America, although this is obviously not true of actual historical works on this subject. Accepting this condition will allow us to formulate certain issues simply, without, I think, begging any serious questions or departing too far from the intent of the historian. It should also be observed that whereas all of the statements that compose a chronicle will be logically singular, some of them will be quite different in character from others. When I call something a chronicle I do not mean that it contains only statements that record historical events in the narrowest sense of that word. Thus, for example, a chronicle of England might begin with statements to the effect that the ancient British residents of England lived in small tribes under chiefs or kings; that they could not read, that they kept cattle, hunted, and fished; that they made baskets and pottery; that they grew barley in some places; that they mined for tin in Cornwall; that they were partially clothed in skins. These statements report what might be called the conditions of life of the ancient British inhabitants of England, and in that sense might be distinguished from a statement that Julius Caesar's army came to England in 55 B.C., the latter being a statement that refers to an event in a narrow sense of that term. Of course, statements about conditions and statements about events or episodes are different in interesting and important ways, but they are both components of chronicles. Statements of conditions tell us what was true of England at certain times just as much as the statement that Caesar came to it in 55 B.C., only the times they refer to are more like generations than years.

If one conceives of a chronicle of England in this way, one may say that a chronicle of England is true just in case its component statements are all true, since a chronicle has been defined as a conjunction of statements. The truth of the chronicle is a function of the truth of its components alone.

4. I turn now to the idea of a history of a subject. A history will in the familiar way be distinguished from a chronicle by the fact that a history employs the notion of explanation. As E. M. Forster has remarked in another connection,[3] a chronicler leads his reader to ask merely 'And then what?' whereas a historian leads him to ask 'So what?' The chronicler is likely to tell us: 'The King of England died, and then the Queen of England died, and then the Prince of England died, and then the Princess of England died. And there endeth our chronicle.' But a corresponding history is likely to read: 'The King of England died, so the Queen of England died of grief. And because he worried so much about the Queen's death, the Prince of England committed suicide; and therefore the Princess of England died later of loneliness. And so endeth our lugubrious history.'

Since a history makes reference to explanatory connections, we may conceive of a history as a logical conjunction of explanatory assertions. One might say that in the simplest case it consists in asserting: 'Because A was true of S at time t_1, B was true of S at time t_2. And because B was true of S at time t_2, C was true of S at time t_3, and so on.' Therefore a history is true just in case its component *explanatory* or 'because' statements are true. Moreover, each one of the explanatory statements implies its own components, that is to say, the statements connected by the word 'because.' If we say in a history of Germany that England declared war on Germany because the Germans had invaded Poland, we imply both that the English declared war on Germany and that the Germans had invaded Poland. For that reason a history will logically imply its associated chronicle but not conversely. By its associated chronicle I mean the conjunction of all the components of the history's explanatory assertions.

The foregoing analysis commits us to no controversial view of the nature of explanatory assertions. Whether they may all be analyzed or supported in the manner advocated by partisans of the so-called covering law, or regularity model, is an independent issue. Whether they are to be conceived as stating reasons or causes or both is also an independent issue. From the point of view of our model it is merely required that they be true. How they are to be analyzed is another matter. And something similar might be said about the nonexplanatory components of chronicles. The problem of how we are to analyze such statements is also different from certain problems concerning the overall structure of a narrative.

5. Even though the question whether a history is true is answered merely by discovering whether its components are true, one may properly raise certain other serious questions which will require examination of more than the truth-value of the components of histories. Historians evaluate each other's works in ways that take them beyond the question of the truth or falsity of the statements composing these works. Hence one of the basic philosophical questions concerning narration is whether assessments of chronicles and histories inevitably fail to be objective by comparison to assessments of the truth or falsity of the component of these chronicles and histories. Thus

we may ask: Does the evaluation of a history of Rome introduce subjective considerations that are not present when we evaluate the statement that Caesar crossed the Rubicon? Suppose that a historian or historical critic interested in the United States of America is presented with several distinct true histories of it in the above sense, and suppose he is asked, as a historian, to choose among them. Having gotten beyond asking whether the histories are true, must he now make an evaluation of a fundamentally different sort, in which his interests and moral values inevitably prevent him from being objective?

In other words, we have been led to consider the question 'What do historians mean when they say that one history of a given subject is better than any other when all of the competing histories are true in the sense of being composed exclusively of true statements?' I do not know whether historians or historical critics are often faced with such a question, for historians may in fact be in that happy situation where they can always eliminate all of the other contenders because the other contenders contain a lot of false statements. But in that case I can think of no other way of raising the important philosophical question than by asking it in hypothetical form: 'What would a historian who had to make such a judgment of superiority mean by it? How would he go about backing up his choice of one from among all of these true histories?'

6. Before we try to deal with this central question of the philosophy of narration, let us try to narrow it down a little further. So far we have seen that every history of a given subject is a conjunction of causal or explanatory statements. But if every history of the subject has this same form, then our effort to choose among rival true histories of S requires us to compare their contents, as it were, and comparing their contents means comparing the *components* of the causal statements in one history with the components of the causal statements in the others. But, as we have seen, the components of the causal or explanatory statements will make up the associated or entailed chronicle. And therefore, from one point of view, the effort to choose from among rival true *histories* of a

given subject reduces to an effort to choose from among the different true *chronicles* entailed by these rival histories. The best history of S from this point of view is that history whose true chronicle of S is best. But how shall we decide that one true chronicle, i.e., one conjunction of *true* singular statements about a given thing is superior to another? This is the problem of selecting *the facts* one incorporates in a narrative, the problem of defending one such selection as against others that are possible.

7. I must digress to point out that by regarding the word 'because' as a regularly occurring constituent of all histories and hence as not affording a basis for distinguishing true histories from each other, I have avoided a whole area of philosophical discussion that may well be ultimately unavoidable. For it might be argued that even though each history will be like every other in containing the word 'because' at stated intervals, and even though the histories containing it are alike in being true, there are important hidden differences, so to speak, between different assertions of causal connection, differences that may well supply a basis for differentiating histories according to merit. A proponent of the regularity theory of explanation who held that it successfully analyzed all causal words might hold, for example, that we should look underneath each of the 'because' statements in order to find the true laws or theories that form their grounds. In which case he might argue that we may find another basis for judging the merits of a history by comparing the merits of its underlying true generalizations or theories, their degree of simplicity, for example. Such an investigation would admittedly take us beyond the evaluation of truth, but might be as objective as the investigation of the simplicity of scientific theories. On the other hand, it might also be held that since the typical explanatory assertion that one thing is the case because another is the case involves selecting one fact among many possible jointly sufficient facts as *the* cause, the probing of the assertions of causal connection might also unearth a variety of value-dominated selection.

It is this area of discussion and debate that I am deliberately avoiding in order to concentrate on another dimension in which truth-transcending evaluation may and does go on. If the task of a historian is, as Samuel Eliot Morison says, to answer the double question 'What actually happened, and why?' [4] we may distinguish the historian's answers to these two distinct questions and assess them separately, at least up to a point. The effort to assess the true theories or laws supporting true causal assertion by examining, say, their simplicity, takes place on one truth-transcending axis along which we can evaluate a history; but the effort to evaluate the history's entailed chronicle, as I have defined that, takes place along another. And there is reason to believe that the truth-transcending evaluation of an answer to the question 'What happened?' is less objective than the truth-transcending evaluation of the simplicity of a scientific theory.

8. After this digression I want to reiterate that even when you narrow down the class of chronicles to those that are entailed by histories and hence are internally connectible,[4a] there will usually be more than one if we define a history of a given thing as we have. It is conceivable, of course, that only one set of statements about the central subject could be constructed into a history as we have defined it, in which case there would be no rival accounts of what happened. But generally speaking this does not take place in historical writing. It is rather the case that for any given subject there are many histories and hence many chronicles which must be compared on some basis if one is to distinguish them in terms of historical merit.

Let me say in passing that I believe that this multiplicity of different true histories will exist even if we decide to limit ourselves to presenting a history of a factor-dominated kind, for example, an economic, or political, or social, or religious history. It is true that many historians take refuge in this kind of narrowing of their task, in the hope that it will limit the class of facts about, say, the United States, from which they must choose. I don't doubt that a narrowing will take place if they limit themselves to a history of an aspect of their central subject. But even such a limitation might not remove the need to choose, say, from among several true *economic histories* of the United States. Historians may cut down on the number of choosable facts in this way, but this does not imply that they can eliminate altogether the need to choose from among true histories.

9. Let us return to our basic question: If we say that one true history of a given subject entails a chronicle which is superior to that entailed by its equally true rivals, what kind of judgment do we make? Different answers have been given to this question, and they may be given labels that conveniently link them to philosophical positions or attitudes of a more general nature. Let us begin with the answer that might be called 'Subjectivism.'

Sometimes the subjectivist says that the best history of a thing entails a chronicle that reports the most interesting facts. I have no doubt that many a narrative has been called superior to its rivals on just this score. Such a narrative tells the most exciting, intriguing, or stimulating true story, and that, according to the subjectivist, makes it preferable to all of the others. The facts need not be those of which the historian approves, but they must move him, titillate him, aggravate him, amuse him, and so on. Sometimes the subjectivist will focus more narrowly on what William Dean Howells called the "smiling aspects of life," and maintain that the superior history of something is simply one which entails a chronicle that records facts about the thing's more attractive features from a moral or aesthetic standpoint. Surprisingly enough, even Henry James encourages such a view of the matter. In his essay on London, although he was not there engaged in writing narrative history, he formulated an attitude that might very well be assumed by a narrator. James observed that London was immense and that:

> one has not the alternative of speaking of London as a whole, for the simple reason that there is no such thing as the whole

> of it. . . . Rather it is a collection of many wholes, and of which of them is it most important to speak? Inevitably there must be a choice, and I know of none more scientific than simply to leave out what we may have to apologize for. The uglinesses, the "rookeries," the brutalities, the night-aspect of many of the streets, the gin-shops and the hour when they are cleared out before closing—there are many elements of this kind which have to be counted out before a genial summary can be made.[5]

The effort to make a genial summary was in James's case that of a commentator on one period in London's history, but one may infer that if he were writing a history of London, its entailed chronicle would be a conjunction of such genial summaries, one for each period or time in London's development. However, although such histories are in principle constructible, they are not easy to construct, and I do not know of any work that comes close to being one. It is, of course, easy to make a *mere chronicle*[5a] of the interesting or the attractive features of a given subject, but for reasons that I need not discuss in detail, it is not easy to construct an internally connectible chronicle and hence a history along such lines. The fundamental point is that interesting facts, like interesting people, may have boring antecedents and boring offspring. And an analogous thing may be said of beautiful facts, since the rose grows in manure.

For similar reasons, it is difficult to construct a connected narrative that entails a chronicle consisting exclusively of statements which all supply admonitory or encouraging information for statesmen. When in his famous Inaugural Lecture J. B. Bury disassociated himself from Cicero's view that history was *magistra vitae,* and from the view of Dionysius that history was "philosophy by examples,"[6] he might well have pointed out the difficulty of constructing a history composed exclusively of statements reporting facts useful to the politician or the poet. In the abstract it seems possible to select such a set of facts and to connect them by explanatory links, but the fact about such facts is that they are not easily forged into the kind of coherent discourse called narrative. In short, a serious objection to subjectivism in the theory of narration is simply that it does not seem to allow us to construct true histories in my sense, and of course false histories are not my concern here.

10. Even if this purely empirical objection to subjectivism could be surmounted, even if narratives could be constructed out of exclusively attractive features of their central subjects, another objection might be leveled against the subjectivist's program. It would come from those historians and philosophers of history who feel that the principle of selection employed by the subjectivist is not that of the student of history, properly understood; who hold that the facts in a history of the United States may and must be selected in ways that are not determined merely by the varying interests, tastes, and practical problems of the historian or his chosen masters. On such a view not enough has been conceded to the demands of objectivity when it is granted that the history's factual and causal statements are objectively true. Such extreme objectivists may assume different philosophical postures, and I shall turn to one group of them now—those who admit that there are true chronicles and true chronicles, but who insist that some express truths that are *deeper* than others. On this view, some chronicles may be said to express the essence of the thing whose history is being written, or at least come closer to expressing it than other chronicles. Such a view, which may be called 'Essentialism,' is poignantly expressed in the following passage from Dostoevsky's novel *The Possessed:*

> Her literary scheme was as follows. Numbers of papers and journals are published in the capitals and the provinces of Russia, and every day a number of events are reported in them. The year passes, the newspapers are everywhere folded up and put away in cupboards, or are torn up and become litter, or are used for making parcels or wrapping things. Numbers of these facts make an impression and are remembered by the public, but in the course of years they are forgotten. Many people would like to look them up, but it is a

labour for them to embark upon this sea of paper, often knowing nothing of the day or place or even year in which the incident occurred. Yet if all the facts for a whole year were brought together into one book, on a definite plan, and with a definite object, under headings with references, arranged according to months and days, such a compilation might reflect the characteristics of Russian life for the whole year, even though the facts published are only a small fraction of the events that take place.

"Instead of a number of newspapers there would be a few fat books, that's all," observed Shatov.

But Lizaveta Nikolaevna clung to her idea, in spite of the difficulty of carrying it out and her inability to describe it. "It ought to be one book, and not even a very thick one," she maintained. But even if it were thick it would be clear, for the great point would be the plan and the character of the presentation of facts. Of course, not all would be collected and reprinted. The decrees and acts of government, local regulations, laws—all such facts, however important, might be altogether omitted from the proposed publication. They could leave out a great deal and confine themselves to a selection of events more or less characteristic of the moral life of the people, of the personal character of the Russian people at the present moment. Of course, everything might be put in: strange incidents, fires, public subscriptions, anything good or bad, every speech or word, perhaps even floodings of the rivers, perhaps even some government decrees, but only such things to be selected as are characteristic of the period; everything would be put in with a certain view, a special significance and intention, with an idea which would illuminate the facts looked at in the aggregate, as a whole. And finally the book ought to be interesting even for light reading, apart from its value as a work of reference. It would be, so to say, a presentation of the spiritual, moral, inner life of Russia for a whole year.

"We want every one to buy it, we want it to be a book that will be found on every table." Liza declared. "I understand that all lies in the plan, and that's why I apply to you," she concluded. She grew very warm over it, and although her explanation was obscure and incomplete, Shatov began to understand.

"So it would amount to something with a political tendency, a selection of facts with a special tendency," he muttered, still not raising his head.

"Not at all, we must not select with a particular bias, and we ought not to have any political tendency in it. Nothing but impartiality—that will be the only tendency." [7]

We may easily express Lizaveta's inclination to think in terms of a presiding spirit by reference to our model. Let us suppose for purposes of simplicity that the rival historians divide their narratives of the subject S into the same temporal periods, $t_1, t_2, \ldots, t_n$. At any given time there are *many* things that *might* be said of *S:* at time t_1 it had features A, A', A'', A''', etc.; at t_2 it had features B, B', B'', B''', etc.; and analogously for time t_3 and each succeeding time. Now let us suppose for simplicity's sake that each of the *histories* to be compared attributes one feature for each given time, and connects each one with a similarly attributed feature for times before or after it. In that case, Lizaveta's idea is that although at any given time Russia may possess a vast number of accidental features, the feature which is recorded in its history, say, *A* for time t_1, expresses Russia's spirit, inner character, or essence at that time.

We have here a philosophico-historical analogue of the ancient doctrine that individuals have essences. The controlling idea is that the historian seizes upon the essence of subject S at time t_1, moves to its supposedly different essence at time t_2, and so on, until a history is produced which entails a chronicle consisting exclusively of statements expressing essences. The doctrine is not strictly classical because it allows that the essence of a thing may change with time. But apart from this it shares a great deal of Aristotle's view that we can present Socrates' essence only by saying that he is a man, and hence with the view that some true singular statements about Socrates have a favored status. I venture to say that in some of its formulations the Marxian view that the history of productive techniques constitutes a superior history of mankind, is dominated by some such notion. And certain historians who say that Europe was essentially characterized by a Renaissance at one time, and at another by an Enlightenment may think along similar lines. Both of these attributions to Europe are seen by such historians as analogous to saying that Socrates is a man, whereas they view alternative propositions about Europe in the same period as Aristotle would have viewed the propositions that Socrates was bald, white, and married to Xantippe. The best history of S, in this view, would be that which is a connected account of the changing essences of S.

One might vary this conception of history by not demanding that such a history be composed exclusively of descriptions which capture the subject's new essence at each time for which a description is provided. Instead, one might say that although a description will be provided for each of the periods into which the historian has divided his account, these selected descriptions need not be said to express the subject's essences during the periods for which they are the selected descriptions. Rather, the superior *conjunction* of such statements of selected features, i.e., the superior chronicle taken as a whole, may be thought of as presenting *the* essential feature of the central subject, even if its conjuncts do not rate this appellation. Whichever of these conceptions is adopted, the essentialist's view is that there is one true statement about the central subject—a long conjunctive statement, of course—which is *the* objectively chosen truth about the central subject, the statement of *what really happened.* Even the most cautious and unspeculative historians are prepared to speak in some such vein of the "line" that the main stream of United States "actuality" has followed.[8] And this image of *the* line, objectively determinable, the one that must be chosen from among all the other lines through the jungle of historical fact, is paralleled in our model by the chronicle or conjunction which expresses the essential truth about the historian's central subject.

11. Whichever variety of historical essentialism is adopted,

it will create philosophical difficulties that are not unlike those to which Aristotle's doctrine of essence is subject, difficulties that I shall not rehearse before this audience. But there *have* been efforts at treating the notion of essence without Aristotelian tears, and so one may well ask whether they may not be relevant to our problem. Here the views of William James suggest themselves almost automatically. In his *Principles of Psychology,* James followed what he took to be Locke's lead in an effort to undermine the Aristotelian view and to replace it by what James called a teleological conception of essence. James argued, in terms that are familiar, that "all ways of conceiving a concrete fact, if they are true ways at all, are equally true ways. *There is no property* ABSOLUTELY essential to any one thing." [9] Therefore, James said, the question "What is *that*?" as the questioner points to a concrete thing may be answered in many true ways, depending on the practical concerns of the questioner or his respondent. The thing upon which he was writing, said James, might be regarded as a surface for inscription, or as a combustible material, or as a thin thing, or as a hydrocarbonaceous thing, or as a thing eight inches by ten inches in size, an American thing, and so on, *ad infinitum. What* one regards it as depends, according to James, upon one's practical concerns, upon what one wants to do with it. And since one can only do one thing with it at a time, James continued, one can regard it in only one of these ways at a time.

It is easy to see the implications of this view of essence for a view of history. In a similar way one might argue that the historian will present that chronicle, that conjunctive singular statement about his central subject, which is related to *his* practical aims as James's regarding his piece of paper as a combustible was related to James's need to light a fire. And here we have the basis of what might be called a teleological view of the superior chronicle of S. On such a view, when we say that a certain account of what happened to S, i.e., that a certain chronicle of S is superior to another, we are speaking elliptically, for what we mean would be more properly expressed by saying that this chronicle is superior to another *relative to a certain* desire to do something to S or with S.

However tempting such a view may be, we are immediately struck by one difficulty in it. James's view may be plausible as an analysis of essence when the object is present to us now, as his piece of paper was to him when he was penning his words. But what about the typical subject of the historian, the dead and buried individual or the extinct civilization? Surely we have no immediate *practical* interest in such entities, that is to say, no interest in doing something overt *to* them or *with* them in the sense in which James had a practical interest in writing on or burning his piece of paper. For this reason a simple transfer of James's pragmatically teleological view of the essence of a thing to the history of a thing cannot be made. Even if James be right in suggesting that categorizing a contemporaneous concrete thing "is first and last and always for the sake of . . . doing" [10] which is overt, we cannot hold the corresponding view about a piece of paper in the distant past or about ancient Greece. So a teleological view which is narrowly pragmatic seems incapable of sustaining an analysis of the essence of, or of the history of a thing which is in the distant past.

We might be tempted to revise the pragmatic view so it no longer says that the superior true history of S is superior because it facilitates action on or with S, the thing whose history is being written, but rather that it is superior relative to our desire to do something which is not necessarily *to* or *with* the central subject of our history. But so long as this action is conceived as practical in the narrowest sense, even if it is not performed on or with the central subject, I cannot see how we can defend this view. Some histories are written without any intention to facilitate practical action of any kind. I do not wish to deny that a reader of a history of ancient Greece *might* learn something of use to him in his efforts to do something to contemporary America or something else in the contemporary world. But I do wish to deny that all historians write histories of ancient Greece with an *intention* that would make it proper to judge the merit of their chronicles by reference to these chronicles' capacity to facilitate a specifiable overt action in the present.

So what is left of the teleological view of the superior history that is modeled on James's teleological view of an individual's essence? We have removed from it the condition that a history is superior only in the degree to which its chronicle facilitates practical action, for we have construed the purposes for which one writes a chronicle and a history in a much broader way than James did. On this more liberal view, a historian of the United States of America may follow any of a number of "lines" so long as he presents a true history in the sense defined earlier. The number of "essential" histories he may tell will be greater than even a Jamesian historian would permit, for his lines of narration may be dictated by goals that are not crudely practical. Provided that he can construct a history in the sense defined, a historian may concentrate primarily or exclusively on the interesting, the genial, or the unattractive features of his subject. And of course he may, if he can, construct a narrative out of them, fill his book with statements that he thinks will guide or influence action in the present. He may even follow the advice of E. H. Carr [11] and write what has been called 'Big Battalion' history, that is to say, select his facts with an eye on the ruling classes or men of the past or the future. I repeat that such histories may not yield internally connectible narratives, but if they do succeed in doing so, I know no absolute way in which the teleological view of history may exclude them without supplying extra advice about permissible and impermissible goals.

A teleologist is now conceived as a philosopher who will apply the word 'history' to any true connected narrative, whatever the principle that guides the historian's selection of facts. And the teleologist does not insist that for each history there be only one principle of selection. In all consistency, he is, or should be, perfectly willing to allow the historian to choose his facts for even one history with eyes on all kinds of considerations, so long as the historian writes true and connected narrative. I dare say that if one were to examine history books with a mind to finding the reasons for the inclusion of their chronicles' true statements, one would in fact find that some are included for reasons of curiosity, some for the beauty of what they report, some for the ugliness of what they report, some for the moral grandeur of what they report, some for the bizarreness of what they report, some for the practical advice, warnings, encouragements they suggest.

12. Where have we arrived in our flight from subjectivism via essentialism? At a view which is not narrowly subjective in the sense of making mere curiosity or mere congeniality the condition of being a historical fact about our central subject, but one which might be called broadly relativistic insofar as it allows the choice of facts to be made with reference to the aims of the historian. And about these aims we have said very little, save that they can be almost anything the historian pleases, and that one or many may guide the construction of a given historical work. But, it might be held, this is the result of beginning with Aristotelian essentialism as the only alternative to a narrow subjectivism and then driving on to relativism via a critique of James's pragmatically teleological view of essence. And this route, it might be argued, is not the only one that may be taken. Instead, we may be urged to take another and more promising route. We should not begin, it might be held, by supposing that the historian seeks a deeper or essential truth about his central subject, but rather that he seeks to approximate *the whole truth* about his central subject. This doctrine we may call 'Encyclopedism.'

The encyclopedist has a goal which must be distinguished from that of the essentialist, especially if we associate essentialism with Aristotle's doctrine on this subject. For Aristotle does not think of statements of essence as conveying *more* than any other statement about the individual, but rather as conveying something which is deeper, as I have said—such that if the individual were not to have it or to lose it, the individual would not be numerically the same individual as it now is. Hence the Aristotelian difference between saying of Socrates that he is a man and saying that he is white. Now it is true that there is a passage in the *Categories* in which Aristotle speaks of an essential statement about an individual as rendering a "more instructive account" of him.[12] But this is where Aristotle is invidiously comparing a statement of Socrates' species, *man*, with one of his genus, *animal*, both of which are what Aristotle calls "secondary substances." It is true that one of these statements expresses more about Socrates than the other, insofar as one of them entails the other and not conversely. On the other hand, when Aristotle invidiously compares *all* secondary substances with an accident like whiteness, he does not say that he who would render a more instructive account of Socrates should say of him that he is a man rather than that he is white. The superiority of the attribution of any secondary substance to Socrates, whether it be *man* or *animal*, over the attribution of an accident like whiteness to Socrates, is not measured by the capacity of the former to say *more* about Socrates in the sense of coming closer to the whole truth about it. For this reason an Aristotelian essence is not what a historical encyclopedist would seek. The encyclopedist, as I have said, aims at the whole truth rather than the essential truths.

But how can an encyclopedist decide which of two rival chronicles comes closest to the whole truth? Presumably by seeing whether one says more true things than another, in the way that 'Socrates is a rational animal' says more than 'Socrates is an animal.' And yet this is not the only or the typical way in which rival histories compete. They don't merely vie with each other in the amount that they can say about their central subject. Even Macaulay, who subscribed to the idea that a superior history should approximate the whole truth, believed that it often happens that one historian "tells less truth than another, merely because he tells more truths."[13] And so the encyclopedist must diminish the size of his goal, following the advice of William James, who wrote:

"Mr. Warner, in his Adirondack story, shot a bear by aiming, not at his eye or heart, but 'at him generally.' But we cannot aim 'generally' at the universe; or if we do, we miss our game." [14] The encyclopedist may continue to disapprove of the subjectivity of the method of Henry James's genial summary, but will now no longer insist that the historian seeks to say as much as possible about his subject.

Yet once the encyclopedist abandons the notion that the whole truth about his subject is what he has his eye on, he must abandon the idea that the feature of the subject he is to report for a given time somehow comes closest to *expressing the whole truth* about the period. Instead, the encyclopedist may adopt a modified encyclopedism, according to which the selected feature is the feature of his subject which most successfully organizes all of the *known* or given features of his central subject at that time, and which may be linked in a narrative with other features similarly selected. He would then, perhaps, be subscribing to what might be called 'scientism' in the manner of J. B. Bury. He would argue that if at any given time we *know* that our historical subject has features A, A', A'', A''', etc. we may select from them one that is central in some objective sense, central in the way that the feature of experiencing a Renaissance or an Enlightenment might be said to be central by comparison to other features of Europe. I have in my own historical work used such concepts on at least two occasions, once when I labeled a certain period in the history of American social thought as characterized by a Revolt against Formalism,[15] and on another occasion when I took my life in my hands and characterized the twentieth century as the Age of Analysis in philosophy.[16] If I understand them correctly, Mr. Walsh has called this organizing process "colligation" [17] and Professor Dray has discussed it in his paper " 'Explaining What' in History." [18]

Let us not enter the difficult problem of characterizing the logical relationship between the colligating feature and the other features of the subject which it colligates, just as we have avoided the discussion of the 'because' in our history.

But we cannot waive the question: Are the features which are usually colligated by historians all the known or given features of their central subject? They are not all of the knowable features, i.e., the features which it is logically possible to know, as we have seen. But I should go further and say that they constitute a class that is smaller than the class of *known* features. Of course, historians working on very remote periods for which there are few remains and documents may try to colligate all of the known features of the subject, just as an archeologist may try to depict an ancient structure on the basis of all of its known features. But this happy embarrassment of poverty is not the fate of all historians. Many historians, I submit, try to colligate features which they select from among the known features as colligable, on the basis of a value judgment as to their importance. In other words, even if we should be able to characterize the relationship between colligating feature and colligated features as "objective," even if we should hold that the logical relation between the statement attributing the colligating features and the colligated features is *like that* of the superior scientific statement to its confirming data or the data it explains, the choice of the data to be colligated will often rest on a value judgment that will sometimes be relative to differing standards of importance.[19]

I am aware, of course, that logicians of historical method who wish to emphasize its similarities with the method of natural science stress the fact that the scientist may become interested in his data for all sorts of reasons that might be subjective and that this does not destroy the objectivity of the statement that the data are explicable in a certain way. And a logician of natural science might argue that the reasons why the data are selected for explanation lie outside the domain of science itself, and hence beyond the purview of the logician interested in the methods of scientific inference and explanation. But even if the logician of natural science be justified in sharply separating the motives or reasons that a scientist has for wanting to explain certain phenomena, and the scientific evaluation of the scientist's proffered explanations of those phenomena, the logician of narration is not always justified in making the analogous separation. In other words, the statement that something is a superior history implies more than a judgment that all of its causal statements are true and that each component of such causal statements presents the best colligation of the features selected for colligation. It also implies a judgment to the effect that those features which are so colligated are in some sense *worth* colligating. A similar judgment of the worthiness of the data to be data, so to speak, may be made when scientists dispute the interest or importance of data that prompt questions of the form 'Why?' but on the whole the tendency of the logician of natural science is to disregard this aspect of the process of scientific thinking as scientifically irrelevant; as having gone on, so to speak, in the private recesses of the scientist's mind prior to his entering the really scientific phase of his investigation, and hence as of no concern to the logician of natural science. But it does not seem to me that the logician of narration can disregard the analogous segment of the historian's thinking as a sort of logically irrelevant overture. For given the process of historical investigation, writing and criticism as we know it, it is surely true that historians do judge each other's works not only with an eye to the truth of factual and causal statements but also with an eye to the importance of the facts colligated. And if we grant that the historian in one phase of his work seeks a feature of a period that will colligate other features of the period that are *important* or *significant* or *worth colligating*, we have not escaped the possibility of relativism.

It will be recalled that we were launched on the most recent phase of our reflections by the advice of the encyclopedist who urged the historian to speak the *whole truth*. But once the encyclopedist's thesis is scaled down to the contention that the historian should colligate that part of the truth about his subject which is significant, the question: "Significant for what and for whom?" must arise. The doctrine of the deeper truth and the doctrine of the whole truth, both of which are adopted by some in order to avoid relativism, seem to lead to the view that to evaluate a historian's answer to the question 'What happened?' along what I have called a truth-transcending axis, we cannot escape the need to take into account the purposes of the historian.

This is really not surprising when we remember that history is an extension of memory, and that memories may be judged not only on the basis of their truth but also on the basis of their worth. 'Has he recorded what is true?' is one question we may ask of a recorder. 'Has he recorded what is worth recording?' is another. 'Has he recorded anything that colligates what is worth recording?' is a third. No adequate definition of a superior history can therefore eliminate a truth-transcending reference to some kind of memorability. A superior history of S is one that contains only true statements mentioning S, which statements record features of S that are worth recording, either intrinsically or extrinsically. And, it goes without saying, different people find different things worth recording, or have different conceptions of what it is to be worth recording.

13. Having said all of this, I must add my awareness of the fact that I may have only scratched the surface of a large and deep problem. For after reaching this point we may still wish to ask whether there is a use of the phrase 'superior history' which is exclusively that of the professional historian, the historian with a large 'H'; a use which, when it is analyzed or clarified, will allow us to pick out some purpose or set of purposes that will distinguish his history from that of any old truthful narrator. A number of preliminary things must be said before facing this question directly. The first is that professional historians write their histories about a limited class of things. Not *any* thing may be a central subject of a historian's history. Historians write histories of nations, civilizations, scientific societies, philosophical movements, revolutions, economies, religions. They don't usually write histories of plants, animals, stars, rocks, or galaxies. So we know that they are

primarily concerned with the social behavior of human beings. However, the problem before us now is not that of defining the class of things or subjects *of which* historians with a large 'H' may write a history. That is a difficult question, and I cannot enter it here. Another question that must be distinguished from the one we have asked, is: What sorts of things does a historian say about his central subject, meaning by that, what *kind* of features does he attribute to his central subject? That too is a difficult question, often discussed by philosophers who ask 'What is a historical fact?' by analogy to those who ask 'What is a physical fact?' and 'What is a biological fact?'

What we have asked is neither of these questions, but rather a question that may be raised even after we have answered these questions about what subjects and what predicates are admissible in histories. Namely: what predicates or features that are admittedly historical should be selected for attribution in a history, whether it be directly, as it will be when Henry James's genial summarizer writes the history, or indirectly, when J. B. Bury's allegedly scientific colligator writes it? Here we are being asked to define a standard of memorability, as I have been calling it, and not to define a class of statements syntactically, as we might be if we were asked the question 'What is a logical truth?' But once we see that we are being asked to supply a *definition* or a *criterion* for something like historical memorability or historical importance, a definition which may be usefully employed by all historians in their effort to write superior histories, we must, I think, say that we cannot supply what is demanded. At least I know that I cannot provide it by reflecting on my own efforts at history, nor can I by reflecting on the office of the historian with a large 'H.'

I know no rock of historical practice or usage upon which to rest some definition of historical memorability. Historians may in one generation band together and by fiat rule out certain kinds of true histories as nonhistories, but I should doubt that they could provide any clear notion of memorability which supposedly flows from the nature of history as a discipline. That is why I find it so strange that E. H. Carr should think that he has extracted the essence of history, "properly so-called," when he suggests that the test of historical importance is relevance to the future triumph of the masses in Asia and Africa. He is of course entitled to think that only such facts are worth recording, but not to think that he is delivering the essential truth about history from Sinai.

Once again we may be presented with a legacy of essentialism, but this time it is not an essentialism concerning individuals but rather concerning universals or concepts. Behind the search for a necessary and sufficient condition for historical memorability, may lie the idea that by reflecting on what a historian is you may derive *the* species of memorability that underlies his writing, that the criterion of memorability flows, as it were, from his essence, qua historian. However, unlike those philosophers who strain at the doctrine that individuals have essences but swallow the doctrine that concepts or offices do, I cannot stomach either of these ancient camels. It is ironical that both of them have sometimes been admired by historians, those traditional refugees from the realm of essences. Yet historians, of all people, should realize that the logic of historical narration has no more room for essences, however subtly introduced, than does the logic of natural science and mathematics.

The main conclusion of this part of my argument is that the objectivity of singular and explanatory statements in history is objectivity enough, and if this be relativism, I am prepared to have the most made of it. Whether the objectivity of singular and causal statements is also effected by a variety of relativism is another matter, with which I have not been concerned.

14. Behind all of my analysis there may seem to lie the assumption that we can always sharply distinguish between the dimension of truth and the dimension of memorability, always take a piece of historical writing and separately answer two separate questions, namely, 'Are the factual and explanatory statements true?' and 'Are the facts recorded by the singu-

lar statements worth recording?' It is easy to do this in the abstract, of course, and to deliver pompous lectures on the difference between saying in an objective vein that statement *A* is true, and saying in a vein that might not be objective, that statement *A* is worth recording in a history. In the abstract, of course, it may be relatively easy to persuade a historian that even if the statement of worth were not acceptable to him—on grounds that ultimately involved his special preferences, interests, and values—the first statement of fact, *A*, by virtue of its objective nature, must command his assent. This is what might be called the 'You may not share my attitudes, but you surely must agree with me about the facts' argument. But we all know, if we have tried to write history, that we do not sit back after every singular nonexplanatory statement we write down, and say to ourselves: "Now, let me see. I know this is true, but is it worth saying and should it be woven into the narrative?" Similarly, those of us who read histories through do not always find ourselves giving two distinct grades, one for facts and the other for memorability. The two assessments often take place in a sort of total way, and they are not explicitly joined by logical conjunction, if I may state the point that way. The process of evaluating a history may often be undifferentiable, and therefore we might not be able to separate out these two elements. Under such circumstances we do find ourselves making a blended judgment which is, as it were, based on a simultaneous estimate of truth-cum-memorability. We feel that the author has written a narrative which, in the light of our acquaintance with the facts and our estimate of their importance, is on the whole good, and yet we can not apportion its merits under different headings, as the old report cards used to do when they gave separate marks for the excellence of the pupil's work, for his deportment, and his effort. We look at the history as whole in the way that Emerson asked us to look at the man and Dewey the child. And this is more likely to be the case the longer and the more complex is the narrative under consideration. One approves of the history because the author seems to look at the evidence with one's eyes and one's heart—I am assuming that one is a fellow-historian who is familiar with the so-called evidence—and to feel about him that he is a kindred spirit, one who would see the same figure as we would in a Rorschach inkblot, or who would first see the duck-rabbit of Jastrow and Wittgenstein as a duck, just as we did every time we looked at it.

Now this is the sort of situation in history that might correspond to two men being asked of William James's piece of paper 'What is that?' and responding in unison 'It's a piece of paper' but not bothering to say what similar interest it was that underlay their jointly making only one of the true statements that might have been made in answer to the question. Just as James would say that they have converging interests without articulating them, so two mutually resonant historians may have a similar value-orientation but not bother to make explicit that shared orientation when they praise each other's work. But the serious question raised by our most recent reflections is whether we can confidently say that *whenever* a historian tells only one of the many true stories he might tell about his central subject and his work is examined by a critic, that critic will praise him in a statement that *must be* divisible or analyzable neatly into a conjunction of assertions—one that says his facts are right and the other that says they are well, wisely, soundly, properly, justly, etc. chosen—whether the statement is so divided or not.

My reply to such a question must be 'No' for reasons that I can only sketch here. Briefly, I say 'No' because I am unable to demonstrate to my own satisfaction that all terms for criticizing a history must either be like the word 'true,' or like the word 'memorable,' or logically decomposable into such terms in a way that would allow another person to agree, as we say, with the factual part of the criticism but not with its non-factual part.

Let me say in conclusion, however, that the fact that we cannot *prove* that all such evaluation of a narrative is so decomposable does not in any way interfere with our knowing that sometimes it can be. And where we can separate out the two elements, it is imperative to do so, for all the general reasons we give for distinguishing the distinguishable, and for those special reasons we have when we seek as much agreement as we can or when we seek to pinpoint disagreements.

NOTES

1. E. M. Forster, *Aspects of the Novel* (New York, 1927), p. 88.

2. See Nelson Goodman, "About," *Mind,* LXX, New Series, (1961), 1–24.

3. Forster, *op. cit.,* p. 130.

4. Samuel Eliot Morison, *By Land and by Sea: Essays and Addresses* (New York, 1953), p. 348.

4a. By an internally connectible chronicle, I mean one whose components can be truthfully linked by the use of explanatory connectives. In other words, it is a chronicle entailed by a true history.

5. Henry James, *Essays in London and Elsewhere* (New York, 1893), p. 27.

5a. A mere chronicle is one that is not internally connectible.

6. J. B. Bury, "The Science of History," *Selected Essays of J. B. Bury,* ed. Harold Temperley (Cambridge, 1930), pp. 3–22.

7. Fyodor Dostoevsky, *The Possessed* (Everyman ed., New York, 1931), I, 114–16.

8. See, for example, Morison, *op. cit.,* p. 357. For a discussion of some problems concerning such a point of view, see my article, "New Horizons in Philosophy," *Adventures of the Mind* (Second Series), eds. Richard Thruelsen and John Kobler (New York, 1961), p. 600.

9. William James, *The Principles of Psychology* (New York, 1890), II, 333; James's italics and capitals. For a more recent expression of a related point of view, see Nelson Goodman, "The Way the World Is," *Review of Metaphysics,* XIV (1960), 48–56.

10. James, *op. cit.,* p. 333.

11. See E. H. Carr, *What Is History?* (New York, 1962), esp. pp. 167–68.

12. Aristotle, *Categories,* 2[b].

13. Thomas Babington Macaulay, "History," *Critical and Historical Essays* (Boston and New York, 1900), I, 245.

14. James, *op. cit.*, pp. 333–34.

15. Morton White, *Social Thought in America: The Revolt against Formalism* (New York, 1949; rev. ed., Boston, 1957).

16. Morton White, *The Age of Analysis: Twentieth Century Philosophers* (Boston and New York, 1955).

17. W. H. Walsh, *An Introduction to the Philosophy of History* (London, 1951), pp. 59–64.

18. William Dray, "'Explaining What' in History," *Theories of History*, ed. P. Gardiner (Glencoe, Ill., 1959), pp. 403–408.

19. For a more "objectivistic" approach, and one which I now think inadequate in certain respects, see my essay "Toward an Analytic Philosophy of History," in *Philosophic Thought in France and the United States*, ed. Marvin Farber (Buffalo, 1950), pp. 705–25. See also "A Plea for an Analytic Philosophy of History," in my *Religion, Politics and the Higher Learning* (Cambridge, 1959), pp. 61–74.

2

On "The Logic of Historical Narration"

LEE BENSON
Wayne University

MY OWN FRAME of reference, no doubt, leads me to believe that Professor White's main contribution to the logic of historical inquiry is to provide concrete support for the familiar observation that historians suffer from, and pay for, their traditional indifference to logical and methodological problems. Specifically, he helps us to see that E. H. Carr in his recent volume of lectures, *What Is History?* got himself into logical difficulties because he gave insufficient thought to the nature of his questions and answers. Since Professor White may not agree with my assessment of his paper, it seems useful to confront directly the arguments he and Mr. Carr present.

First, Mr. Carr: Notoriously, titles of essays, papers, lectures, and books sometimes are chosen for reasons not entirely relevant to their contents. Mr. Carr, however, not only called his series of lectures *What Is History?*, he asked precisely that question in the first sentence of his first lecture. Moreover, he asked it in one form or another, repeatedly, throughout his lectures.[1] Thus, we might be tempted to conclude that, "What is history?" was the question which really concerned him and to which he really addressed himself. For example, he presented this dictum on the proper study of past human behavior:

> History properly so-called can be written only by those who find and accept a sense of direction in history itself. The belief that we have come from somewhere is closely linked to the belief that we are going somewhere. A society which has lost faith in its capacity to progress in the future will quickly cease

> to concern itself with its progress in the past. As I said at the beginning of my first lecture, our view of history reflects our view of society. I now come back to my starting point by declaring my faith in the future of society and in the future of history.[2]

In that passage, and in others, Carr seems to be trying to supply what Mr. White has characterized as "a *definition* or a *criterion* for something like historical memorability or historical importance, a definition which may be usefully employed by all historians in their efforts to write superior histories. . . ."[3] Thus, if we were to accept Carr's own definition of his task, namely, to answer the question "What is history?" we might say that his answer derived from a natural law doctrine of historiographic significance. For Carr's formulation of his argument makes it possible to paraphrase him as follows: Independently of men's wills and judgments, there naturally exist in the universe some criteria of historiographic importance. These criteria are, to borrow from Mr. White's recent essay on the revival of natural law doctrines, "universally binding, certain, rationally established by the inspections of universals, essences, or meanings. . . ."[4]

If Carr really wanted us to understand him as presenting a natural law doctrine of historiographic significance, it would be appropriate for Mr. White to invoke against him the logical objections he invokes against all propositions derived from natural law theories. True, Mr. White fails to indicate explicitly that Carr is his main target. Surely, he does so implicitly, however, by singling him out to dismiss the possibility that a criterion can be found for something like historical memorability or importance:

> I know no rock of historical practice or usage upon which to rest some definition of historical memorability. Historians may in one generation band together and by fiat rule out certain kinds of true histories as nonhistories, but I should doubt that they could provide any clear notion of memorability which supposedly flows from the nature of history as a discipline.

> That is why I find it so strange that E. H. Carr should think that he has extracted the essence of history, "properly so-called," when he suggests that the test of historical importance is relevance to the future triumph of the masses in Asia and Africa. He is of course entitled to think that only such facts are worth recording, but not to think that he is delivering the essential truth about history from Sinai.[5]

Game, set, and match—apparently to Mr. White. When the term "history" connotes the study of past human behavior, there is no such thing as history independent of men. What then is history? History is what historians do—as physics is what physicists do, geology what geologists do, economics what economists do. It is critically important and cannot be overemphasized, however, that both the subject matter and the aims of economists, for example, are relatively similar, when compared to the range of subject matter and aims of men called historians. Thus, compared to historians, economists tend strongly to do more or less the same things, and so do physicists, geologists, and the members of all other disciplines included in the natural and social sciences. In other words, one major difficulty that arises when we discuss the logic of historical narration is that we use the same term, historian, to designate men who actually deal with incredibly diverse phenomena and who actually want to achieve incredibly diverse aims. If I understand Mr. White correctly, he argues that no criteria exist for judging work as superior which would logically compel historians who wish to do superior work to study more or less the same aspects of past human behavior or try to achieve more or less the same aims. I agree, although it seems to me that he makes what is, after all, a simple point, in unnecessarily lengthy, elaborate, and confusing form.

Except on the ground of arbitrary value judgment, we have no logical basis for ranking a historian as intrinsically superior to a chronicler. Similarly, we have no basis for ranking a true history—whatever we mean by that term—of one kind of past human behavior as superior to a true history of another kind of past human behavior, e.g., for ranking a true history of changes in the possession and form of political power in the United States from 1789 to 1961 above a true history of changes in women's clothing in the United States from 1789 to 1961. And yet, and here I suspect is where Mr. White and I part company, it seems to me that Carr would also agree that judgments of the relative superiority of true histories are intrinsically arbitrary. In fact, that seems to me what Carr wanted to say, but did not say clearly.

In context, Carr's "history properly so-called" passage (which I quoted above and which Mr. White rather freely paraphrased) more or less acknowledges that his conception of superior history represents an arbitrary value judgment. That passage is preceded by three sentences. Taken together, the three sentences and the passage previously quoted form the concluding paragraph of his lecture, "History as Progress." The paragraph begins as follows:

> I return therefore in conclusion to Acton's description of progress as "the scientific hypothesis on which history is to be written." You can, if you please, turn history into theology by making the meaning of the past depend on some extra-historical and super-rational power. You can, if you please, turn it into literature—a collection of stories and legends about the past without meaning or significance.[6]

Those sentences can be faulted on the ground that Carr used a debating trick to belittle men who differ with his value judgments about what historians should do. The critical point is, however, that he first indicated awareness that arbitrary value judgments determine what historians do, and only then went on to becloud the issue somewhat by saying: "History properly so-called can be written only by those who find and accept a sense of direction in history itself."

Mr. White's paper helps us to see that Carr's lectures lose some of their effectiveness because, as Carr presented his argument, he confused what he believes historians *should* do with what he *believes* historians *must* do. He said that he would answer one question, "What is history?" but he actually answered a radically different question, "What should historians do?" Moreover, his attempt to answer the question, "What is history?" led him to commit the same sin of reification that he so forcefully chastised historians for committing when they forget that history is made by men.

For example, Carr observed that "when we speak in abstract terms of the tension between liberty and equality, or between individual liberty and social justice, we are apt to forget that fights do not occur between abstract ideas." [7] Exactly. But that same line of reasoning leads to the conclusion that the old question, "What is history?" is a bad old question and should be dismissed from serious consideration. It is a bad question because when we ask it we convert an abstract concept, "history," into a concrete, self-developing, organic entity. Carr knows, of course, that history is what historians say it is. He succumbed to reification, I suggest, because historians are neither trained to, nor accustomed to, think carefully about the logic of historical narration. Thus, in my own area of substantive interest, American Civil War causation, relatively little progress has been made, in part because historians insist on pitting "the North" against "the South," and insist on asking a metaphysical question, "What caused the Civil War?" rather than the real-word question, "Who caused the Civil War?"

I may be wrong in speculating about why Carr succumbed to reification, confused radically different questions, and thereby weakened and obscured his "essential" argument. No matter. Once we agree that his lectures were really intended to answer the useful question, "What should historians do?" rather than the useless question, "What is history?" it seems to me that his argument becomes somewhat more compelling. Rather than try to support that assessment, however, it seems best to focus on the problem directly posed by Mr. White and suggest that discussions of the logic of historical narration require us to distinguish among four different types of questions:

(1) What have different historians done in specified times and places? (2) What are different historians now doing in specified places? (3) What *can* historians do? (4) What *should* historians do?

Clearly, in principle, answers to the first two questions require little more than factual, nonexplanatory statements; they do not require us to engage in epistemological discussions. Unless we simply wanted to indulge quarrelsome propensities or play intellectual type games, when we got down to cases, that is, specific times and places, we should not find it impossible to agree on criteria that would permit us to identify historians. And, I venture to predict, if we made systematic studies of what historians have done and are now doing, we would find that no basis exists for edicts that seek to limit historians to one kind of subject matter, one kind of activity, one kind of aim. "All systematic and responsible historiography would show" that neither individualizing historicist nor generalizing social scientist must a historian *try* to be. Some historians have tried to generalize in order to achieve their primary aim, a fuller, richer understanding of the unique and singular; other historians have tried to understand the unique and singular, in order to achieve their primary aim, credible generalizations about the behavior of men in society.

To reconstruct what historians have tried to do poses relatively simple problems compared to the third and fourth questions posed above. Contrary to Mr. White, I believe that the question, "What can historians do?" is the critical one now confronting philosophers and historians interested in the logic of historical inquiry. To answer that broad question, we have to grapple with such questions as these:

What do we mean by a true explanation of past human behavior? (Mr. White, I assume, does not mean to imply that he has satisfactorily answered the question by saying that a true explanation is one whose components are true.) If we know what we mean by a true explanation, are we entitled to say that historians can objectively satisfy our requirement for true explanations, or are subjective relativists correct when they claim, as Louis Gottschalk does, that assessments of the relevance and significance of data, must, in the nature of things historical, be left largely to personal judgment? [8] Have criteria been developed, can criteria be developed, which would permit us reasonably to assign relative weights to the different "factors" we say determined a specific event, or sequence of events? Can historians effectively use contrary-to-fact conditional statements? Do different kinds of past behavior pose different kinds of logical problems and require us to develop different kinds of logical explanations?

Obviously, unless we agree on the kinds of questions historians can answer truthfully, the kinds of behavior they can explain objectively, the procedures they can use justifiably, we cannot usefully begin to argue about the questions historians *should* answer. We might agree with Mr. Carr, for example, that it would be desirable to answer certain questions, but regret, alas, that he is mistaken to think we can answer them.

If I accurately reconstruct Mr. White's strategy, he deliberately bypassed the question, "What can historians do?" to call attention to the arbitrary nature of Mr. Carr's answer to the question, "What should historians do?" That strategy seems to me to reverse the logical order of procedure, but suppose we accept it. And suppose we agree that historians can truthfully answer a variety of questions that require explanatory statements, including the questions that Mr. Carr wants historians to answer.

Granted that nothing in the nature of the universe entitles us to say that someone who provides a true history of political power in the United States has done work *intrinsically* superior to someone who provides a true history of women's clothing in the United States. Must we end our analysis where Mr. White ends his and thus use rigorous logic to arrive at the absurd conclusion that no objective basis can be found to rank true histories? I do not think so. We can, for example, go on to recognize that different historians have different kinds of aims and focus on different kinds of substantive problems.

We can, in other words, set up a typology of historians and thereby bypass Mr. White's logical cul-de-sac.

Mr. White makes some use of E. M. Forster's observations on the novel, but fails to note that the latter found it necessary to create a typology of novelists in order to discuss the question, "What is the novel?" The most useful way to talk about the novel, Forster said in effect, is not to talk about novelists indiscriminately. Instead, one must identify and group together "novelists who are looking at life from much the same angle. . . ." [9] He explicitly used this method for the same reason that I urge its necessity in discussions of historians, namely that he had to deal with an extraordinarily diverse group of writers, all entitled to be called novelists.

"What is a novel?" Forster asks. And then he answers and dismisses that question with a finality that historical critics would do well to emulate:

> Any fictitious prose work over 50,000 words will be a novel for the purposes of these lectures, and if this seems to you unphilosophic will you think of an alternative definition, which will include *The Pilgrim's Progress, Marius the Epicurean, The Adventures of a Younger Son, The Magic Flute, The Journal of the Plague, Zuleika Dobson, Rasselas, Ulysses,* and *Green Mansions,* or else will give reasons for their exclusion? [10]

For our purposes, it is unnecessary to present here a comprehensive, logically consistent typology of historians, grouped according to their different aims and problems. Surely we can agree, however, that men accurately classified as historicists and sociological historians, respectively, do not want to achieve the same aims, do not try to do the same things, do not focus on the same problems, and are, therefore, really noncomparable historians, just as Forster suggests that Henry James and H. G. Wells are noncomparable novelists.

To avoid misunderstanding, let me note that I am using Hans Meyerhoff's definition of a "historicist." Historicists, he observes:

> aim to portray the bewildering, unsystematic variety of historical forms—people, nations, cultures, customs, institutions, songs, myths, and thoughts—in their unique, living expressions and in the process of continuous growth and transformation. . . . For them the special quality of history does not consist in the statement of general laws or principles, but in the grasp, so far as possible, of the infinite variety of particular historical forms immersed in the passage of time.[12]

A legitimate aim for a historian, although it happens to be one that I fail to share, and temperamentally fail to sympathize with. Intrinsically, however, it is neither *more* nor *less* legitimate than the aims of a sociological historian like Mr. Carr; aims which I do happen to share and, temperamentally, find more congenial and inspiring. Mr. Carr states his aims somewhat differently in different places, but this quotation is enough for our purposes. "To enable man to understand the society of the past and increase his mastery over the society of the present is the dual function of history." [13]

Granted that we are not entitled to rank a true history of Soviet Russia written by Carr above a true history of American women's clothing by a historicist—except on the admittedly arbitrary ground that the first is more likely than the second to deepen men's understanding of how best to go about shaping their societies and their lives. Does Mr. White contend that those two true histories would serve equally well to achieve that objective? If he agrees that we must differentiate historians according to their aims, does he contend that criteria cannot be found that would permit us to rank one historicist's true history as superior to other historicists' true histories, one sociological historian's true history above other sociological historians' true histories?

Suppose we abandon Mr. White's strategy of discussing hypothetical histories on the ground that it is too abstract to illuminate the logic of historical inquiry. Suppose, instead, we tried to adapt to the problem Mr. White poses, the empirical method which Clive Bell, the English art critic, used to answer the question, "What is civilization?" Bell's method was to "assume, on the strength of a consensus of educated opinion which amounts almost to unanimity, the high civility of three different societies," Athens of the fifth and fourth centuries B.C., Italy of the late fourteenth to early sixteenth centuries A.D., France from 1660 to 1789. He then identified what he took to be the common characteristics of those societies and concluded that men who wished to be members of highly civilized societies should strive to have their societies embody those characteristics.[14] Does Mr. White intend to say that no possibility exists that we could use some variant of Bell's method, or develop any other method, to find reasonable criteria of superior *historicist* work, superior *sociohistorical* work, or other *specified types of historical work*?

In conclusion, I should like to restate my belief that the question Mr. White invites us to focus upon is not, *at present,* a very useful one, particularly since he poses it in a fashion that forces us to agree with his negative conclusion that no true history *intrinsically* is superior to any other true history. Rather than follow Mr. White's invitation to enter a logical cul-de-sac, it would be more useful, I believe, for philosophers and historians to work together to identify, order, and try to solve the logical and methodological problems that actually confront historians when they try to explain different kinds of past human behavior. Mr. White's strategy of bypassing those problems neither disposes of them nor helps eventually to solve them—it only distracts us from them.

NOTES

1. E. H. Carr, *What Is History?* (London, 1961), p. 1, *passim.*
2. *Ibid.*, pp. 126–27.
3. Morton White, "The Logic of Historical Narration," this volume, *supra,* sec. 13.
4. Morton White, *Religion, Politics and the Higher Learning* (Cambridge, 1959), p. 124.

5. White, "The Logic of Historical Narration," *supra*, pp. 26–27.

6. Carr, *op. cit.*, pp. 126–27.

7. *Ibid.*, p. 28.

8. Louis Gottschalk, *Understanding History* (New York, 1950), pp. 205–206.

9. E. M. Forster, *Aspects of the Novel* (Harvest Book ed., New York, n. d.), pp. 14–15.

10. *Ibid.*, pp. 5–6.

11. *Ibid.*, pp. 14–17.

12. *The Philosophy of History in Our Time . . .*, ed. Hans Meyerhoff (New York, 1959), pp. 9–12.

13. Carr, *op. cit.*, p. 49.

14. Clive Bell, *Civilization* (Penguin Books ed., Great Britain, n. d.), pp. 28–29, 30–44.

3

Objectivism in History

MAURICE MANDELBAUM
The Johns Hopkins University

PROFESSOR WHITE'S PAPER is one on which it is a pleasure to comment, not only because of its clarity but because of its scope. What he says is not only relevant to recent discussions concerning historical explanation, it also takes us back to a number of earlier discussions of historical methodology and to a number of problems concerning objectivity and historical truth. I think that the fact that he has placed these issues within a single context may be fruitful for future discussions of all of them. Furthermore, the major portion of Professor White's paper, dealing with various alternatives with respect to objectivity and truth, is both original and suggestive. While I shall have a good deal to say in criticism of the conclusions he draws, I should first like to indicate what I think is particularly helpful in those of his observations which are directly relevant to questions of methodology and to the role of explanation in history.

Professor White's paper begins by harking back to the familiar distinction between chronicle and history. To my knowledge, no one has previously used the distinction so fruitfully, and I think that what he says is basically sound.[1] However, I believe that there are certain points at which we must be cautious if we are not to be led astray in making use of his distinction; while what I shall be saying about these points suggests the need for certain emendations and additions, I hope that with respect to them I shall not be making any suggestions with which Professor White would disagree.

There are two criteria which Professor White uses in distinguishing between chronicles and histories. First, he holds that the statements which make up a chronicle are not explanatory statements (i.e., they do not use terms such as "because"), but are statements which merely refer to a particular event or set of events. Histories, on the other hand, not only contain factual statements, but attempts to explain the facts to which they refer by stating connections between them (i.e., they connect two or more statements of fact with a word like "because"). Second, it follows from this difference that the truth of a chronicle is to be estimated solely with respect to the question of whether its individual component statements are true; whereas, if each factual statement within a history were true, the historical account might nonetheless be false at a number of crucial points because the connections asserted to hold among some of these individual facts might not have obtained. Though I have stated these two criteria with less exactitude than has Professor White, I have not sought to emend them in any way.

The first and most obvious point which I wish to make with respect to this distinction is that Professor White has clearly seen that every historical account, in contrast to chronicles, seeks to explain something. It will have been obvious from his paper that he would not wish to define "explanation" in any tendentious fashion: the linkages which he finds essential to history could be of any of a variety of kinds, or could be of some one kind only. By temporarily removing the question of explanation from questions concerning the relations of historical explanation to other forms of explanation, he may have done us a service. At the least, he has stated the question of what constitutes explanation in history as a question to which an answer is to be sought through examining works regarded as histories, rather than through discussions of the general theory of explanation. To be sure, I would hope that such an examination would prove that historians necessarily use general laws in their proposed explanations, and I see no reason to suspect that Professor White has renounced his own earlier belief that this is true. However, Professor White's present treatment of the question is one which suggests that the answer to such a question is only to be found through looking at what historians do, and that, I believe, is as it should be. Furthermore, it seems to me a distinct advantage of Professor White's account that, unlike some of his predecessors, he has not assumed that statements concerning connections between facts are somehow necessarily less objective than are statements that such and such specific individual events occurred.

I come now to a point at which we must, I think, be careful to avoid misconstruing Professor White's account: what he says about the *logical relations* between history and chronicle must not be taken as defining the *actual procedures* which it is proper for an historian to follow in his inquiries. The fact that a history cannot be true if its "associated chronicle" is not true, does not entail that anyone can, or that anyone should, attempt to establish a set of isolated facts before making any explanatory assertions about them. However, it is not uncommon to find that handbooks of historical method talk as if this were the ideal way for historians to proceed. An extreme example of this opinion is to be found in Langlois and Seignobos, who assumed that before the construction of any narrative could take place, the historian must have established a set of isolated facts through the criticism of documents, that "Historical construction has thus to be performed with an incoherent mass of minute facts, with detailed knowledge reduced as it were to a powder." (*Introduction to the Study of History*, [New York, 1903], p. 214.) However, these authors failed to tell us how it was possible for historians to embark on a criticism of documents without first assuming themselves to be in possession of a good deal of knowledge concerning the matters to which these documents purported to refer. The blunder inherent in the Langlois-Seignobos view seems so obvious that one is amazed to find it frequently repeated. However, Professor White's analysis permits us to comprehend the origin of their blunder: these methodologists have clearly seen that no history is true if its individual factual assertions are false, but they have taken this *logical* relation to be determinative of the method which historians should follow. Professor White is guilty of no such confusion. However, just because he has stated the logical point so forcefully, it seems to me desirable to insist that this *is* a logical point, not a methodological one.

I now come to a point at which I feel obliged either to add to, or to emend, Professor White's account of the explanatory assertions which are to be found in histories. You will recall his lugubrious historical account: "The King of England died, so the Queen of England died of grief. And because he worried so much about the Queen's death, the Prince committed suicide; and therefore the Princess later died of loneliness." (Cf. p. 6 of his paper.) However, you will also recall that earlier in his paper (p. 4) Professor White had said: "I shall begin by assuming that every history is a history of some entity which existed for a reasonable period of time, that the historian wishes to state what was true of it. . . ." Now, if we ask what is the enduring entity to which Professor White's lugubrious history had reference, or (better put) what is the central subject of that history,[2] I suppose that the answer is clear: it is the reigning house of England during a certain period of time.[3] What I wish to point out, and to insist upon, is the fact that the existence of a central subject constitutes one of the forms of linkage among the events entering into any particular history, and Professor White does not make this fact clear.[4] In his discussion of the explanatory linkage between the various assertions which are present in an historical account, Professor White has stressed the sequential, causal linkage between one asserted fact and the next, but he has not explicitly mentioned another form of linkage: that which binds asserted facts into one history because they have in common the property of being parts or aspects of that which is the central subject of the history. The difference in these two forms of linkage may be illustrated in the following way.

Someone may tell the following story: "The King of England died, so the Queen died of grief, and so the Royal Chamberlain arranged the funeral. Because of the funeral, traffic was blocked, and my bus was delayed. Because I came home later than usual, I missed seeing my friend before he left London." Let us assume that in this account each of the factual statements is true, and let us also assume that each of its causal explanatory statements is also true. Nonetheless, it is not the history *of* anything: it has no central subject, and we should certainly be inclined to ask what "point" it had. If it is taken as an explanation of something which concerns my relations to my friend, the story need not have begun before the fact that (because of the funeral) my bus was delayed: neither who arranged the funeral, nor why the Queen had died, constitutes a proper part of *this* story. But if the subject of the story is something relevant to the royal dynasty, the delay of my bus and my failure to see my friend are irrelevant. Yet, to repeat, in such a case the chronicle represented by the above conjunction of statements is true, and each of the causal attributions may also be true.

Now, I should not expect Professor White to disagree with me in rejecting the preceding account as a history, for not only does he say, as we have seen, that a history must have a central subject, but he is also willing to distinguish between "mere chronicle" and the sorts of chronicles which are directly related to historical accounts: the latter too, I would assume, must have a controlling theme of some kind in order that they should be "internally connectible." (Cf. pp. 10 and 12 f.) However, there is an important lesson which I think can be learned from my absurd example: in practice, an historian sets about to write an account of some central subject, and individual persons or events become part of his historical narrative only because of the relations in which they stand to this subject. If this be true, the *sole* linkage within an historical account is not the sort of sequential causal linkage which Professor White explicitly discusses: there is also another type of linkage, namely that which connects part to whole.

To illustrate this sort of linkage, and to show its independence of the sequential causal linkage (whose presence in many accounts I by no means wish to deny), let us revert to Professor White's own lugubrious history. Let us suppose that this account has as its central subject the royal dynasty over a certain period, and that it has been told in order to make comprehensible the fact that the Black Usurper assumed the throne when he did. Now, the story of the dynasty, as a dynasty, would have been the same had the Queen died of pneumonia rather than of grief, or had the Prince been assassinated rather than having committed suicide, or had the Princess abdicated without designating a successor instead of dying of loneliness. If the historian is answering the question of how the Black Usurper was able to assume the throne at this time, the answer may (in some cases) be precisely the same regardless of the specific causal linkages which led to the extinction of first one and then another of the members of the royal family. To illustrate this point with a straightforward example: consider what happens if we seek to trace the history of a particular technological development in a particular industry over a specified period of time. The explanation of this development may lie in a series of inventions, some of which were not in fact causally related to one another at all, although each of them was causally related to the technological development of the industry. Thus we may see that the serial linkage of elements may not in all cases be essential to the explanation which we offer of a particular historical change. This point, I should say, constitutes a supplement to what Professor White has stated; it is not intended as a denial of the fact that causal linkages of a serial sort also exist, and that they are of great importance in historical accounts.

I wish to turn now from a consideration of questions associated with Professor White's discussion of the difference between history and chronicle to his discussions of questions concerning historical truth. To be sure, Professor White tells us that he will be restricting his discussion to problems concerning "the truth-transcending dimension" of historical accounts. I do not particularly object to his phrase when it is used as Professor White uses it, and when it is not allowed to prejudice any questions as to what constitutes a more or a less adequate historical account. All that Professor White apparently wishes to do is to limit his discussion to questions concerning the adequacy of alternative historical accounts, after one assumes that each of these accounts contains only true statements about individual facts and connections among facts. This is an important problem, and there is certainly no reason why Professor White should not turn his attention directly to it, rather than first raising questions as to how, if at all, we can establish that the facts in a particular account did occur, and that they were connected with one another in the ways attributed to them by historians. Personally, I am not sure that when the latter questions are discussed, they will be found really to be different from questions concerning the adequacy of alternative narratives, and I am not sure that Professor White himself would be certain that an ultimate distinction can here be drawn. (Cf. sec. 14 of his paper.) However, as will become apparent, if I were to connect the two problems it would be by assimilating the so-called truth-transcending question to questions of factual truth, whereas Professor White would probably be inclined to move in the opposite direction.

Now, Professor White's way of phrasing the problem of what criteria are to be used in evaluating alternative narrative accounts of the same subject is to ask what criteria there are for selecting one entailed chronicle rather than another as basic to the history which is to be written. As Professor White recognizes, this is simply another way of saying that the question is one of *selection:* it is a question of which among alternative possible sets of facts an historian should select in constructing his account of the past. (Cf. pp. 8–9.) When the matter is put in this more conventional form (that is, in terms of selection), I think that one can immediately see that there are some misleading aspects to the question. By discussing these first, we may be in a position to see that Professor White's own way of putting the question is also not without its difficulties.

If one asks which among alternative sets of facts an historian should select in writing his account of the past, I think it should be clear that if he took it to be his task to give an account of "The Past" he should not make any selection whatsoever. However, no historian does in fact take as his subject matter "The Past": he has some more specific central subject, such as the history of the United States, or of Western science, or of Christianity, or (in most cases) of some far more restricted topic, as the central subject concerning which he is writing an account.[5] To be sure, embraced within the field of facts which together constitute the total past of the United States, or of any other such subject, there are far more facts than any historian can know, or if he knew, would have time and space to chronicle. Therefore, it is truly said that he must select from among the whole field of facts which are connected with his subject matter, and what is included in his account is but a small proportion of these facts. However, to say *merely* this is to put the matter in a quite misleading way: it is to suggest that if he *could* do so, it would be proper for an historian writing about the United States in a certain period of its history to chronicle every event which took place within the borders of the United States within that period, or which was causally connected with any one of those events. This, however, is simply not true. When we are writing a history of the United States we are writing a history of a particular social entity, and geological events, or thunderstorms, or the like, may have no place in such an account. Furthermore, there is the matter of "scale" to be considered.[6] As long as we are dealing with *the United States* as the central subject of our account, many of the events in the life of most of its individual citizens, as well as many events associated with its state and municipal governments, will be wholly irrelevant to that account. Those individuals who feature in an historical account of the United States do so because they are causally related to (or because they are taken as typical of a whole group of persons who are causally related to) the specific events which constitute the large-scale events in the development of the subject of the account.

Professor White's way of phrasing the issue of selection

and its relation to the adequacy of an historical account is one which can actually help us avoid the gross error which I have been discussing, namely, the error of thinking that any historical account should embrace every facet of (or every detail connected with) those events which occurred at a definite place over a specified period of time. However, it does not seem to me that Professor White himself uses his way of putting the matter to its full advantage. I think his failure to do so lies in a failure to emphasize the fact that every history has a delimited scope. When he speaks of an entity such as the United States as being the subject of two or more historical accounts, he seems to me to slip into the error of assuming that because two historians have written works contributing to our knowledge of the United States, the central subject of their two narratives is actually the same. But this is not necessarily the case. For purposes of illustration, let us suppose one historian to be writing the history of the relation of the federal government to commerce, and another to be writing the history of this country's industrial development. Admittedly, there are close relationships between these two histories, and there are many points at which historians writing about these topics will chronicle the same facts. It is precisely for this reason that I have chosen this example. However, it should be clear that in spite of this fact, and in spite of the fact that both accounts are concerned with the United States (and not with the history of Germany), the two accounts are clearly about different things. To put the matter succinctly but crudely, the fact that the same proper name designating a specific nation appears in the title of many different historical works does not imply that these works have the same central subject. It is no more surprising that when historians write about different features which are present in American society the chronicles entailed by their narratives should be different, than it is surprising to find that when one historian writes about pre-Civil War history and the other writes about the United States in the twentieth century, the chronicled events in these two accounts should also be different. Similarly, when two historians work on totally different scales, one dealing, say, with the maneuvering that preceded the passage of a particular bill in the Congress, and the other with the place of this bill in a whole series of bills dealing with the same subject, it should certainly not be expected that the entailed chronicles would be the same.

Let us now assume that Professor White will grant us a right to make these finer discriminations concerning what constitutes the central subject of a particular historical account. And let us also assume that he will not have disagreed with what has been said concerning differences in scale which are to be found in various historical works. If these points are granted, it is no longer obvious that there will be alternative histories, each of which has the same central subject, and each of which entails a wholly true chronicle, but each of which gives us a different narrative. I do not say that there *may* not be cases in which such alternative histories are to be found, but the more explicitly one denominates what particular facet of a particular subject one is taking as his central subject, and on what scale he will be working, the less frequently such alternatives are *likely* to be found. I do not mean to suggest that the problem with which Professor White was wrestling will have been exorcised by the preceding remarks. Even if there were *never* a case in which there were two or more competing histories, each of which entailed a true chronicle, historians might still continue to argue which of two accounts was the more *significant*. Professor White's relativism consists in holding that such a question can only be answered in terms of what each finds to be more worth remembering.[7]

I think there is another criterion which is actually used in attempts to determine which of two historical accounts is the more significant, although I would not wish to deny that some historians may sometimes have been willing to accept the criterion Professor White proposed, and the relativism which it entails. The additional criterion to which I wish to call attention is not, however, located on "a truth-transcending axis": it is the criterion of which factors are the most important factors in historical change. If one is, for example, a Marxist, certain subjects will not be viewed as important matters for historical investigation, whereas other subjects will be those concerning which it is important to seek knowledge. The choice, however, will not be along a truth-transcending axis: it will be a question of what explanatory hypotheses are the most fruitful in history. And if I am not mistaken it is in terms of theoretical considerations such as this, and not in terms of alternative accounts of what is "worth remembering," that most present-day historical disputes concerning alternative accounts are actually waged.

If this be true, then we can see that the problem of "essentialism"—although in another guise—is still with us: the theories of Marx or Ellsworth Huntington, or even Toynbee, cannot be gotten rid of by criticizing the Aristotelian doctrine of essences, for these historians purport to say what is essential in history in terms of a general explanatory sociology. Each of them may be wrong, but if this is the case then each is wrong because of the inadequacies of his generalizations, and this fact cannot be established except in terms of an examination of the relationships which have actually obtained in the past: the question is not one of "significance" in some nontheoretical sense.

Professor White's criticism of subjectivism, as well as his criticism of the Jamesian form of the teleological criterion, are criticisms which I of course welcome. However, the main point of my remarks, as will now have become clear, is to defend what I should be willing to call a modified encyclopedism: the historian's task is to approach as nearly as is possible to understanding and narrating the whole truth about man's past. However, I should of course reject the notion that any one historical work has this as its object. Just as the best encyclopedias are not written by a single man, so it is necessary for there to be a cooperative effort of tremendous proportions to win for us any very accurate and broad-ranging knowledge of even some tracts of that past. However, as historiography has developed we have become increasingly aware of its cooperative nature, and of the necessity for narrowing our scope and phrasing our problems more precisely. Thus the ideal is a body of independent narratives dealing with different aspects of the human past at different times and places, and dealing with these in both the large and in the small, with all of these accounts not only not contradicting one another, but actually reinforcing each other. As is clear, this is one form of encyclopedism, and it can of course also be characterized as an unmitigated objectivism. However, I find nothing in Professor White's paper that has forced me to relinquish this ideal.

NOTES

1. Professor White's use of the distinction is reminiscent, of course, of the manner in which Croce used the same terms. Cf. B. Croce, *History, Its Theory and Practice,* tr. Douglas Ainslie (New York, 1921). However, the Crocean mode of drawing the distinction was so closely tied to Croce's own assumptions regarding knowledge that it is considerably less useful than Professor White's more neutral characterization of the difference between chronicle and history.

To be strictly accurate, however, the contrast should not simply be between "history" and "chronicle," for chronicles (in a strict sense) are but one of the varieties of recording the past which differ from "history" as either Croce or White would use that term. Cf. Ernst Bernheim, *Lehrbuch der historischen Methode* (Leipzig, 1908), ch. 1, sec. 2, on the various forms of "referierende Geschichte."

2. I am inclined to think that the term "central subject" which Professor White also uses (cf. p. 5 and *passim*) is preferable to either "entity" or "event," a term which I formerly used. I suggest this because we do have histories of what would not normally be called "an entity" (e.g., a military history of the Civil War), and we also have histories of what would not ordinarily be called "an event" (e.g., the history of the reigning house of Great Britain). I shall therefore borrow the term "subject" (meaning thereby "central sub-

ject," as Professor White uses that term) in order to replace either "entity" or "event."

3. I should suppose that we can consider this as a "central subject," although Professor White may be using that term in a more restricted sense, since he says that histories having "a central subject" are merely one species of histories. When he compares such histories to *Moll Flanders* one might think that "central subject" is to be taken as being confined to those cases in which a narrative centers upon one person only, but then his lugubrious history would not have a central subject, and he has promised to confine his attention to histories of this species.

In the absence of express statements to the contrary, I shall take it that a dynasty (or the like) can be used as an example of "a central subject" in an historical account.

4. To be sure, in his more formal statement of what constitutes a history, Professor White does make an implicit reference to the fact that he is concerned with the history of a particular subject, by using the symbol "S" as he does (on pp. 6–7) in the following schema: "One might say that in the simplest case [a history] consists in asserting 'Because *A* was true of *S* at time t_1, *B* was true of *S* at time t_2. And because *B* was true of *S* at time t_2, *C* was true of *S* at time t_3, and so on.' "

5. It will be recalled that both Carl L. Becker and Charles A. Beard assumed that history deals with the total human past. This was one of the most potent sources of their relativism, since if the historian's selection of facts must be made from among *all* things said and done in the past, and is not confined to those which are directly relevant to a particular subject matter, it is difficult to see how any standard of selection other than one dominated by the historian's own interests can be applied.

Professor White's way of formulating the problem of selection avoids making this the obvious conclusion to be drawn from the fact that historians are necessarily selective in their accounts of the past.

6. I originally borrowed this concept from the doctoral dissertation of K. Milanov, who is presently teaching at the University of Tasmania. Cf. my *Problem of Historical Knowledge: An Answer to Relativism* (New York, 1938).

7. I confess to surprise at finding Professor White (on p.25) suddenly introducing the notion of "memorability," which has far

closer affinities to existentialist ways of interpreting what is involved in historiography than it has with positions which one would expect him to adopt. For my part, I find it misleading to speak of history as "an extension of memory" unless the historiographer has himself lived through or has witnessed the events which he records. While I know what it means to say 'I remember my third-grade-teacher,' and also that 'I remember that my sister had an auto accident' (which I didn't witness) and that 'I remember that my father was angry at her because of it' (which I certainly did witness), I don't know what it means to say that I "*remember*" that I was born at my parents' home, and not in a hospital, although I do know from the record of my birth that this is true.

PART II

The Problems of the Working Historian

4

Some Problems of a Working Historian

LEO GERSHOY
New York University

PROFESSIONAL HISTORIANS have enjoyed no immunity against disagreement over the postulates of their craft and the procedures to be followed in overcoming inherent perplexities. One way of solving problems was to carry on with day-by-day work and ignore their existence. This approach has been followed, but one cannot recommend it as definitive. Another, also long pursued, was to turn to philosophy for aid if not for consolation; and philosophers of history as well as philosophically-minded historians, it must be granted, have generously offered detailed analyses of the nature of the problems along with learned suggestions for their solution. Those suggestions, for a variety of reasons, have not invariably been accepted. Thus, while disagreement exists within the ranks of historians, something less than an entente cordiale prevails between them and philosophers.

This is a regrettable state of affairs, for the indebtedness of practicing historians to philosophers of history is great. As he goes about his day's work, the historian is drawing, even when he is least conscious of it, upon someone's theory of history. The philosophy may be Hegel's, though I am disinclined to believe it. Most certainly in this year of 1962, it is not Ranke's assumption that the historical facts, patiently amassed and critically tested for their accuracy, would speak for themselves and tell the historian and his readers how things actually happened and thereby what they meant. The professional American historian draws his conceptual sustenance, if not directly from Dilthey, Croce, and Collingwood, more likely from the native version of their relativism in Becker and Beard. And a sane and reasonable relativism, Becker's in particular, it remains, a generation after its enunciation.

Nor could one honestly deny that the great philosophers of history have been catalysts of historical consciousness. One may decry the grandiose systems they have built, their doctrinaire proclamations of laws, and the inevitabilities that they insinuate or overtly state, the dangers to which the abuse or even the use of their doctrines can lead history. Yet we owe much to them. Without the seminal suggestions, say, of a Karl Marx on the relations between economic realities and the superstructure of institutions and culture, without Tocqueville's sustained inquiry into the possibilities and the limitations of historical prognosis, without the exhilarating insights into human behavior and cultural and societal development of a Vico or a Toynbee, the awareness of the historian concerning his subject would be considerably leaner than it is. They are vital to the existence of working historians. Each philosopher in his own way has enlarged understanding of the human action and behavior which are the stuff of history.

As for the inherent problems of historical writing, the presentation of the procedures followed by a professional historian and the difficulties that he encountered in one particular inquiry will assuredly illustrate some of them. It may also, past experience notwithstanding, provide a point of departure for narrowing the area of disagreement among historians and between historians and philosophers. In any case, discussion of those problems is at least appropriate to a meeting of the Institute of Philosophy which is focused on the relations between the two disciplines of history and philosophy.

I decided, in speaking of "Some Problems of a Working Historian," to speak of the historian whose ways I knew best, that is myself. That the experiences of a towering practitioner of the craft are more interesting is indisputable, but I shared them only vicariously. So, paraphrasing Jean-Jacques Rousseau, I asked why should I go in search of Tocqueville to find out the perplexities that history put forth before me. I had studied and written about the large movement of the French Revolution and the antecedent period of the Old Regime. Most recently, I saw through the press the biography of a little-known figure of the eighteenth and nineteenth centuries, Bertrand Barère, in which I gave primary emphasis to his career during the Revolution. I chose to illustrate the procedures followed by one working historian, and the difficulties that attended those procedures from that field of professional activity.

Let me speak first and at some length about that hardy perennial, the historical fact, since all discussion of procedures and problems derives from settling the question of what constitutes the raw material of historical inquiry. My first interest in Barère was a seemingly simple query about the validity of an interpretation that he was a cowardly opportunist and a trimmer sucked into a fierce power struggle in which he displayed a skill amounting to genius in jumping unerringly on the bandwagon of the stronger. This judgment I first found in Lord Macaulay's essay on Barère in the *Edinburgh Review* of April 1844, and I questioned it from the start, probably for no other reason than that it was so intemperate in its expression. However, preliminary sampling of what a few other historians had written revealed that it was a dominant interpretation. Still unconvinced, I turned to the systematic bibliographical aids and guides to get the titles of published works on the subject as well as references to unpublished manuscripts where the facts were stored. Those facts were in the published debates of the several assemblies of which Barère was a member, in committee and club records, in newspaper accounts, diaries, memoirs, letters, and the like. Needless to add, there were references to a ponderous array of secondary sources, such as general histories, specialized monographs, and memoirs of contemporaries with whom Barère was in one way or another associated.

As I next proceeded to discharge my professional obligation of fixing in mind, or at least in notes, which of those facts were textually accurate and correctly dated—far from a simple matter since many of them were overlaid with legend and distorted out of resemblance to what had occurred—I soon saw that there were far more of them than I could handle without being overwhelmed by sheer weight of numbers. Not wishing to be swamped in a sea of statements, I did what everyone in real life does when he wishes to know what he is about, I set out to make a selection of facts significantly related to my inquiry.

That too was no simple matter. There were of course patently significant facts in Barère's career that he himself recognized as such, thus making it awkward for researchers to think otherwise. Such as, for example, casting his vote in January 1793, for the death of the former King Louis XVI whom earlier he had warmly praised; voting on June 2, 1793, for the arrest of the Girondins with whom he had once been close; shifting in July of the same year from a policy of co-existence with the great powers to one of all-out war; and his fateful break with Robespierre on 9 Thermidor. But there were scores of other facts, also indexed in the series of parliamentary debates or cited elsewhere, whose significance challenged easy evaluation. I was learning that without a criterion of selection, that is, a tentative hypothesis concerning Barère's particular involvement with the facts, I was effectively compounding confusion. I was unable to decide what data were relevant and in what context and what were not relevant.

Empirical investigation was teaching me that though the available data were potential raw material for the historian, and some of it essential, it did not by itself constitute history. I was learning that historical facts were statements or affirmations that certain events had taken place which I had the option to use or not use. There was no hard, irreducible cluster that had to be taken in toto. I could exercise a discretionary selection. Pragmatically speaking, historical facts, however numerous and detailed, did not take on significance for me until by using them and not ignoring them, I made them come to life. In that figurative sense I created them. Their existence could not be denied, but it was my selection that brought them into the world of history by lodging them in my mind for the purposes to which I intended to employ them. Without my consciousness that they were historical facts relevant both to Barère and me, they did not assume effective existence and there was in effect no Barère problem for me to examine. It did not exist by itself in the subject matter. Barère was the subject of those facts; he was at the same time the object of the reconstitution that I was making of their sequence and their meaning. By selecting those historical facts and not others, I was reweaving in my mind a fabric of events whose occurrences they affirmed and establishing a dialogue between them and myself. I was committing myself. This was as true for Barère's own affirmations about what he did and said and thought as it was for those made by other participants concerning his actions.

My difficulties did not end here. There were in all instances multiple affirmations that a particular occurrence had taken place, such for example Barère's voting to have Louis XVI guillotined. To decide that some of the later statements were totally worthless or almost so presented no problem. They were so far removed in time or place from the occurrence itself as to justify the tired quip that though history never repeated itself, historians frequently repeated each other. Nor was there any real problem in deciding that some of the affirmations made by participants themselves were at least of debatable value. Such was clearly the case when one came upon statements in which fervent royalists passionately damned Barère's behavior in the tragedy of the king's execution or intemperate Paris sans-culottes hailed it.

There was another order of difficulties, a more sophisticated problem, concerning historical facts, even those found in the primary sources where Barère's own words in speeches from the floor, proclamations to the nation, and committee reports were recorded. I had to go beyond certifying them for textual accuracy. I had to bear in mind that the statements he made concerning his actions were already processed in his conscious mind or by his unconscious emotions, or both, and sometimes processed more than once. In 1793, for example, when he voted to have Louis XVI executed, Barère had publicly called the ex-king a traitor, rhetorically proclaiming that kings did not belong to the human race; years later, in writing about the same event and behavior, he explained that condemning the king was "a sad duty disagreeable to [my] heart." He may have been sincere in the first instance or truthful in the second. For my immediate purpose it does not matter which. What does matter is that on both occasions he was part of the historical process. He was discussing and viewing it from a particular angle of vision, from the point that he then occupied in the moving procession of historical change. He was looking at it through his own prism of thought and belief, just as I was examining him through mine.

In part the Barère prism was compounded by the facets of his personality, by the qualities of his mind and heart. It was compounded also by impersonal forces larger than himself in which he was somehow caught up, he himself not knowing perhaps how much. And in 1792–1793 powerful mass movements and mass emotions certainly existed which gave a kind of determinist propensity toward bringing the king to trial and proving him guilty of counterrevolutionary intelligence with the enemy. So the undisputed fact that Barère voted as he did had to be interpreted and explained both in the context of his personality and the circumstances of the powerful emotions, drives, pressures, and organizational activities of Montagnard deputies within the National Convention and Parisian sans-culottes outside it, all of whom were bent on the king's death.

Nor was that all. He had not always been linked in personal association of thought and purpose with those forces. Hence to comprehend as fully and deeply as possible the fact of his action, I had to broaden my inquiry in two ways: first, to have it include those larger forces and second, to attempt to understand what there was in his prior experience and development that led him to associate himself with them and the sponsors of those forces. Barère as the object of my reconstituting his past was turning out to be a far more complex problem than he first seemed when I took on the original task of understanding his behavior. My inquiry had taken on broadened dimensions and was presenting greater perplexities than I had first imagined.

Moreover, as I began reviewing the procedures followed by many historians of the last century and a half who had written about Barère, that review empirically confirmed what common sense had already suggested, that those historians were also in the thick of an evolving interplay between selected facts and guiding hypotheses. Like participants, like Barère, like myself, they too were involved by their conscious thoughts or their unconscious emotions or by both. The interplay reflected, in some instances more and in others less, the societal and ideological circumstances of their present. Like all other historians, I too was reconstituting the past by putting the present into my research. And from all that I was moving toward the conclusion that Raymond Aron in his *Introduction to the Philosophy of History* (first published in French in 1938) and E. H. Carr, in his stimulating lectures, *What Is History?* (1961), expressed without aid from me or vice versa, that history was "a continuous process of interaction between the historian and his facts, an unending dialogue between the present and the past." I was finding out that though historical facts constituted a hard core in "a surrounding pulp of disputable interpretations," as Sir George Clark put it, the reverse was paradoxically not less true. Without accurate and verifiable historical facts, interpretation was empty; without hypothesis, the facts were blind.

Take by way of concrete, if complex, illustration of this contention a pivotal moment in Barère's revolutionary career, the crisis of Thermidor, Year II (July 1794). On that occasion he aligned himself with a loose and somewhat unsavory coalition of anti-Robespierrists whose only tight point of agreement was their determination to topple the Incorruptible from power. They were successful in that resolution, and Robespierre was overthrown on 9 Thermidor. By many historians it was held that Barère joined the plotters at the last moment, not because he shared their design, but because he then realized that they would win out. The hypothesis that guided my explanation was different and less angular. It ran somewhat as follows: before he took his final stand, Barère had tried to mediate a bitter dispute within the Committee of Public Safety in order to maintain its unity and effectiveness of action. He had also endeavored to ward off attacks that other avowed enemies of Robespierre outside the Committee were making on him. Reluctantly, because he convinced himself, little by little, that breaking Robespierre's hold over the Committee was more desirable than having the Incorruptible dominate it, he opted for the former. Once he made his decision, he joined with the opposition and played an active and important part in Robespierre's downfall.

Did that hypothesis, as it finally fashioned itself, exist in my mind? Of course it did, and my subjective point of view entered into it. Did I, in formulating it, exclude or falsify the evidence? I do not think so. I had begun by positing one principle of explanation based upon empirical data and concurrently selecting and analyzing evidence on the basis of that tentative hypothesis. But as I went along in my inquiry, I found that I was observing the old evidence differently because I had meantime come upon revealing clues concerning Barère's behavior that I had not previously noted. I had initially noted that Barère repeatedly maintained on the floor of the National Convention that all was harmony in the ranks of the policymakers. I had also observed Barère publicly praising Robespierre as "a great republican," whose "patriotic reputation [was] justified by five years of toil and [adherence] to unshakable principles." But additional investigation disclosed the absence of harmony in the Committee; it also disclosed a Barère who was covertly edging his way to a position against the man whom he was openly praising. I modified my first hypothesis concerning the springs of his behavior. By fusing new hypothesis with the data, I found myself observing the circumstances of my problem differently. I was still viewing Barère through my filter, but my filter was now different.

Was my procedure an instance of an irresponsible subjective relativism which made the conclusions reached by any historian as valid as those reached by any other historian? I am not prepared to agree that this is so. It was not violating the canons of scientific method. The logic of my inquiry was not fundamentally different from that of the scientist. Like him, I was relying upon singular statements; like him, I was tacitly assuming that there were empirical regularities in occurrences and that explanation of those regularities was based upon an assumed causal dependence within the component parts of a situation or development. The elements constituting my filter or prism could be tested like any scientific explanation for accuracy, cogency, and logic.

While the knowledge that the historian derives from historical facts is of a different nature than the knowledge that the scientist obtains from his instruments and his procedures, the most scientifically conducted research cannot transcend an intrinsic margin of uncertainty in his interpretation. In that respect the historian is a little in the position of the subatomic physicist whose knowledge of the phenomena he investigates cannot entirely be divorced from the character of the instruments used to obtain it, and where he cannot determine accurately both the position and the momentum of the electron at the same time.

But how much certainty does remain and how much of that certainty concerning a unique situation can be generalized? Does history have room within it for the kind of generalization that science makes? As a professional historian I was primarily concerned with the particular situation of Thermidor. Like the scientist, however, though in ways peculiar to my own discipline, I could not escape generalizing either overtly or by implication. I could not help wondering how much of the stuff of every conciliator and mediator there was in Barère and how much Barère there was in all of us. The dangers of generalization, I think one will agree, are not less for an historian when he goes beyond the particular and the unique than they are for other human beings. Each advance in understanding the human situation brings with it a frustrating warning of how little we actually understand of what happened in the past and why it happened as it did. The fresh insights that we obtain from psychologists, from sociologists, from economic historians, are tantalizingly paradoxical in revealing the existing limitations of understanding. How much do we know, for example, of the nature of thought and behavior, of the psychological-biological-physical-chemical bases of individual action and speculation? To what extent is human behavior the result of drives, how much or how little is it a homeostatic, self-regulating, developmental process tending to reach and maintain a core of norms and procedures established in the protoplasm? I do not have to lacerate the flesh and stress the fact that I share the ignorance of qualified investigators. But the conclusion to note is not the limitations of understanding, rather that each advance still does increase the possibility of fuller understanding of the nature of individuals and the situations in which they find themselves, hence adds to the possibility of more valid generalizations. The enlarging experience of history, as it makes use of those advances and employs new auxiliaries, builds a bridge between the unique situation and situations not yet existent.

As I deployed between my present and Barère's past, between the unique occurrence and its meaning for today and tomorrow, I found the particular and the general forming a whole. The particular was Barère's course of action. The general was the question of how men similar in their nature and placed in roughly comparable situations were likely to act. In reflecting on the general problem, I drew upon what Barère did in Thermidor, what he had done in the crisis of June 2, 1793, and on what he did on the occasion of the trial of the king. I also drew upon the experience of earlier would-be pacificators of history, such for example, as the *Pacifiques* in the religious wars of the sixteenth century. I also looked back to the Barère experience from the dilemmas of hopeful mediators in the tensions of the cold war of today.

Obviously, the particular judgment I made that a network of relations impelled Barère to attempt to preserve governmental unity by sacrificing Robespierre is not a generalization concerning individuals in a crisis which is valid in the sight of eternity. More or less similar combinations of circumstances impelled conciliators to act differently in the past; they may also impel would-be mediators today and tomorrow to act as Barère did. No situation is ever exactly comparable with another, no facts identical. The limits of generalization, even more of prediction, are palpable. Generalizations are bound to be incomplete and inexact. Yet for all that, something durable and constant does remain. There is no guarantee that the generalization concerning Barère's behavior will retain worth or value for the future. No past has a fixed, definitive future; the future evolves from the processes of history. Generalizations drawn from Barère and his situation in the power struggle do not inform us in advance how mediators will act in a contemporary power struggle. They can have no universal validity nor absolute predictive certainty. They do, however, suggest the range of the possible. In them there is a conditional validity, a working measure of probability. They may prove useful and valuable; at least they are legitimate.

One may again ask at this point if my argument does not make the reconstitution of the past a hopelessly subjective affair, dooming in advance all efforts toward an objective search for truth. Does it not virtually compel the historian—and his bewildered reader—to cry out with Carl Becker, half ironically, half despairingly: "O history, how many truths have been committed in thy name!" My answer to such a query would be no. I believe that research so conducted maintains the possibility of coming as close to objectivity as the writing of history inherently permits. It permits the historian to get all the truth possible and adequate for him within the commitment that he has made. It does not inhibit him, himself, from checking "scientifically"—let us use the accusing word—on what he is doing. It places no prohibition on his fellow workers to test his research—the facts that he gathers and the criticism of the data, the hypothesis he employs and the presentation that he makes—to test it for accuracy, cogency, and logic.

I was aware that my inclination to think rather well than ill of much that Barère did or endeavored to do was rooted in the values of my personal experience. No reminder was needed to inform me that other historians were not guilty of sharing that predisposition. Nor did I have to remind myself that my selection of significant facts was also and somehow a function of a larger body of ideas, tenets, rationalities and irrationalities, and values of the communal culture of which I was a part. But in that very awareness was there not a kind of built-in check and control upon my working practices? Did not that self-consciousness strike a line through the "No" of the "No Exit" sign over my subjective universe? Did it not also open up to me the possibility of utilizing additional insights available to the historian from the contemporary understanding of human behavior that advances in psychology, social theory, scientific knowledge of the physiological and chemical structure of man afforded, even to have myself psychoanalyzed for Clio's sake? It does not follow that the historian takes advantage of those opportunities to cut himself loose from his personal moorings; it does follow that he may rise above himself and to some degree hold himself and his subject-object at arm's length. And when he does not, even when he does, he always has his professional colleagues to apply the criteria of scientific research to his deficiencies.

By way of making the theoretical argument specific, did I maintain or achieve objectivity and detachment as I set up a pattern of action in which I found a cause-consequence relationship in Barère's actions? Take the situation which reached its denouement on June 2, 1793, when he acquiesced in the arrest of the Girondin leaders. In common with all historians from the very beginning of historical inquiry, I postulated without demurrer that human behavior was determined by causes and that those causes in principle were ascertainable. Though David Hume devastatingly proved a long time ago that that belief could not be validated by unassisted reason prior to experience, nevertheless it was a belief necessary to all scientific thinking. Without that postulate the historian also could not function. Since he could not postulate a universally unchangeable pattern of causation which would explain satisfactorily every comparable situation, he looked for a pattern in the particular occurrence that was the object of his inquiry. In that way I set up a configuration of causal sequences for Barère's behavior in the event that occurred on June 2, 1793. The items that made up this configuration were not of equal importance. I set up a hierarchy of significance and I established priorities.

I was aware that I was not obliged to seek all the historical facts that were theoretically available and that I could not give a total explanation even if they did lie at hand. I was aware also that in that texture of June 2 I introduced my knowledge of his antecedent efforts to keep the unity of the National Convention intact by achieving a synthesis of belief and action among the bourgeois revolutionary deputies of that assembly. I drew upon such historical facts as his attempts to dissuade the Girondin spokesmen from establishing an armed guard in Paris ostensibly to protect Paris from its irresponsible sans-culottes, his maneuvers to prevent the impeachment of such anti-Girondin leaders as Robespierre and Danton, his futile endeavor to minimize the fears and the revulsions of feeling that welled forth when Louis XVI was guillotined. Into my pattern there also entered his many other endeavors, immediately before June 2, to save the Girondins in spite of themselves from a fate which their political ineptitude was bringing closer. And into it went my appreciation of his ultimate conviction that to give up the obstructionist Girondin leaders was the price that had to be paid to keep the assembly in control of the revolutionary movement.

By following that conduct did I observe or move toward objectivity? Here, well-qualified workers would give the answer, but whatever the answer would be in this particular instance, I would maintain that the procedure qua procedure did not deny me the opportunity to do so. Without violating the agreed upon canons of research, the method in itself did not preclude detachment or impair the possibility of rising above the limitations of personal involvement. It wove a pattern of causal interpretation. If anything, it postulated a high degree of determinism in Barère's actions, which the historian observed but did not create or superimpose upon the occurrences. Moreover, in recognizing a determinism of cause and effect, it did not go to the extreme of predicating inevitabilities. It left room for the unforeseen, the contingent, the haphazard, the accidental. All participants, and Barère not least, were free at crucial or decisive moments not to do what they did do. Within the large confines of determinism the actors were free. "Necessity and irresistibleness," to use Tocqueville's phrase, were not one and the same. The Girondins might have benefited from free will to exercise the prudence and the wisdom that they did not. They need not have suffered from the freedom of displaying such staggering recklessness at the crescendo of their struggle with the Jacobins as threatening to raze Paris to the ground. Barère was free to remain linked to the end with the cultivated men whose society he enjoyed instead of sacrificing the Girondins to their folly for what he deemed a greater good. A philosophy of inquiry that recognizes a determinist causal pattern in occurrences and allows for the contingent, even for irresponsible free will, transcends subjectivism. It is as scientific, objective, and detached as history by its nature can be.

In reviewing the problems that confronted me as a working historian, I concluded first, that the approach to their solution which I would still call relativist was inescapable, and second, that one *could* move toward "the edge of objectivity" or even beyond. I could not isolate my research from the insights that the sciences and the social sciences are now providing for a deeper and richer comprehension of the human condition. As has been true since at least the time of Aeschylus, the historian still drew sustenance from the wisdom of the great creative writers. It was not a scientist who first probed into the Oedipus complex. The historian has at his disposal today instruments and techniques which add new dimensions to his understanding the behavior and the motives, reasoned and irrational, of individuals and the groups of which they were parts. Far more than was the case with their predecessors, historians today are offered opportunities for moving toward a detachment that the limitations of critical awareness had frequently denied them in the past. I would not willingly place myself on record as saying that historians will invariably avail themselves of the newer opportunities of escaping the dangers inherent in the highly personal nature of the colloquium between the historian and his facts, or that they can now triumphantly transcend the inherent limitations of the dialogue between the past and the present. I would prefer to say that they are given a greater chance to do so and that their failure to take advantage of these opportunities can be more readily established by historians within the fold and philosophers outside than was true before.

This confidence in the greater possibility of a harmonious understanding among historians as well as between working historians and philosophers of history may be naïve. But it was rather reinforced by this self-inquiry than born of it. Perhaps this confession explains why I nourish what may be a delusion. I never wholly agreed with the pessimists of the guild who, now for a whole generation, have been shaking their heads sadly over the plight of history, seeing its long domination as an intellectual discipline, the intellectual discipline, ended. It cannot be denied, of course, that there is lessened public confidence in history as an all-embracing explanation of human developments and change in a time-space continuum. The long debate between present-minded and past-minded historians, which one could follow in the pages of the professional journals, revealed the shortcomings of the historians' methodology without arriving at fresh approaches on which they could all agree. It is also true that many younger historians, retreating in intellectual confusion from the spectacle of their mentors engaged in heated and not overwhelmingly edifying disputation, became bewildered and skeptical. Bereft of philosophical certainty and justification for their work, they carried on their assignments, hoping perhaps that by not taking thought themselves, they would add cubits to their stature and that somehow all would come out well at the end. There was agreement with many thoughtful critics that in a rapidly changing world for which history gave no satisfactory explanation, the bases and the premises of existing historical thought had to be thoroughly reconsidered, lest other disciplines took over by default, leaving history to itself as a jigsaw puzzle without solution or a nightmare from which readers would seek to escape.

All that could not be gainsaid. But the tide of despondency, it seems to me, has turned; historians have been taking steps forward toward the asked-for reconsideration of their postulates. If by itself the flow of highly specialized postdoctoral monographs is not prima facie evidence that the younger generation of researchers is less bewildered than it ought to be, the stream of essays, articles, and books on the nature of history and the avid interest of readers in such writings, suggests that historians have grown out of the age of philosophical innocence. They are consciously and systematically searching for an area of agreement concerning the problems immediate to their research. More than searching, they are converging upon mutually acceptable answers to the questions about the kind of knowledge that the historian seeks and the nature of the data that he uses. They seem to be in closer agreement than they were, say, even only thirty years ago, on the relation between the hypotheses they posit and the empirical facts they assemble and examine. The limitations of objectivity are understood as they have always been understood or sensed by historians and, sometimes eloquently, sometimes harrowingly, illuminated in the writings of the great men of letters. Yet, the possibilities of detachment within the ancient discipline of history are more consciously apprehended.

The dual nature of that old discipline as art and science, personal involvement and objective inquiry, interplay between the past and the specious present, remains what it was when Herodotus first began to practice it: remains what it was, but more fully understood, more sensitively felt. The Golden Age of history may still lie ahead.

A SELECTED BIBLIOGRAPHY

Becker, Carl L. "Detachment and the Writing of History," *Atlantic Monthly,* CVI (1910), 524–36.

———. "What Are Historical Facts?" *Western Political Quarterly,* VIII (1955), 327–40.

———. "Everyman His Own Historian," *American Historical Review,* XXXVII (1932), 221–36.

Berlin, Sir Isaiah. *Historical Inevitability.* Oxford, 1954.

Bloch, Marc. *The Historian's Craft.* New York, 1953.

Carr, E. H. *What Is History?* London, 1961.

Collingwood, R. G. *The Idea of History.* Oxford, 1946.

Dray, William. *Laws and Explanation in History.* Oxford, 1957.

Gershoy, Leo. *Bertrand Barère: A Reluctant Terrorist.* Princeton, 1962.

Hexter, J. H. "The Historian and His Day," *Political Science Quarterly,* LXIX (1950), 219–33.

Hodges, H. A. *The Philosophy of Wilhelm Dilthey.* London, 1952.

Holborn, Hajo. "Wilhelm Dilthey and the Critique of Historical Reason," *Journal of the History of Ideas,* XI (1950), 93–128.

Marrou, H. I. *De la connaissance historique.* Paris, 1956.

Meyerhoff, Hans (ed.). *The Philosophy of History in Our Time.* New York, 1959.

Nagel, Ernest. *The Structure of Science.* New York, 1961.

Seidenberg, Roderick. *Posthistoric Man.* Chapel Hill, N.C., 1950.

5

Relativism and Some Problems of Working Historians

ERNEST NAGEL
Columbia University

LIKE OTHER intellectual workers, professional historians are rarely self-conscious about the organizing concepts or the principles for assessing evidence which they habitually employ in their discipline. To be sure, historians have written extensively on the specialized techniques of their craft as well as on the general problems that arise in the external and internal criticism of documents and other remains of the past. Nevertheless, serious discussions of such broad questions as the structure of historical explanations, the grounds upon which they are warranted, and in particular the logic of causal imputation in historical research, have in the main been carried on by professional philosophers or philosophically minded students in other branches of social inquiry. When historians do express themselves on such issues (usually on ceremonial occasions), they are therefore likely to voice philosophical ideas imbibed by chance during their school days or in their desultory reading, but which they have seldom subjected to rigorous criticism in the light of their own professional experience. At any rate, this hypothesis helps to explain the radical skepticism (or "relativism") professed by many contemporary historians concerning the possibility of objective knowledge in their discipline, despite the fact that in their substantive historical analyses they do not practice what they preach.

Professor Gershoy's instructive and gracefully written account of the considerations that controlled the researches incorporated in his recent biography of Bertrand Barère is a notable exception to these general remarks. The main concern of his paper is the relativity of historical knowledge. He describes himself as a "sane and reasonable relativist," attributing his moderate relativism at least in part to the influence of his teacher, the late Carl Becker, but claims nevertheless that objective knowledge is within the historian's effective reach. However, he does not assert these views without examination, but advances them as reasoned conclusions based on an analysis of the procedure he followed in his study of Barère. Although his reading of Becker's relativism as "reasonable" seems to me overgenerous, I am in substantial agreement with Mr. Gershoy's conclusions as well as with the general tenor of his argument, and it would serve little purpose in the present context to express my dissenting opinions on issues not strictly relevant to his central theme. On the other hand, it may be useful to clarify Mr. Gershoy's moderate relativism by asking how the objective but relative knowledge of the past, which he thinks the historian can attain, differs from objective knowledge *simpliciter,* without the qualification of being only relative. I will therefore devote the first part of my comments to this question. In the second part I will note briefly some problems of historical inquiry which Mr. Gershoy has not discussed, but which because of their importance deserve careful study.

1

Since Mr. Gershoy's analysis is intended to reveal as well as to support his moderate relativism, let us examine the successive steps of his inquiry as he presents them, in order to identify whatever may be distinctively "relativistic" in historical investigations that is manifested in them.

a) He begins his presentation by recording his early doubts about the dominant interpretation of Barère as a cowardly opportunist, doubts which eventually assumed the form of the problem of "understanding Barère's behavior" that initiated his own inquiry.

b) Mr. Gershoy next reports some of his efforts to ascertain which of the alleged facts concerning Barère's specific actions (upon which the dominant interpretations of the latter's character are based) are supported by reliable documentary evidence; and he makes clear the various difficulties he faced in this undertaking.

Thus far, at any rate, I can find nothing "relativistic" that sets off historical investigations from any others. Thus, while Mr. Gershoy's inquiry was addressed to the solution of a particular problem, all inquiries are initiated by unsolved questions, even if the circumstances under which particular problems are generated vary with individuals and disciplines. Furthermore, although reliable evidence for factual claims is often unavailable or incomplete, this is true in every area of study and not only in history, but is manifestly not *always* true; for despite Mr. Gershoy's difficulties on this score, he appears to have no doubt that many claims concerning Barère's behavior and thought constitute unqualifiedly objective knowledge.

c) Mr. Gershoy points out that even when he satisfied himself as to the solidity of such facts about Barère, he did not consider all of them, but selected some and ignored others in the light of what he calls a "tentative hypothesis concerning Barère's particular involvement with the facts." Moreover, he observes that such facts "did not assume effective existence," until he recognized their relevance to his hypothesis.

However, although the fact that the historian selects even his "raw materials" on the basis of explicit or tacit assumptions is commonly cited as evidence for the distinctively "relativistic" character of historical reconstructions, it is not clear just how that evidence supports this conclusion. No inquiry in any discipline can possibly concern itself with the inexhaustible totality of specific facts belonging to its subject matter, so that the selection of some facts and the ignoring of others is a characteristic of all investigations and not only of historical ones. In Mr. Gershoy's inquiry, moreover, the principle of selection (or hypothesis) was admittedly tentative; and it was therefore presumably a conjecture which could be confirmed or refuted on the basis of evidence that can be established *independently* of the hypothesis. It is more difficult to test such hypotheses when investigators are not explicitly aware (as Mr. Gershoy apparently was) of the assumptions controlling their selection of facts; but in this case also, the selections can nevertheless be challenged in the light of explicit hypotheses that can be tested. Accordingly, the selection of facts even in historical inquiry is ultimately not a wholly arbitrary matter, which reflects nothing but the personal or social biases of the investigator, but is in principle capable of objective assessment and correction. Nor can Mr. Gershoy's claim that the facts he selected did not assume an "effective existence" until he became conscious of their significance, be construed as an argument for relativism. For his claim is only an emphatic assertion that the selected facts could be used by himself in resolving the problem of his inquiry only after he had grasped their import, and he obviously does not (indeed, could not) mean that he actually created those facts when he recognized their relevance.

d) Something more pertinent to relativism appears in Mr. Gershoy's account of the next step in his inquiry. He reports his discovery, to which he assigns great methodological importance, that Berère's statements about his own actions cannot be taken at face value but have to be construed as products of Barère's conscious and unconscious processes—that is, as statements about what he did and thought which Barère made from a certain historical perspective. Accordingly, rather than accepting Barère's statements as unvarnished and unbiased *descriptions*, they must be viewed as *interpretations* of what actually happened, and hence as assertions embodying various beliefs and preconceptions Barère held as a child of his time. Mr. Gershoy generalizes the point of this discovery and maintains that, like the statements of Barère and of other participants in the events in which Barère was involved, the statements of all later historians of Barère's actions (including the statements of Mr. Gershoy himself) reflect the "societal and ideological circumstances of their present," so that historians succeed in reconstructing the past only "by putting the present" into their researches.

However, the significance which Mr. Gershoy attaches to his discovery is not entirely clear. On the one hand, he seems to be maintaining no more than that although the task of establishing the reliability of factual claims contained in documents is more complex and perplexing than is often assumed, the complexities do not preclude the possibility of objective knowledge concerning the alleged facts. For example, his assertion that Barère's statements about his own actions reflect the effects on Barère of the circumstances under which those actions occurred, obviously imputes a causal (and apparently a distorting) influence to certain events in the past upon Barère's view of those events. In consequence, Mr. Gershoy's account of his discovery assumed that this causal imputation is objectively grounded, for otherwise he would have no foundation for his claim that he made the discovery; and he says nothing in this context to place in doubt the possibility of establishing such causal imputations in general, even if on frequent occasions statements about causal relations may lack adequate support. Moreover, the prima-facie intent of this account is to show that in view of the causal influences upon Barère, the latter's statements about his own conduct must be used with great caution as evidence of what he actually did. Mr. Gershoy is here certainly not questioning the possibility that objective knowledge of Barère's conduct is attainable. On the contrary, the context of these remarks requires that he be understood as saying that the difficulties noted do not in principle exclude the possibility of obtaining firmly grounded and reasonably accurate knowledge of Barère's actions—for example, perhaps by examining and comparing a sufficient number of statements by Barère and other contemporary witnesses of the latter's behavior, and making suitable allowances for the distorting effects of various influences upon the authors of those statements.

On the other hand, Mr. Gershoy's account of his discovery

can also be construed to mean that since in their reconstructions of the past historians have their base of operations in the present, their statements embody the biases of their social class and particular intellectual climate, so that the statements are not timelessly true or false, but are "historically conditioned"—i.e., that the degree of validity their statements possess is in some sense "relative" to the place and period of their origin. Something like this view is suggested by E. H. Carr (to whom Mr. Gershoy refers) when he declares, "Before you study the history, study the historian. . . . Before you study the historian, study his historical and social environment." (E. H. Carr, *What Is History?* [New York, 1962], p. 54.) But even on this construction, Mr. Gershoy's account, and in particular his assertion that the historian puts his present into his researches into the past, is eminently sound, if its claims are the innocent ones that the past can be viewed only through the eyes of the present; that historians bring to their study of the past the knowledge available to them in the present; that the standards a historian employs in assessing the evidence for a proposed historical reconstruction are standards of validity regarded as sound in the present; and that historians are therefore exposed to the danger (and indeed, are often victims of it) of imparting into their reconstructions unwarranted assumptions derived from their involvement in the events of their own historical period, anachronistic interpretations of human actions in the past, erroneous explanations of past events because of the limitations of present knowledge, or otherwise dubious statements which may be supported by evidence consonant with some currently accepted canons of validity, but which are unsatisfactory in the light of more rigorous and reliable standards. However, none of these truisms is applicable exclusively to historical inquiry, none of them is ground for believing that the errors and biases of which historians may be guilty are in principle uneliminable, and even if they are taken in conjunction they constitute no reason for denying that objective historical knowledge is possible.

In any event, Mr. Gershoy's "relativism" would not be "sane and reasonable," and his standpoint would be radically incoherent, were he to maintain that, in view of his discovery, no statement about the past can conceivably be simply true or false, and that the factual validity of any such statement varies with the historical circumstances in which it is made or its merits are considered. Although I do not fully understand what is being said by those who profess a relativism of this extreme kind, let me recall a familiar, but in my judgment fatal, difficulty in it by noting some consequences entailed by E. H. Carr's dictum quoted above, if this dictum is taken literally. According to Carr's injunction, the factual merits of a historical essay can be evaluated only if we first study the historical and social environment of the historian who wrote it. But if the historian flourished in the past, how can we study his environment and its influences upon him, except by studying some historical work on this subject? And if the historian is one of our contemporaries, how can we find out anything about his environment, except by either studying some contemporary analysis of that environment or undertaking by ourselves an independent historical study of the contemporary scene? In either case, however, we must at some point judge the factual worth of a historical reconstruction without first studying the historian and his environment (and hence must reject the version of relativism under discussion), or else embark upon an infinite regress whose only fruit is a skepticism so thoroughgoing that it destroys even the ground upon which this form of historical relativism is asserted to rest.

e) The culminating step in Mr. Gershoy's inquiry, as reported by him, was the introduction and elaboration of a hypothesis, differing from the commonly accepted one, to explain Barère's conduct in the Committee of Public Safety during the Thermidor crisis—a hypothesis which he finally enlarged into an overall interpretation of Barère as a man who was at heart a social reformer inclined to moderation, rather than a revolutionist without personal integrity. According to the usual view of Barère as a cowardly opportunist,

Barère joined the opposition to Robespierre at the last moment because he recognized that the opposition would be victorious in the struggle, and he acted so as to be on the winning side; but according to Mr. Gershoy, Barère voted against Robespierre only after futile attempts to mediate between the parties in the conflict, because he became convinced that the desirable objectives of the Revolution would be better achieved by Robespierre's defeat than by the latter's continued domination of the Committee. Mr. Gershoy notes that after this hypothesis occurred to him, he found himself "modifying" and "observing differently" the "facts" he had previously gathered and examined; and he suggests that this experience is but another illustration of the principle, advanced by many physicists on the basis of their interpretation of quantum mechanics, that "the observer is also part of the observed." Moreover, although he conducted his inquiry on the assumption that human behavior is determined by discoverable causes, he reports that he felt no obligation to find all the theoretically available determinants of Barère's behavior, and also that he recognized his inability to give "a total explanation" of that behavior even if he had found all those determinants. The upshot of Mr. Gershoy's reflections is that while his investigation does not exhibit Barère's actions as "inevitabilities," so that his explanation of Barère's conduct contains "an inescapable margin of uncertainty," such a margin is present in the conclusions of all scientific inquiry, and the procedure he followed in establishing his explanation is therefore "not an instance of irresponsible subjectivism."

Mr. Gershoy's reference to the Copenhagen interpretation of quantum mechanics seems to me of only doubtful relevance to his analysis; and I also find the account of his inability to provide a "total explanation" of Barère's behavior too brief to be clear. Moreover, he is disappointingly silent on the crucial question (to which I will return in the second part of my comments) of why he believes that his own explanation of Barère's conduct is better supported by the available evidence than the usual explanation. Nevertheless, there is nothing in what he does say that sets off the methodological difficulties he encountered as a working historian as radically distinct from those which confront students in other domains. His account makes evident that historians engage in research in order to solve particular problems, that in the course of their investigations they select and reinterpret data in the light of assumed knowledge as well as tentative conjectures, that they are subject to the risk of committing various kinds of errors in the conduct of their inquiries, and that no demonstrative certainty can rightly be claimed for their conclusions. However, if subscribing to the belief that these features characterize every scientific inquiry suffices for being designated as "a sane and reasonable relativist," it is unlikely that many contemporary scientists fail to qualify for this title.

2

It is clear from Mr. Gershoy's paper that his study of Barère involves many claims concerning the causes and effects of various particular occurrences. However, although he undoubtedly believes that in asserting them he is not expressing his personal vagaries but is basing them on competent evidence, he does not discuss how he established his causal imputations, or how he can distinguish between genuine and spurious causal claims. The absence of any examination of this question is a serious limitation of his defense of his reasonable relativism. For the question is centrally relevant for understanding the operations of the working historian, and it bears directly on the nature of the objectivity which Mr. Gershoy thinks historians can achieve in their inquiries. Indeed, if it could be shown that the causal imputations historians constantly make have no objective foundations, an extreme form of subjective relativism would in my opinion be inescapable. The question is notoriously difficult, admittedly unsettled, and cannot be handled adequately except at great length; and the following brief comments are intended only to note some of its complexities and to persuade historians that it merits their serious attention.

To avoid misunderstanding, let me repeat that the question under consideration concerns the grounds for *particular* causal imputations in historical studies, rather than for causal *laws.* Like everybody else, historians take for granted a host of *general* causal propositions, some of which are the explicitly formulated conclusions of the natural and social sciences, while others are the products of common-sense experience—for example, numerous causal laws of physics or economics, or much less precise generalizations such as that those who possess power over men tend to be corrupted by it. However, although historians assume such laws in their inquiries, they usually accept them as established in some other branch of inquiry, and are not expected by and large to be able to marshall the detailed evidence on which the assumptions presumably rest. On the other hand, it is a recognized task of historians to explain various features of particular happenings by exhibiting those features as causally related to other particular occurrences. In performing this task historians certainly employ causal laws. However, while historians are not primarily responsible for the validity of such laws, they are concerned to show that the particular causal imputations they make with the help of those laws really are sound—for even if the validity of the laws a historian assumes in his explanation is beyond reasonable doubt, he cannot assume, without further ado, that the conditions for applying the laws to some actual case are realized, and he must therefore provide evidence that his particular causal imputations are not mistaken. For example, it may be true that in general men who are dominated by passionate hatred try to injure the object of their hate; but it does not follow that because a given individual is known to hate another who suffered some deliberately inflicted injury, the given person actually inflicted the injury. The issue at stake is whether historians have ways of establishing such particular causal assertions on objective grounds.

Writers on historical method frequently disregard the obvious fact that there are many sorts of historical works, and that the occurrences narrated or explained even in works of the same sort are not homogeneous in kind but fall into distinguishable types. In consequence of such neglect, their analyses overlook the variety of logical problems which confront the working historian, and fail to codify and explicate the different logical techniques for assessing evidence in historical research. The controversial and relatively primitive state of much of the literature on the logic of causal imputation in history is an especially unfortunate result of this neglect. For example, many writers maintain that such imputations are purely subjective judgments, which cannot be evaluated in the light of objective evidence. However, they often make this claim largely because they do not distinguish between various types of factors to which historians ascribe a causal influence, tacitly assume that there is only one technique for identifying causes, and find that in historical inquiry this special technique is rarely if ever applicable to the type to which they mistakenly assimilate all causal factors.

Accordingly, an adequate analysis of the warrant for causal statements in history ought to begin with a systematic classification of the kinds of occurrences which historians attempt to explain causally, as well as of the types of factors to which they assign causal roles. Such typologies are not at present available, although some suggestions for constructing them can be found in the relevant literature. For example, if the discussion is restricted to human history, the objects of historical concern appear to fall into two main divisions: the actions of particular individuals, and the aggregative actions of groups of men; and a further distinction, which cuts across this classification, can be conveniently made between actions requiring relatively little time for their performance, and actions that are of considerable duration and that may be spread over a sizable region of space. Again, if we lump together and put to one side the various nonhuman events and circumstances recognized by historians to affect human life, the factors commonly invoked by causal historians as causal determinants of human actions can be classified under the following major heads: prior actions by individuals or groups;

the "reasons" or aims professed by individuals when pressed to account for their conduct; the motives that serve as springs of individual action; the acquired dispositions or habits of individuals; social customs and traditions; and the structure of social institutions and formal organizations. This list of possible causal factors is at best only a sketch, but it is long enough to make evident that the nature of the evidence required to support particular causal imputations must undoubtedly be quite different for different items on the list.

In any event, three questions basic to the logic of causal imputation in history must be mentioned.

a) Can the *existence* of an item alleged to be a causal determinant of some past action be conclusively established? Most historians would probably agree that the answer is in principle affirmative, although they would undoubtedly also add that because of practical difficulties in obtaining the requisite evidence, there is frequently insufficient ground for affirming with confidence the existence of such items. On the other hand, there is considerable dispute as to whether certain factors commonly designated as "subjective states" (e.g., reasons, motives, and dispositions) can properly be regarded as causal determinants; and some students also doubt whether the existence of such states can be objectively warranted, despite the fact that reliable techniques for doing just this have been developed and are currently widely used in empirical social research.

b) Taking for granted that the answer to the first question is affirmative, can compelling evidence be supplied for the claim that the item whose existence has been established really *did* operate as a causal determinant for the particular action under examination? This question must not be confounded with the previous one, and an affirmative answer to the first does not automatically assure an affirmative answer to the second. For example, it may indeed be the case that a given individual has a certain reason for acting as he did; it may nevertheless be erroneous to conclude that he acted as he did *because* of that reason, since it may not be generally true that such a reason is invariably accompanied by such an action, or that such an action never occurs in the absence of such a reason. Thus, suppose it is beyond dispute that a certain individual had a strong sexual passion for a particular woman, and that he subsequently married her. However, he may not have married her because of his sexual desire for her, even if he believed that this was the reason for his doing so. For although strong sexual attraction often leads to marriage, it does not do so always; and the man may in fact have married his wife because of her fortune, for which he may also have had a strong desire. Accordingly, the second question can be put into the following schematic form. Suppose that an action *A* often but not invariably follows upon the occurrence of one or the other (or both) of the characteristics *B* and *C*, and that an individual (or group of individuals) *x* performed *A* on a given occasion *t*. Assume first that *x* is known to have possessed *B*. Can an objective basis be supplied for the claim that *B* was a causal determinant for *x*'s action on occasion *t*? Assume next that *x* is known to have possessed both *B* and *C*. Is it possible to show that *B* rather than *C* was a causal determinant for *x*'s action on that occasion?

Historians rarely concern themselves with the second question in either of these two forms, whether explicitly in their discussions of historiographical problems or implicitly in their publications of substantive historical researches. As has already been mentioned, Mr. Gershoy's account of his own study of Barère contains no consideration of the question, despite the fact that the issues raised by the question are crucial for his claim that his interpretation of Barère's conduct is not just a personal preference. For this claim is not well taken unless his researches enabled him to establish two points: that Barère was at heart a moderate social reformer; and that it was this attitude rather than a disposition to cowardly opportunism which determined certain actions of Barère, such as his vote against Robespierre in the Committtee of Public Safety. Mr. Gershoy presents much evidence in support of the first point, and we may assume, if only for the sake of the argument, that he has established it beyond reasonable doubt. But this still leaves unsettled the second point, and I have been unable to find either in his paper or in his book, *Bertrand Barère,* a clear presentation of the evidence on which he rests his case for it. The assumed validity of the first point (i.e., that Barère was at bottom a moderate social reformer) is not incompatible with the supposition, affirmed by the dominant interpretation of Barère, which Mr. Gershoy rejects, that he was also a cowardly opportunist, so that Barère may in fact have had both of these dispositions. Accordingly, if Barère did have both of them, since either disposition (so it could be argued on the basis of our general experience) is often manifested in conduct similar to Barère's behavior, Mr. Gershoy is required to show, in order to establish his thesis, that one disposition rather than the other was actually operating as a causal determinant in the relevant instances of Barère's actual behavior. In short, the assumption that Mr. Gershoy has supplied firm ground for the first point is tantamount to saying that he has succeeded in giving an affirmative answer to the first of the above two questions; but it is not obvious to me that he has been equally successful in providing an affirmative answer to the second question. It is therefore not irrelevant to the problems of working historians to suggest that this second question deserves more study from them than it has thus far received.

Although there are serious difficulties in establishing particular causal imputations in history, some of the alleged ones seem to me spurious. Of the spurious difficulties, perhaps the most frequently cited one denies the possibility of supplying objective grounds for such imputations for the reason that history is not an experimental science. The historian, so the objection runs, deals with occurrences that, by definition, are unique and are no longer in existence. In consequence, their causal determinants cannot be isolated and identified by experimental means, since experiments are possible only if more than one instance of the phenomenon studied is available, and in any case experiments cannot be performed on things in the past. However, while this account of some of the conditions for experimentation is undoubtedly sound, it holds equally well for many domains other than history—for example, for investigations in the natural sciences directed to ascertaining the causes of particular events, such as quite specific landslides or fires, as well as for situations involving the discovery of the causes of specific human actions, as in criminal investigations. But despite the fact that these inquiries are not strictly experimental, it would be absurd to deny that reliable statements about causal relations can be made in them. Accordingly, the objection reveals only insufficient familiarity with the logical techniques employed in the sciences and everyday affairs for establishing particular causal hypotheses. However, I cannot on this occasion examine any of the genuine difficulties involved in attempts to provide objective support for such hypotheses in history, and can only state my belief that they are not insuperable in principle though frequently insoluble in practice.

c) The third question is no less crucial than the first two, but can also be discussed only briefly. Since historians do not (and in the nature of the case, cannot) state the complete set of sufficient conditions for any event they undertake to explain, but address themselves only to those of its causal determinants which they think are the "more important" ones, can such judgments concerning the relative importance of causal factors be supported by objective considerations? To avoid misunderstanding the point of the question, it perhaps needs mentioning that certain causal variables do not *normally* enter into historical explanations, even though their importance would probably be acknowledged by most historians, simply because these factors (e.g., physical or biological determinants of human life, often called "exogenous variables") are traditionally or conventionally regarded as falling outside the historian's professional concerns. However, the question is *not* about the grounds for the omission of such exogenous variables from historical explanations—for the omission is usually the result of a tacit division of labor between historians and other inquirers, and in point of fact historians frequently introduce exogenous variables into their explanations, as when the occurrence of a heavy rain is mentioned to account for the course of the battle of Hastings. The question *is* about the grounds on which historians assume certain *endogenous* variables (i.e., variables which are recognized to fall into the historian's province) to be more important than other endogenous variables—for example, about the basis for the claim made by some historians that the economic conflicts between the North and South were a more important cause of the American Civil War than were their moral differences over the issue of slavery. This last example suggests a further clarification of the question. The question must be understood to assume that the historian knows that the event he is studying has a number of causal determinants, *all* of which are strictly indispensable for its actual occurrence; and the issue raised by the question is whether, in asserting that some item in this set of determinants is more important than the others *also* in the set, he is saying anything that can be evaluated as true or false in the light of objective evidence.

The question nevertheless remains ambiguous, even after these explanations, because the term "important" as used by historians is not univocal, and its several relevant senses must therefore be first distinguished. However, none of the possible interpretations of the term can be listed here. In any event, the real difficulties facing attempts to answer the question begin only after these ambiguities have been removed. For, although judgments concerning the relative importance of various causal factors can be given verifiable meanings, so that such judgments can in principle be made to rest on firm evidential foundations, in practice the pursuit of the requisite evidence for achieving this goal is rarely easy and is frequently unsuccessful. But these fragmentary comments on a crucial question must suffice to indicate that more problems lie in the path of the working historian than he usually suspects, and that objective knowledge in history is not to be had for the mere asking.

6

The Problems of the Working Historian: A Comment

BERNARD BAILYN
Harvard University

PROFESSOR GERSHOY, in his paper on the problems of the working historian, has reached conclusions with which I both agree and disagree.

He has asked, first, "what constitutes the raw material of historical inquiry?" His answer is: facts, which are pieces of information, themselves inert and meaningless, charged with significance by the inquiring mind of the historian noting their relevance to the matter at hand. In this sense the "effective existence" of facts is a creation of the historian's consciousness. He has considered, second, the double question of the extent to which history is a science and the degree of objectivity that historians can achieve. His conclusion is that historians can "come closer to the objective procedures of the modern scientist than the relativist critics of Ranke had imagined possible," for though the historian's hypotheses are subjective in that they "exist in [his] mind" and though "the knowledge that the historian derives from historical facts is of a different nature than the knowledge that the scientist obtains from his instruments," nevertheless historical investigation is not so very different from scientific investigation: the scientist too makes hypotheses with his mind and he too does not obtain 100 percent certainty in his conclusions. As for the related question of how far one can generalize from the historical particular to the general and hence use history as the basis for predicting the future, Professor Gershoy answers that while generalizations from history have no "universal validity or absolute predictive certainty, they do . . . suggest the range of the possible" and furnish "a working measure of probability." In conclusion, Professor Gershoy describes himself as an optimist concerning the present tendencies within the discipline of history. He believes that younger historians, despite the gloomy things that have been said about them, are in fact agreeing more and more on "answers to the questions about the kind of knowledge that the historian seeks and the nature of the data that he uses," as well as on "the hypotheses they posit and the empirical facts they assemble and examine." There is, he feels, a growing sophistication among historians concerning causation and determinism, free will and inevitability, the unique and the general.

I find myself on the whole in agreement with these conclusions. I too believe that historians are capable of achieving a large measure of objectivity and impartiality; I too believe that raw data become effective facts when they are seen to be relevant by the historian's inquiring mind; and I agree that the discipline of history is flourishing, and that gloomy predictions about its future are unjustified.

What I disagree with is something more basic than these points. I wonder whether, if what one is concerned with is the actual problems of the working historian, he should be talking about such matters as these at all. I believe Professor Gershoy to have been too generous to a certain tradition in defining what the problems of historical study are. For there is a variety of problems involved in historical investigation, and while they are all in some way related to each other, there are yet significant distinctions among them. These distinctions are especially important when it is "the working historian" one is talking about. Problems of objectivity and subjectivity, the involvement or detachment of the inquiring mind, the nature of facts, and the predictive value of historical knowledge are obviously exciting and fruitful subjects for anyone, philosopher or historian, to consider. But they fall more naturally and immediately into the provinces of thought of the working philosopher, of a certain type of interest, than of the working historian. Let me put it more bluntly and personally. Like many historians, I have had a good deal of interest in these questions; and I have pursued them as far as time and ability have allowed me to. But insofar as my concern has been with understanding, teaching, and writing about what has happened in the past, I have never once felt it necessary to work out precise answers to such questions—questions of objectivity and subjectivity, the nature of fact, etc.—in order to advance my work in history. It may well be that that is too bad for me, that I am just a bad example, that I am intellectually insensitive, and that I would write better history if I spent more time on such matters. The last of these points, at least, I am quite sure is not true. What is more important is that though I have often discussed with other historians such matters as Professor Gershoy has presented, I have never yet heard from them, either, a statement to the effect that their work in history has been affected one way or the other by such considerations.

Let me be clear about this. I am not questioning the value of these problems as such. They are of course part of an important philosophical inquiry, and they are involved in the premises and in the ultimate conclusions to be drawn from historical knowledge; but the study of history is different from the study of the premises of historical thought no matter how intimately the two are related, and history is not, at least as most of us think of it, concerned with ultimate truth.

But why insist? The questions Professor Gershoy has discussed are of obvious importance in certain areas of thought even if they are not the problems of the working historian, and they undoubtedly involve the cosmic periphery and the elemental assumptions of the historian's work even if not its ordinary substance. The distinction is worth insisting upon, I believe, because if we accept the convention that these are *the* systematic problems that relate to historical study, we exclude from the consideration they deserve those other problems—humbler, perhaps, less ultimate, but more immediate problems—which historians must, in some way or other, solve in order to proceed with their work, and which they do in fact solve by extemporizations of varying degrees of crudeness. I realize that not all aspects of historical study need to be, or sensibly can be, dignified by "philosophical" analysis. But since I do not know what the boundaries of philosophy are and believe that philosophers, if not philosophy, can help the historian think more clearly and systematically about the questions with which he is daily confronted, I think it might be profitable if I attempted to sketch here, in a very tentative way, what I consider the problems of the working historian to be.

The work of the historian seems to me to group itself into three phases; and I would place the everyday problems he faces within these categories.

I. The first and, I would say, the least understood if not the most important, phase of historical study is the selection of topic.

The choices of topic modern working historians make appear to be based on observations of three distinct though partly overlapping kinds.

a) Historians decide to study and write about something because they observe that in the present state of the historical literature there is a *need* for such work, a need in the sense that a proper utilization of known resources has not been made. It might be observed, for example, that many valuable monographs and articles have been written on the French Revolution since George Lefebvre's survey was written; this new knowledge available to the specialists, one decides, should now be resynthesized with the old and a new master survey produced. Or, again, there might be a *need* for a textbook in economic history because none exists and one is needed for classroom use. Or one observes that there is a *need* for a good short narrative of the War in the Pacific, or of the Great Crash, or of Jefferson's public career—a need in the sense that the existing knowledge has not been made conveniently or properly available, and that there would be profit (in various senses) in making it available.

b) A second group of topics seems to be defined not by these considerations—considerations that we may call matters of strategy, academic, literary, even social or political—but by observations concerning the state of historical knowledge itself. These are topics that are suggested by what appear to be *gaps* in our knowledge: the consideration, for example, not that a book should be written because our knowledge has not been properly assembled or presented to best advantage, but because we do not have the knowledge of the subject that we wish to have. The motivation here is to learn something new and to present this new information; but the precise issues are not defined. There are no specific questions and no hypothetical answers. Thus the motivation for writing a narrative of a battle may be simply to discover what happened in it; to find out how it was that the victors won it. Or, again, one decides to do research and writing about Wilson's Administration because we are ignorant of it, and any thorough, clear narrative of it will be valuable because it fills an important gap, an evident vacuum.

c) A third group of topics is defined by what I would like to call true historical problems. I mean by true historical problems questions raised by the observation of (1) anomalies in the existing data, or (2) discrepancies between data and existing explanations. An example of the first would be the observation that in 1700, tobacco marketing in the Chesapeake area was handled by consignment to merchants located mainly in London; in 1760, much of it was handled by factors who lived in the colonies and were agents of firms largely located in Scotland. Why the change? The observation of the difference creates a problem of explanation, to solve which one undertakes research and writing. An example of the second type—a discrepancy between existing explanation and the data at hand—would be the following. For many generations, the American Revolution was explained as the spontaneous, unanimous uprising of a liberty-loving people against the heedless, not to say tyrannical, action of a power-hungry administration. But then it is discovered that many leaders in the colonies did not rise up as they were said to have done; indeed, a large number was openly sympathetic with the English actions, and they had the support, tacit or overt, of an estimated one-third of the population. Obviously, there is a problem here: either the Americans were not all liberty-loving, or the ministry's actions were not so heedless or tyrannical as they were thought to be, or perhaps the whole formulation is wrong; perhaps other considerations than tyranny or liberty were primarily involved. Let the subject be studied anew, then, and a more reasonable explanation given.

Needs, gaps, and *problems:* these three categories of topics obviously overlap. But they are perhaps distinctive enough in essence to serve as a starting point for more systematic thought than I believe has yet been given to the nature of historical topic-selection and problem-posing. For not every project we can conceive of that involves historical data is worth pursuing; not every question is a good one. What is the difference between a good historical problem and a poor one? Is there such a thing as a *false* historical problem? What are the criteria for deciding? Most practicing historians know a good problem when they see one; but they have acquired this knowledge from experience alone, and much of that experience is repetitious and wasteful. An efficient conceptualization would help, not in a cookbook sense by dictating the selection of problems to the historian, but by sharpening his awareness of the logic of the work he engages in and by informing him, in shorthand, of the experience that has so far been accumulated in pursuing it. One of the greatest values of the doctoral dissertation, it seems to me, is the almost universal experience gained in the process of writing it of discovering that one has given the right answers to the wrong questions. But such education, essential at one stage, becomes paralyzing if continued indefinitely.

Precise, orderly thought applied to this question would be more valuable to the working historian than volumes of speculation on whether it is conceivable to know the past, or what is the nature of a fact.

II. The second phase of the working historian's activity is the gathering of information: that is, *research*. Here again some systematic thought would be useful. Historical research is an analytical process. It is not, like most research in sociology or social psychology, a matter of creating the data one wishes to have after having defined a problem, expecting that analysis will follow; and it is not, hence, mechanical. It is the opposite of mechanical. It is a matter of creatively thinking one's way through a body of information. *Creatively* in the sense that the historian's great problem is deciding what to reject and what to accept as relevant to the subject he studies; and the determination of relevance can be a subtle process indeed. It has often seemed to me that the historian's research is analogous to the operation of a radar machine: he sends out hundreds of probes into the material and flashes the results back, searching for recognizable patterns. Like the radar operator he shifts his focus to take account of the location and configuration of the patterns he sees forming. This is so not only for the social historian; it is only more complicated for him since the events he depicts have structures that are more deeply submerged than those of the events that biographers or political historians usually describe. Much in historical work can be mechanized, and should be, but research must remain essentially this kind of creative process, a process in which the student, his radar wide open, probes the data with his mind, searching for patterns, for relevance, for significance. Often in the process the investigation becomes transformed. What starts as a gap becomes a true historical problem. Indeed, what starts out as a *need*, projected as a large-scale survey, can easily turn into a *gap* and end up as a *problem*, the solution to which may be properly presented in a pinpoint monograph.

But what are the broad problems worth the philosopher's attention in this connection? One seems to me to be preeminent.

In all their research, in their gathering of data, historians face the problem of the sufficiency or insufficiency of proof.

What do historians in fact mean when they say their research has proved something? Often I think they mean only that most qualified historians, given the same information they have examined, would arrive at the same conclusions they have arrived at. But this is more a psychological reflex than a logical explanation. The logic of proof, even in the humble sense in which the historian actually deals with it in his everyday work, would seem to be complicated. Do not the forms of proof differ, for example, according to the types of events we are talking about? Is not a different kind of proof required to demonstrate that Roosevelt died on April 12, 1945, than to prove or disprove Halévy's argument that the rise of Methodism accounts for the failure of a social revolution to take place in eighteenth century England? Are not the forms of proof different in the case of a specific, deliberate act whose evidences are strictly limited, from one which involves the attitudes of masses of people over a long period of time where the evidence is so voluminous that no historian can possibly exhaust it? What proof is there for the accounts historians give of the spirit of an age, the style of a society or a group—accounts like David Cecil's first chapter in his biography of Melbourne, that brilliant piece of impressionism called "The World"? Are the citations in Huizinga's *Waning of the Middle Ages* anything but illustrations of a series of conclusions beyond proof? Yet is not his book historical writing of the highest quality?

III. The final phase of the historian's work is the presentation of his material. The problems here are the most obvious and the least unusual of all those he deals with. But though they are unlikely to appear at first glance to be "philosophical" in character, they are no less susceptible than the others, I believe, to careful analysis at a high level of generality. I would like simply to mention, very briefly, two illustrations of the kind of difficulties the working historian faces in this connection.

The *choice of words* is crucial if only because it affects

the way in which the historian handles the problem of *distance.* Where does he stand in relation to the reader on the one hand and to the personalities and events he is describing on the other? Modern sociologists and psychologists, curiously enough, talk a great deal about themselves; that is, they report to the reader what they did in their study and what they discovered. Their writing does not consist solely and strictly of statements about the people or situations they have examined. The statements of this nature that they make most often include passages about themselves, about their methods, experiments, and reasoning. But the historian, like the novelist, writes sentence after sentence, descriptive or analytical, of those other people or situations. His effort is to keep the reader's mind constantly and evenly focused on the historical situation, not on his own; and his success in this can depend to a considerable extent on the kinds of words he chooses. An excessively subjective or connotative word can suddenly dislocate the author in relation to his reader and his subject by injecting the author's personality and forcing the reader to jump from one world to another. This, for example, explains the jarring effect of the single word A. L. Rowse uses to modify the final noun in this characteristic sentence about the English Puritans: "Leicester was on their side, and kept in with them, and spoke their somewhat nauseating language."

Much could be said about this question of word-choices as they relate to the historian's stance: the distance he assumes from the reader and from his subject. It is a problem that students of linguistic exposition are no doubt familiar with. But historians are not commonly aware of it; they do not sense the implications it has for their whole undertaking.

The use of figurative language in historical exposition also presents problems the working historian faces constantly. In what ways are metaphors and similes useful in historical prose? At times, when they are extended and used with great skill, as in Tawney's *Religion and the Rise of Capitalism,* one has the feeling that historical conclusions are being expressed in figurative language that could be expressed in no other way. But can this be justified? Are not metaphorical statements beyond validation?

One could speak similarly of problems of the tone and the economy of language, and of a number of other questions that relate to *presentation*. But the point I hope is clear. The way in which a historian presents his information, the way in which he relates expository flow to the discrete pieces of knowledge he has available—all of this constitutes an important area of problems he faces in his everyday work. It too is worthy of systematic consideration.

PART III

Patterns in History

7

The Historical Explanation of Actions Reconsidered

WILLIAM DRAY
University of Toronto

IN THE LAST ten years or so a good deal has been written by analytically-minded philosophers about the nature of historical explanation. The discussion has centered in particular upon the question whether, and if so to what extent and in what way, such explanation involves, requires, or entails corresponding empirical laws. Less than five years ago, in a monograph entitled *Laws and Explanation in History,* I offered a contribution myself to what was then already a discussion well under way. If I now essay some further remarks on the subject, my excuse must be that, to judge from what is being read at philosophical conferences and written in the journals, the controversy has not yet lost its interest.[1] In addition, I welcome this opportunity to try to take account of some of the criticisms that have come my way, and to contrast a position I should still want to defend with a number of interesting alternative views which have recently been advanced.

In the present paper, I hasten to add, I shall not attempt to defend all the main contentions of the monograph referred to. My concern will be limited to a single, but I think central, issue: the question of the analysis to be given of characteristic explanations of the actions of individual historical agents. This does not mean that I believe that only individual human actions are subject matter for historical explanations properly so-called; indeed, I should agree with Professor Maurice Mandelbaum that individual actions as such are below the threshold of proper historical interest; they enter history only insofar as they have "societal significance."[2] But even those who would insist that the unit of historical study is a social rather that human individual, would seldom deny that explanations at the level of talk about nations, institutions, and movements usually involve the historian in explaining the actions of particular men and women. It is characteristic of historical inquiry to explain social occurrences piecemeal. Without wanting to raise here the question of the exact logical relation between assertions about social events and about the actions of human individuals, I shall therefore proceed on the assumption that, although no consideration of the historical explanation of such actions could claim in itself to offer a comprehensive theory of "the nature of historical explanation," it will at any rate deal with an important aspect of that larger problem.

My procedure will be to state first, in section I, the theory of explanation which has given rise to most of the discussion of the present problem—a theory which, as previously, I shall call by the inelegant and also somewhat misleading name, "the covering law theory."[3] Having stated it, I shall contrast it with what I should myself want to say about typical historical explanations of actions. In sections II and III, I shall go on to consider some objections to my claims, and to review, necessarily briefly, six alternative positions, none of which seem to me to be fully acceptable. Finally, in section IV, in the hope of clarifying the issue further, I shall call attention to certain relationships between my own analysis and some larger philosophic issues.

I

The classical statement of the covering law theory is to be found in Professor Carl Hempel's article, "The Function of General Laws in History."[4] The central claim there advanced is that to explain an occurrence is to show that a statement asserting it is deducible from (1) certain statements of antecedent or simultaneous conditions, and (2) certain empirically testable universal laws or theories. Unless the *explanandum* is in this way logically entailed by what is offered as *explanans,* Hempel would say, the alleged explanation is, at best, incomplete—a mere approach to an explanation. This account of the logical structure of explanation is offered as applicable generally, regardless of subject matter, and hence as applicable to reputable historical explanations too. What explanation *means,* it would seem, is showing the deducibility of what is to be explained from something else in accordance with universal "covering" laws.

Those who agree with Professor Hempel about the universal applicability of such a theory of explanation, do not usually quarrel with the judgment that most of the explanations actually offered by historians in the course of their work fail to satisfy its demands. From such an admission, however, they would draw conclusions, not about the cogency of the covering law model, but about the looseness of ordinary historical practice. Other philosophers have argued that such a discrepancy between logical theory and historical practice is a sign of an illegitimate "a priorism" on the part of the Hempelians. Their claim would be that, in the case of a "going concern" like history, the task of philosophers is not to *stipulate* a meaning for "explanation," but to elicit it from practice generally agreed to be acceptable within the discipline concerned. If historical practice does not conform to covering law theory, then so much the worse for the theory.

Now it seems to me that each of these positions has a certain kind of right-mindedness about it. I should not myself want to limit the philosopher's task to a mere *description* of what historians do. His job, as Professors Arthur Danto and J. H. Pitt insist, is to explicate, not to duplicate; we expect from the philosopher a "rational reconstruction" which may not, in every instance, coincide exactly with what a practicing historian does.[5] On the other hand, to point out that practice deviates widely and stubbornly from a logical theory at least creates a presumption against the latter; it raises with some urgency the question *why* there should be such a gap between the formula and what it supposedly explicates. I want to argue that the trouble, in the present case, is that what historians usually *mean,* in offering an explanation of a human action, simply does not coincide *conceptually* with showing an action's performance to have been deducible from other conditions in accordance with empirical laws. What is lacking in covering law theory, it seems to me, is sensitivity to the *concept* of explanation historians normally employ. A "rational reconstruction" may indeed properly deviate from practice. But we must be careful that such deviation is not due to its being the wrong *kind* of reconstruction.

Let me try to sketch briefly what I take to be the conceptual foundation of most explanations of human actions in history. The function of an explanation is to resolve puzzlement of some kind. When an historian sets out to explain an historical action, his problem is usually that he does not know what reason the agent had for doing it. To achieve understanding, what he seeks is information about what the agent believed to be the facts of his situation, including the likely results of taking various courses of action considered open to him, and what he wanted to accomplish: his purposes, goals, or motives. Understanding is achieved when the historian can see the reasonableness of a man's doing what this agent did, given the beliefs and purposes referred to; his action can then be explained as having been an "appropriate" one. The point I want to emphasize is that what is brought out by such considerations is a conceptual connection between understanding a man's action and discerning its rationale. As Professor Hook once put it, there is a difference between showing an action to be peculiar and showing it to be confused.[6] There is similarly a difference between showing an action to be routine and showing it to have point.

Explanation which tries to establish a connection between beliefs, motives, and actions of the indicated sort I shall call "rational explanation." The following is a particularly clear example of it. (I hope I may therefore be pardoned for using an example I have used before for the same purpose.)

In trying to account for the success of the invasion of

England by William of Orange, Trevelyan asks himself why Louis XIV withdrew military pressure from Holland in the summer of 1688—this action being, he tells us, "the greatest mistake of his life."[7] His answer is: "Louis calculated that, even if William landed in England there would be a civil war and long troubles, as always in that factious island. Meantime he could conquer Europe at leisure." Furthermore, "he was glad to have the Dutch out of the way (in England) while he dealt a blow at the Emperor Leopold (in Germany)." He thought "it was impossible that the conflict between James and William should not yield him an opportunity." What makes Louis' action understandable here, according to Trevelyan, is our discovery of a "calculation" which was "not as absurd as it looks after the event." Indeed, the calculation shows us just how appropriate Louis' unfortunate action really was to the circumstances regarded as providing reasons for it. In fact, of course, the king, in a sense, miscalculated; and his action was, in a sense, not appropriate to the circumstances. Yet the whole purpose of Trevelyan's explanatory account is to show us that, for a man in Louis' position, with the aims and beliefs he had, the action was appropriate at least to the circumstances as they were envisaged.

For explanations of the kind just illustrated, I should argue, the establishment of a deductive logical connection between *explanans* and *explanandum*, based on the inclusion of suitable empirical laws in the former, is neither a necessary nor a sufficient condition of explaining. It is not necessary because the aim of such explanations is not to show that the agent was the sort of man who does in fact always do the sort of thing he did in the sort of circumstances he thought he was in. What it aims to show is that the sort of thing he did made perfectly good sense from his own point of view. The establishment of such a connection, if it could be done, would not be a sufficient condition of such explanation either, since it would not itself represent the relation between the agent's beliefs and purposes and what he did as making the latter a reasonable thing to have done.

I might perhaps add—to avoid possible misunderstanding

—that the issue between the appropriateness of applying the covering law and rational "models" to such cases has nothing to do with the question whether historical explanations are to be given in terms of people's "ideas" or in terms of "objective" conditions of their natural and social environment. For Professor Hempel, unlike certain materialist philosophers of history, would allow that the explanation of action is peculiar, at least in the sense of usually and properly making reference to the motives and beliefs of the agents concerned. He would admit, I think, that in offering explanations of the *doing* of actions, by contrast with, say, their success or failure, it is not *actual,* but *envisaged,* states of affairs to which we need to refer. Apart from this, however, explanations of action are, for Hempel, "not essentially different from the causal explanations of physics and chemistry." [8] For "the determining motives and beliefs," he says, ". . . have to be classified among the antecedent conditions of a motivational explanation, and there is no formal difference on this account between motivational and causal explanation." In view of what has been said about nondeducibility of the *explanandum,* it should be clear that my quarrel with this is that it does get the form, not the content, of rational explanations wrong.

II

A number of critics have found something to disagree with in the account I have just given of rational explanation in history. The objections which have come to my attention can conveniently be treated under four heads. The first, and perhaps least important, is that few, if any, historical explanations would get very far if it were necessary to discover the calculation of the agent. For, as Professor Nowell-Smith has objected, if we find that our historical agent did not go through the relevant calculation, then the explanation would thereby be falsified.[9] And he seems to assume that few such agents would very often have acted in such a self-conscious, intellectualistic manner.

Now I should certainly agree that there will be many actions in history for which no such calculation can be found; and the difficulty of finding them does call attention to a limitation of the scope of such explanations. Nor should I want to rule out a priori the possibility of some such actions being explained in other ways. It may be, however, that the very word "calculation" is misleading in this connection. For what makes an action understandable rationally, is not necessarily a set of propositions which the agent recited to himself. Our understanding of his action may arise out of our perception of a rational connection between an action and the motives and beliefs we ascribe to the agent without any such psychological implications. What is claimed is rather that understanding of what he did is achieved by ordering such ingredients, once made explicit, in the *form* of a practical calculation. The philosopher's point is one about the kind of logical relation which must subsist between *explanans* and *explanandum*. Interpreted in this nonintellectualistic fashion, the scope of the rational explanation of actions in history will be far from insignificant. I should expect it, indeed, to be operative in most of the explanations given by narrative historians.

A second objection amounts to the suspicion that the scope of such alleged rational understanding is in fact so broad as to be trivial, and possibly also dangerous. For understanding, as I have described it, may appear to be indistinguishable from that activity, after the event, which we refer to pejoratively as "rationalization." "We all know," observes Professor John Passmore, "how hollow-sounding are the explanations of our conduct we give to other people." [10] It is "as if they were constructed to satisfy our audience rather than as explanations of our actions." The historian will similarly be inclined "to make of our behaviour something much more a matter of principle than it actually is."

Now once again, I should not want to deny the danger to which the critic points. But I should regard his objection as calling into view a special hazard of any search for the reasons of actions—a way in which rational understanding can go wrong—rather than to something which rules out the possibility of rational understanding as such. The claim that the perception of appropriateness is the historian's usual criterion of understanding was, after all, a claim of conceptual logic. Its acceptance does not imply that whenever we think we know what an agent's reasons were, we *really do* know. What it implies is a conceptual connection between the claims to understand an action and to perceive its rationale; and this is a matter of correctness of *form* in explanation. Correctness of form, however, is obviously not a guarantee of correctness of content; and a similar point could, with equal propriety, be made about explanation on the covering law model. For the latter, we need to know universal laws; but can we be so certain that we have discovered them—particularly in historical cases where (unlike the thoroughly interconnected and theoretically grounded laws of physical science) they will be simply generalizations from experience?

The third objection is more troublesome; yet I think it too can be met. In this case the objector admits that our claim to understand an action is often conditional upon our discovering the agent's reasons for acting. But this, he points out, is very different from perceiving the *rationality* of the action; for the latter involves our *endorsing* the agent's reasons as *good* reasons. Thus Mr. P. F. Strawson observes, with regard to my claim that we *do,* in some sense, have to "certify" the agent's reasons, that although I condemn "anything which stops short of this as spectatorism in history," he thinks "anything which goes as far as this makes history impossible." [11] It is true that my saying only that the reasons must be good ones "from the agent's point of view," and that the appropriateness of his act is to be assessed only in relation to the circumstances as *he* envisaged them, goes some way toward meeting the objection. But the critics will deny that it goes far enough. For there are "differences of intelligence, temperament, ability and character," Strawson reminds us, as well as of beliefs and purposes. And human action can fall short of an ideal of rationality because of defective *judgment,* as well as defective *information.*

Now there is certainly something correct about this line of criticism, but I do not think it destroys the position I am trying to maintain. For it is obvious that we cannot claim rational understanding of the making of a logical error, any more than we can claim such understanding of a physical failure to implement a decision. Since both of the latter sorts of things can sometimes be explained, it follows that the present criterion of understanding cannot be the only one, even in history. And it was not my intention to claim that it is. My claim is only that the criterion of rational appropriateness does function for actions not judged to be defective in various ways; and that it sometimes *is* found to be applicable. And I add that when we do employ this criterion, we cannot help certifying the agent's reasons as good ones, from his point of view, for doing what he did. That is what is *meant* by "following his argument" or "seeing the relevance of the considerations he took into account." It is out of a very proper recognition of this fact, it seems to me, that controversial theories of "empathy" in history derive their plausibility, for there is an important sense in which the claim to understand implies a claim to be able to "rethink" the thoughts of the historical agent. And one cannot rethink a practical argument one knows to be invalid.

The fourth objection accepts the contention that understanding of actions is achieved by knowledge of the agent's reasons, but denies that the assertion that he acted for these reasons can be made without committing the historian to the truth of a covering law. For once it becomes clear that what the historian needs to discover is the agent's *actual* reasons, and not just *good* reasons there might be for acting as he did, it will be alleged that, if the explanation is to be justified, we shall need to know some generalization to the effect that an agent who has such actual and good reasons will act as this agent in fact did. As Nowell-Smith has put it: if we argue that the agent acted as he did because he went through a certain rational calculation, our evidence will have to include general knowledge of how such men behave when they so calculate.[12] Thus even if it is true that actual reasons must also in some sense be good reasons, if they are to be explanatory, it may be claimed that there is the *additional* requirement that good, actual reasons be linked to the actions being explained by covering empirical laws.

Now it does not seem to me that when I say "He did so-and-so because he thought so-and-so," my use of the word "because" commits me to any such thing; and I cannot agree that my evidence for the statement must include the kind of general knowledge indicated. It should be noted, in this connection, how especially implausible it would be to claim that this is required by what I mean by such "because" statements, when the actions which I claim to be able to explain are my own. For in my own case, too, I distinguish between finding reasons which would justify my action, and getting straight the actual reasons for which I acted; and when I do the latter, I do not need to know that all men like me, or even I myself on all similar occasions, act in the way I do on this occasion, for good, actual reasons. The claim I would make to be able to act *arbitrarily*—i.e., contrary to good reasons which I actually acknowledge to be so—would in itself make it impossible for me to agree with the present objection. For what I mean by such "because" statements when they are self-applied, is also what I want to mean when I explain the actions of others on the rational model.

The exact force of Nowell-Smith's objection is in any case not entirely clear, in view of some further remarks he makes. For he seems to allow that, in "one sense of explain," we *do* explain an action if we show that what the agent did was "the rational thing for a person so situated to do." But this, he continues, does not explain *why he did the rational thing*—why he acted in accordance with the good reasons he had. To answer the latter question, Nowell-Smith says, we should need to cite some such "platitude" as that "rational men who have worked out appropriate plans tend to act on them unless prevented"; and "it is this sense of 'explain,'" he claims, "that the covering law theory was designed to analyze." I must confess that I cannot see that in making this distinction Nowell-Smith really disagrees with me. For to characterize in this way a difference between explaining why the agent did an *act as specified* and explaining why he did *the rational thing,* it is surely implied that rational explanation, short of appeal to the platitude, can be *complete of its kind, or at its level.* And nothing I have said about it need be taken as ruling out the possibility of giving explanation (at the second level) of a man's acting rationally at all. We might, for example, explain the present rationality of a person's actions by referring to the causal efficacy of a certain sort of shock treatment he has undergone since last we saw him. One might still have doubts as to whether such explanations, if they could be given, would consist of showing anything more than the satisfaction of a certain necessary, rather than sufficient, condition of acting rationally. But that issue would be beside the present point. And the kind of explanation involved would in any case be rarely required in history.

I might add that another critic, Professor J. Cohen, scores a good point in this connection, by quoting against me the remark that in history there operates as a "standing presumption" the "general belief that people act for sufficient reasons." [13] The fact that such a presumption might be regarded as trivial is, as he says, irrelevant; the question is whether it is *logically required* by what was above called the first level of explanation of actions in terms of actual, but good, reasons. My reply must be that my declaration of the presumption of rationality was incautiously strong. It is true that it was only stated as a "presumption," and was really intended only to reinforce the claim that historians give priority to the search for rational explanations over nonrational ones. The important point is that any such "presumption" does not rule out the possibility of there being an indefinite and variable number of cases to the contrary. Nor does it imply that cases to the contrary will be explicable failures to act rationally. There is no assumption in history (as there may be in physical science) that everything is, in principle, explicable. Any "presumption of rationality" is thus logically quite different from what methodologists and logicians would mean by a covering empirical law.

III

There are a number of philosophers who would not accept the analysis I have given and tried to defend in the preceding sections, who would nevertheless agree that there is something wrong with the covering law model as originally formulated, if it is to be an elucidation of the logical structure of explanation in history. What generally drives them to this conclusion, I think, is a problem which Sir Isaiah Berlin has expressed thus.[14] If we challenge an historical explanation by asking for the law which renders it deductive, we can usually, in fact, think of some fairly plausible universal generalization which would bring the proffered explanation into line with the requirements of the model. By any ordinary standards, however, the inductive warrant we could claim for the laws we could, with a certain amount of ingenuity, in this way often provide, is not very strong. More significantly, it is generally much less strong than our confidence in the explanation given. We are thus left with the paradox that, on covering law theory, good explanations have to be represented as deriving logically from questionable laws.

In the face of this paradox, and despite the supposed obviousness, a priori, of its original claims, a number of proposals have been made for the modification of the covering law model, while retaining its central idea. In particular, it has been suggested that something less than a law, in the sense of "a statement of universal conditional form," may give force to an historical explanation. In this section, I want to take note of six different ways in which it has been suggested that laws may be weakened or defective and still perform their explanatory role. For it may be argued that it is with reference to the resulting, modified versions of the covering law theory, rather than the austere original, that the need for recognizing a "rational" model of explanation, in the case of actions, should be judged. No thorough examination of any of the six alternatives can be attempted here, although I shall make some remarks about each of them. I hope at any rate to say enough to make it profitable for us to carry the discussion of them further.

The first is a view which I shall associate with the names of Mr. Patrick Gardiner and Sir Isaiah Berlin (although it is not the only view held by either of them on the subject). Both of these authors link the difficulty of representing historical explanation as deductive, in the full Hempelian sense, with the fact that the language of historical description is not that of a technical discipline like physics or psychology, but is the language of the plain, if educated, layman. Nor do they regard this as a defect of history, for it is, they would say, a *requirement* of the study if consumers of history are to grasp what is produced. The concepts of ordinary language, however, are notoriously loose and vague, and these features are consequently features also of any general laws formulated in terms of them. Words like "revolution" or "conquest," Gardiner points out, do not have precisely defined rules of application; indeed, their meaning may even change through time.[15] Similarly, although Berlin accepts the claim that all historical judgments "embody" generalizations, he adds that "few are sufficiently clear, sharp, precisely defined to be capable of being organized in a formal structure which allows of systematic mutual entailments or exclusions. . . ."[16]

Berlin sometimes offers an additional reason for resisting the covering law model in any strict or literal version. This is the claim that ordinary language is not only vague, but also ineradicably *evaluative.* The whole language of human action is bound up with its user's appraisal of what is done, and uncertainty as to whether a concept applies, therefore, may be due to differences of evaluation, not only to genuine indeterminacy of meaning. Some philosophers of history, like F. A. Hayek, Leo Strauss, and Peter Winch, would go further and say that the very notion of an historical or social fact is, in its ordinary sense, a quasi-evaluative notion.[17] Any laws into which such notions are to enter would consequently be evaluative too.

Now it does not seem to me that what Berlin and Gardiner bring out in this way, even if true, represents any insuperable obstacle for the claims of covering law theory as a "rational reconstruction." For it surely follows that, since the historian's explanations employ the same language as the laws, any looseness introduced by the language will affect the explanations too. The really puzzling argument, however, is one which represents a good explanation as resting on poor laws. To argue that only vague or evaluative laws function in a vague or evaluative inquiry, is surely to *accept* the covering law model as the statement of a functioning logical ideal. And this presumably is all that a Hempelian would want to claim —although he might regret that historians should care more about speaking to the general public in its own language than giving completely adequate explanations.

A second and more radical way of trying to meet the original difficulty concentrates, not upon the language, but upon the subject matter of history. It agrees that either the subject matter itself, or the state of inquiry into it, is such that plausible universal laws can seldom, if ever, be discovered, so that if explanations are to be given at all, we must make a virtue of necessity, and abandon the strict *deductive* criterion. A straightforward version of this position is to say that *statistical* as well as universal laws may explain what falls under them. From a statistical law we cannot, of course, deduce the occurrence of a particular event or action to be explained; but we can at least show it to have been probable. We might therefore claim to be able to explain it *inductively*. Such a modified analysis, it might be claimed, would apply to all those cases of explanation in history for which we could formulate a plausible general statement incorporating some such qualification as "usually" or "for the most part." For the notion of a statistical law here is simply the notion of a generalization which asserts a connection, not between *all* cases of what is specified by *explanans* and *explanandum*, but between a certain *proportion* of them. And such a law could, of course, be vague or precise, stating either that most, or a certain definite percentage, of cases were connected. A modification of the covering law model along these lines was suggested by Hempel himself, even in its earliest formulations; and it has also recently been advocated by Professor Nicholas Rescher.[18]

Now the modification of the original claim involved in the abandonment of the deductive criterion and the acceptance of statistical laws seems to me quite a major one from the standpoint of conceptual analysis of explanation. For the new claim is not, presumably, simply that a *partial* explanation, or a mere *approach* to explanation, can be given by this means (a doctrine which would not go beyond Hempel's theory of the explanation "sketch"). The claim appears rather to be that an event can be *completely* explained (although perhaps in a different sense) without subsuming it under a universal law licensing its deduction, and consequently without showing that it had to happen. One may perhaps wonder whether the withdrawal of what was at first received as obvious is anything more than a convenient stipulation of a new meaning for "explain." One may wonder, too, how acceptable the concession really is to those who were at first attracted to the covering law model because of its logical elegance. Professor Michael Scriven, I suspect, speaks for many of them when he objects to the way particular occurrences "rattle around" in statistical explanations.[19] It was a strength of the deductive theory, he observes, that it focused attention on precisely what was to be explained. Statistical laws, however, are compatible with both the occurrence and nonoccurrence of what they are supposed to explain; they "abandon the hold on the individual case."

It may be of interest, in this connection, to note that in spite of its not being deductive in Hempel's sense, a *rational* explanation actually has a better claim than a statistical one to meet Scriven's objections against explanation which appears to lose its grip on the case. For although a rational explanation does not show that a particular action had to *occur,* it may show (in a rational sense of "had to") that a particular action *had to be done.* I say only "may" because I do not think that the puzzlement which leads a person to ask why someone did something is, even in the rational sense, always expressible as "Why did he *have* to do that?" Sometimes all we really want to know, when we ask for an action to be explained, is how it could have seemed rationally possible or "all right" to do it; and here an issue like that between deductive and inductive approaches to the covering law model arises *within* the class of rational explanations. When we do ask why an action had to be done, however, an answer bearing directly on the case is often possible—an answer involving the rational ruling out of all possible alternatives. There is no counterpart of this in the assertion of a purely statistical connection.

A third sort of modification of the covering law model has been suggested by Professor Scriven himself.[20] Scriven's proposal takes its rise from the difficulties already sketched: first, that universal laws elicited from most historical explanations are doubtful; second, that a mere statistical law, since it fails to rule out the nonoccurrence of what is being explained, fails to explain why *it* happened rather than something else. Scriven's solution is to attribute the implicit generality of an historical explanation to a type of general statement which is neither of these sorts, but a kind of logical hybrid, with (he would claim) the important advantages of each.[21]

Thus, to use a simplified version of one of his examples, if we ask why William the Conqueror did not invade Scotland, and answer that it was because he had no desire for additional lands, we may say that the explanation is grounded in some such truism as "Rulers don't normally invade neighbouring territories if they are satisfied with what they have." Such a generalization, Scriven insists, would clearly not be *intended* to be taken as unequivocally ruling out all cases to the contrary; yet it says more than that rulers *seldom* do this sort of thing, as a truly statistical generalization would do. It makes a stronger assertion than this because it represents what is specified by the law as the normal or standard case, to which any counterexamples stand as strange exceptions. Scriven calls such a generalization "normic." It allows us to *deduce* the occurrence of what is to be explained, provided we have no reason for thinking the circumstances extraordinary. Such generalizations often betray their special sense, he says, by containing one or other of a number of normic "modifiers": words like "ordinarily," "typically," "properly," "naturally," "under standard conditions"—the logic of which, Scriven argues, is quite different from "all," "most," or "some." He cautions us, however, that not every generalization employing such modifiers is asserted with true normic force, and that some generalizations omitting them may yet be asserted with such force. Correct diagnosis thus often requires close attention to the context.

The problem, of course, is to get clear just how we are to operate with the notion of "exceptional conditions," and how we are to represent, not only as justifiable, but even as fully intelligible, the distinction between apparent counterexamples which do, and which do not, falsify a normic generalization. For Scriven does not deny that such generalizations are empirical assertions, and they must therefore be falsifiable in principle. It seems to me that, when pressed, such generalizations are in danger of sliding in one of two directions. They will tend either toward an ordinary universal or statistical law, or toward what might be called the agent's principle of action, as it would function in a rational explanation.

It is Scriven's contention that a knowledgeable and skillful practitioner of a discipline (whether it be history or medicine) knows how to handle normic statements because, although he cannot spell out in advance all the sorts of things that would count as exceptional circumstances, he at least grasps the principle at work: the network of exceptions, he says, is "complex but understandable."[22] In this connection, Scriven makes a good deal of the learned capacity or trained judgment of the historian, about which little more can be said; and perhaps he is right in thinking that no adequate account of the nature of historical explanation can be given without some reference to such a notion. But even if we accept the claim that the network can be known without being articulable, it is difficult to see that any logical novelty is introduced which would give normic generalization, so conceived, a different force from universal or statistical laws. The problem would appear to be only that of saying in full what the "understood" generalization is.

There are hints, however, in what Scriven says about the "norm-defining" function of such generalizations, and about their dependence upon the historian's judgment, that they may be logically peculiar after all, in not being straightforwardly empirical generalizations. It is notable, for example, that in offering a very miscellaneous list of the kinds of statements that may have to be interpreted normically, Scriven includes "rules, definitions and certain normative statements in ethics" (although he rather mysteriously refers to the latter as normic statements operating in "other fields").[23] It seems to me that in its explanatory role, a statement like "Rulers do not normally invade neighbouring territories if they are satisfied with what they have" may quite intelligibly be interpreted as stating a "norm" in the sense of reminding us of what it is reasonable to do—and thus, of course, of what people in fact do, *except* when they act foolishly, ignorantly, arbitrarily, and so on. So interpreted, the explanatory function of the normic statement would be to display the rationale of William's noninvasion of Scotland. And this would assimilate explanation in terms of normic generalizations to what I have called the "rational" kind.

A fourth and equally interesting attempt to provide a more plausible type of explanatory law for historical cases has been elaborated by Professors N. Rescher, C. B. Joynt, and O. Helmer.[24] According to these authors, although historians do often use universal laws brought in from the various sciences, both natural and social (chiefly to establish the "boundary conditions" for action), they also themselves *discover* generalizations of a logically different sort. As part of their own proper inquiry, historians are said to formulate, not general laws, but restrictive generalizations, limited by spatiotemporal considerations, but fully valid and lawlike within them. Examples would be: "Officers of the pre-Revolutionary French Navy were selected from those of noble birth," or "Heretics were persecuted in seventeenth century Spain." [25] What makes such generalizations of special interest in the present context is their relation to a certain characteristic objection of historians, when presented with the original claims of covering law theory. This is the objection that universal laws would commit them to making unsupported claims regarding what happens in unexamined regions of historical space and time. Explanations given in terms of *limited* generalizations would employ only general knowledge of the kind historians would claim to have—namely, knowledge of "the period."

It might be added that Rescher also points out that most limited generalizations actually in use in history are loose in the more familiar sense of admitting counterexamples, although not too many—*within* their proper sphere of application. This admission raises no special problem for him since he allows that statistical laws and probability hypotheses, when known, can also function in an explanatory role. The point of importance here is that such generalizations could in principle be perfectly general, in the sense of not allowing any counterexamples within the limited scope of their application; and they would thus, although themselves not strictly universal, afford *deductive* explanations in favorable cases. In considering the Rescher-Joynt-Helmar thesis as making a novel point, by contrast with others noted in this paper, we may therefore concentrate upon the claim they make regarding restricted generalizations which are nonstatistical.

Now the most natural interpretation to place upon the examples noted is that they are really *summative* generalizations. The form of any explanation given in terms of them might therefore be thought to be like that given in terms of drawing a red ball from a bag when it is pointed out that only red ones were put into the bag in the first place. One could hardly deny that this would be to give an explanation, although it might be doubted that such explanations would be of any importance in historical studies. It might be claimed, at any rate, that the explanation has greater force than, say, a derivation from a mere statistical, although otherwise unrestricted, generalization. And there doubtless are true summative generalizations in history: for example, "All the Reformation Parliaments were packed," a statement which would presumably be asserted on the basis of independent knowledge of all of them. But the present authors explicitly repudiate such an interpretation of the restricted generalizations in view. For these are said to apply to unexamined cases as well as examined ones; and they also have counterfactual force. They apply not only to known French naval officers and Spanish heretics, but also to unknown ones, and to ones who might have existed but didn't.

When we ask, however, on what basis we can assert them, limited generalizations, like normics, seem gradually to dissolve into something more familiar (although it is not entirely clear why they have to). This comes out especially in the discussion of a favored example (which unfortunately is not itself the explanation of an action): the explanation of the defeat of Villeneuve at Trafalgar, in part by reference to the generalization, "In seafights, 1653–1805, large formations were too cumbersome for effectual control." [26] We can have confidence in this, we are told, because of our general knowledge of the state of eighteenth century naval ordnance; our knowledge of the latter reinforces the mere generalization by showing *why* the regularity holds in the period and area indicated. What we have, in fact, is a "transitory regularity," which is itself explicable in terms of universal regularities, in conjunction with local conditions. The crucial point for the interpretation of the Rescher-Joynt-Helmer doctrine is whether the limited generalization would be explanatory even if no such link with universal laws were known. Do we at any rate need to have this further information to know what the spatio-temporal limits of the limited generalization are? To make either admission would surely be to concede all that an exponent of the original covering law theory would require. And as far as I can see, these authors concede it. The only caveat, as in the case of Scriven's normics, concerns the inarticulateness of the knowledge of supporting generalizations. There is only "a vague knowledge of underlying regularities."[27]

A fifth sort of modification of the covering law doctrine which has been proposed tries to take account of the resistance of historians to admitting universal empirical laws by narrowing the extent of their alleged commitment in still a further way. This is the suggestion that, in the case of the explanation of an individual human action, at least, the general statement providing the link between what is explained and the motives and beliefs which explain it, need only be a "lawlike" statement, formulated to apply to a range of actions of a specified *individual.* The doctrine in question entered current discussion in philosophy of history as an application of Professor Gilbert Ryle's account of dispositional explanation in *The Concept of Mind.* Ryle pointed out that dispositional statements we make about individuals—for example, character statements like "Disraeli was ambitious"—are "lawlike" in licensing singular hypothetical statements of the form, "If Disraeli sees an opportunity to obtain a position of leadership, he will take it." Unlike true laws, however, they make no assertion connecting *kinds* of beliefs or motives (or people) with *kinds* of actions. If they are explanatory, statements which are defectively general in the dispositional sense, like Rescher's limited generalizations, would appear to be especially useful in historical studies. For it is a commonplace that it is dangerous to generalize about individuals in history. The historian must, as Strawson puts it, get to *know his man,* which is, he says, quite different from knowing "platitudes about men in general."[28] To know one's man is, in this view, to discover the dispositional complex we call his character. We can then, it is claimed, explain what he does as *characteristic* of him.

It is clear that a dispositional statement about an individual is not itself a law. The question arises, however, whether we can assert such statements without committing ourselves to, or deriving them from, laws. Ryle has declared that we can; he has even claimed that we learn dispositional truths about particular things, even in the study of nature, *before* we know corresponding laws. It is unfortunate that his best-known example is poorly selected for illustrating this claim. For if I try to explain the shattering of *this* pane of glass when hit by a stone, by saying it was brittle, it is hard to see how I could have known this apart from general knowledge of the properties of glass. I certainly could not have experimented relevantly in the past with this particular pane. In other cases, however, where prior manifestations of a disposition would not entail destruction of the object, it does not seem out of the way to say we could have such knowledge. And we could similarly discover that a particular person was disposed to act in a certain way by noticing the way he has acted already in relevant circumstances.

It has been argued, however, that there is a logical peculiarity of *human* dispositions which brings any such claim into question. In introducing the dispositional model into the discussion of explanation in history, Gardiner made a great deal of Ryle's own admission of the looseness of the prediction of action which is licensed by dispositional statements about people. Ryle puts the point by saying that human dispositions are highly determinable rather than determinate; there are usually a number of alternative ways of actualizing them, so that knowing a man's dispositions is not necessarily being able to predict in any detail what he will do. Professor Jonathan Cohen has argued that this complexity of human dispositions may well maneuver the historian giving dispositional explanation into assuming universal laws.[29] Cohen's point is that if the statement, "Disraeli was ambitious," licenses us to expect, not a specific expression of ambition previously noted in his behavior, but only one or other of quite a number of alternatives, then if we are going to base our explanation of Disraeli's attack on Peel in 1847 on our knowledge that he was ambitious, we need something more to warrant our inference than our having found Disraeli acting ambitiously in *other* ways in the past. We need to know that he is disposed to act ambitiously in this particular way as well. Cohen suspects, therefore, that the historian, in giving the explanation, really assumes some such universal law as that a person who is disposed to act ambitiously in some ways is disposed to act so in others as well. Such an argument, it should be noted, does not show that what is *asserted* by the dispositional statement about Disraeli is a universal law, or even that it could not be *established* by observing Disraeli's past behavior alone (provided that he had already acted ambitiously in the requisite number of ways). It does suggest, however, that in typical cases in history, what is asserted may *in fact* rest on assumed universal connections.

Still a sixth type of modification has been suggested by some other philosophers. Professor Charles Frankel, for example, having accepted from Hempel the conclusion that the failure of historical explanations to display a tight covering law pattern may often be due to their offering incomplete explanations, goes on to distinguish between this kind of deviation and another not attributable to the historian's not finishing what he begins. Historical explanations, Frankel claims, may fail to be deductive (and hence lack predictive force) because they state only certain *necessary* or *essential,* not sufficient, conditions of what occurred. This also happens in other domains, he reminds us, but when it does, the stating of sufficient conditions still remains the ideal of explanation. In history, on the contrary, stating certain necessary conditions often "seems fully to satisfy our demand for an explanation." [30] To give such an account, especially as part of tracing the necessary stages in a process, according to Frankel, "is one of the stable and accepted meanings of 'explain'"; and it would therefore be incorrect to regard it as in any proper sense incomplete—

a mere "explanation sketch." We must realize "that not all satisfactory explanations supply us with exactly the same type of information, and that not all requests to have something explained are unequivocal requests for a single kind of answer."

An explanation in terms of necessary or essential conditions does not aim to represent the *explanandum* as deducible from the *explanans*. It nevertheless, Frankel goes on to say:

> rests as much as does a fully predictive explanation on tacit or expressed generalizations. Otherwise we could not distinguish between a mere succession of events and a series of connected events. For it is only in terms of generalizations to the effect that events of a given type do not take place unless they are conjoined with other events of a given type that we are able to say what we mean by an "historical process." . . .

In his general account of *genetic* explanation, Professor W. B. Gallie says much the same thing. If an historian explains the rapid rise of Christianity by referring to its possession of the proselytizing platform of the Jewish synagogue, he points out, this does not commit him to arguing that the development was either necessary or probable. The force of the explanation is rather to show how Christianity got its opportunity. An everyday example of the same pattern would be the explanation of an angry retort by reference to the taunt which evoked it. Once again, there is no claim to show the retort to be deducible or predictable. It is rather that *but for* the taunt, "the statement would remain unintelligible in the sense of lacking an appropriate historical context." [31]

Professor Gallie has been criticized for assuming that we could have knowledge of a necessary condition of an occurrence which is logically independent of knowledge of its sufficient conditions, and hence for implying that we could ever offer a properly warranted explanation of the so-called genetic type without filling out antecedent conditions and laws to the point where we have the materials for a covering law, deductive explanation.[32] I cannot see why we should deny that we can discover, empirically, laws of the form, "Only if so-and-so then so-and-so," which could warrant the assertion of mere necessary condition in a particular case. Nor does it appear questionable that knowledge of such conditions alone may in some contexts be explanatory. They are especially likely to be explanatory, it might be added, when the puzzlement giving rise to the demand for explanation is of the kind most naturally expressed in such questions as "How could that have happened?" where it seems at first that a certain essential condition was not fulfilled.

All I should want to point out is that, in explaining *actions* nondeductively in the rational way, it is no more required that we establish certain antecedent conditions, such as the agent's motives or beliefs, as necessary by virtue of corresponding "only if" laws, than it is that we establish them as sufficient conditions. It is enough that what provides the agent with a reason for acting be a *rationally* necessary condition—that is, that it be shown that without it, he had no reason to do what he did. It is not required that we show that he *could not* have acted in the same way without having that reason. It has already been argued that, when we show that an agent *had* to do what he did because there was no reasonable alternative open to him, we do not commit ourselves to representing his action as predictable from the fact that he had sufficient reason for performing it. Similarly, in the present case, when we show that but for the taunt, the agent would have had no reason for his response, we do not commit ourselves to representing the taunt as *retrodictable* from the fact of his angry remark. The proposed weakening of the covering law model to include explanations in terms of "laws of necessary condition" is thus still not sufficiently radical to encompass the relevant forms of the rational explanation of actions. It does, however, so far as it goes, indicate a genuine way in which the claims of the original model can go wrong.

IV

This completes our brief review of some of the more important proposals which have been made for modifying the covering law theory. In every case, what we are offered seems to be a concession by logical theory to the realities of historical knowledge. These concessions, as we have seen, are of logically different sorts; and there may be better reasons for accepting some of them than others. It might be noted, however, that although the various deviations from the original conception of what would count as a covering law were presented as *alternatives,* they are not (with the possible exception of statistical and normic generalizations) *exclusive* alternatives. It has, in fact, already been pointed out that some of the authors treated represent explanatory laws in history as being "defective" in two or more ways at once. It might be added that anyone who accepted the legitimacy of each type of modification separately, could also accept them as functioning together: one might conceive of an explanatory law which fell short of the ideal in all six ways at once. It might assert *vaguely* that the beliefs, purposes, and actions of a certain *individual* are *normally* connected, in a certain *proportion* of cases, in a restricted *geographical area* and during a limited *period,* in such a way that *but for* his having those beliefs and purposes, the actions would not be performed.

A philosopher who was prepared to recognize such a maximally modified "law" as satisfying the demand for generality in an historical explanation, could certainly not be accused of failing to keep theory in touch with practice. And it might very well be that a sufficient accumulation of such modifications would break down completely the usual resistance of historians to admitting that the particular explanations they give either explicitly contain, or implicitly commit them to, a law or laws. The commitment, after all, can come to look pretty innocuous. Yet, for reasons which I sketched in the first section of this paper, it seems to me that it is misleading to say that even the most innocuous law is what gives typical explanations of action in history their force. To point out that an action which puzzles us falls under a law of any kind—even if this is true—is to make a claim in the wrong "universe of discourse" for the answering of typical "why" questions in history.

It may perhaps be useful, in concluding this paper, to try

to link this position with some considerations arising out of broader philosophical questions. There are two points I should especially like to touch on. The first is the relation between the acceptance of the rational model of explanation and the holding of a libertarian metaphysical position. The second is the relation between the giving of rational explanations and a certain view of the nature and purpose of historical inquiry.

Let me confess that I do in fact hold a libertarian position, and that I think the rational model of explanation to be of special interest to anyone who does. It is of interest because it shows a way in which explanation can be given in history which is logically *compatible* with indeterminism regarding human actions. The incompatibility of representing actions as both free and explicable has often been asserted. But if the contentions of this paper are correct, this doctrine holds only for explanation on the covering law model, with an assertion of a deductive connection between an action and its explanatory conditions.

In saying this, it should be clear that I am not *arguing* for the acceptability of the rational model of explanation from libertarian metaphysics as premiss. I am arguing on conceptual grounds that there is a meaning of "explain" which is already current in history, as well as everyday affairs, which does not entail determinism. I should like to point out also that I am not arguing from the possibility of giving rational explanations to the truth of libertarianism. For I cannot see—as some like Professor Winch apparently believe [33]—that the giving of a rational explanation excludes the giving of a covering law explanation; that rational explanation entails *indeterminism.* I cannot see that we need agree even with what appears to be Professor Donagan's view on this: that rational explanations would at any rate have *point* only so long as we cannot give law-covered explanations of the same things.[34] The two sorts of explanations are better regarded as belonging to different logical and conceptual networks, within which different kinds of puzzlement are expressed and resolved.

I have suggested that the compatibility of rational explanation and libertarianism may provide some philosophers of history with a justifiable motive for emphasizing the conceptual differences between such explanation and the covering law model in all its forms. There is also, however, a reason for accepting the rational model, and believing that it *should* function in historical inquiry, which ought to appeal to determinists as well. This claim will put me at odds with any philosopher who, having accepted the compatiblity thesis, argues that since explanations which are logically "tight" are obviously superior to "loose" ones, whatever the reason for the looseness, covering law explanations are clearly to be preferred wherever they can be given; so that it would be legitimate to hope that a "defective" rational model in history would gradually be replaced by something better. I want to argue that even if covering law explanations were always available, it would still be valuable and proper to explain the actions of historical agents in the rational way.

My reason for saying this arises out of an answer I think we should give to the question: What is the study of history for? Certainly one reason people study history is the hope of gaining knowledge of past human activities which may help them in coping with present problems. And, as in the study of nature, it would often be very helpful indeed to be able to explain and predict on the covering law pattern. As Professor Donagan has on more than one occasion eloquently urged, the possibility of pursuing such a study with very significant success still remains to be shown; and he is surely right to say that it would be foolish to abandon "antinomian" social inquiry, which has been going on for centuries, on the mere *promise* of something "better." [35] I should like, however, to push this point a little further. For it seems to me that, even if a "science" of history employing covering law explanations were well advanced, there would *still* be no good reason for abandoning an inquiry giving nondeductive, rational explanations, and very good reason for continuing it—if necessary, alongside the other.

For what drives us to the study of history, as much as anything else, is a humane curiosity: an interest in discovering and imaginatively reconstructing the life of people at other times and places. To discover and understand their life, we need to be able to do more than regularize, predict, and retrodict their actions; we need to apply to those actions the categories and concepts of *practice;* we need to take a view of them, as R. G. Collingwood might have put it, *from the inside.* Even if we are not libertarians, we are ourselves, and believe others to be, agents; and even if we accept the possibility and usefulness of covering law explanation for some purposes, we may still surely share the desire to extend such understanding and evaluation of human life *from the standpoint of agency.* The slogan, "Historical study is vicarious experience," like all such slogans, fastens on only one facet of the truth. But it *is* a facet of the truth, and one which covering law theorists are likely to ignore.[36] What we should be careful to remember is that history is not only (possibly) a branch of the science of society, but is also (actually) a branch of the humanities. My chief complaint against acceptance of the covering law doctrine in history is not the difficulty of operating it, in either fully deductive or mutilated form. It is rather that it sets up a kind of *conceptual barrier* to a humanistically oriented historiography.

NOTES

1. Over Christmas, for example, while Professor Hempel, in his address to the Eastern Division of the American Philosophical Association in 1961, was discussing the explanation of rational actions (an address which I was unfortunately unable to consult in preparing this paper), Professor A. Donagan was arguing before meetings of the American Association for the Advancement of Science against the application of Hempel's model to precisely that kind of subject matter. For those who stayed home, there was Professor Maurice Mandelbaum's article in the January issue of *History and Theory* entitled, "Historical Explanation: the Problem of Covering Laws."

2. *The Problem of Historical Knowledge* (New York, 1938), p. 9.

3. It may be misleading in seeming to imply that explanation

should employ a *single* law linking *explanans* and *explanandum.* It also fails to distinguish (as Professor Donagan has done) between claiming that explanation must be deductive and that it must employ universal laws: either of these criteria might be satisfied independently.

4. Reprinted in *Theories of History,* ed. P. Gardiner (Glencoe, Ill., 1959), pp. 344–56.

5. A. Danto, Review, *Ethics* (July 1958), 299. J. H. Pitt, "Generalization in Historical Explanation," *Journal of Philosophy* (1959), 579–80.

6. "A Pragmatic Critique of the Historico-Genetic Method," in *Essays in Honor of John Dewey* (New York, 1929), pp. 163–71.

7. *The English Revolution* (London, 1938), pp. 105–106.

8. C. G. Hempel and P. Oppenheim, "The Logic of Explanation," reprinted in H. Feigl and M. Brodbek, *Readings in the Philosophy of Science* (New York, 1953), pp. 327–28.

9. Review, *Philosophy* (April 1959), 170–72.

10. Review, *Australian Journal of Politics and History* (1958), 269 ff.

11. Review, *Mind* (April 1959), 268.

12. *Ibid.*

13. Review, *Philosophical Quarterly* (April 1960).

14. "History and Theory: The Concept of Scientific History," *History and Theory,* I, 1 (1960), 19.

15. *The Nature of Historical Explanation* (Oxford, 1952), pp. 53, 60–61.

16. *Historical Inevitability* (London and New York, 1953), p. 54.

17. See *The Counter-Revolution of Science* (Glencoe, Ill., 1952); *Natural Right and History* (Chicago, 1953); *The Idea of a Social Science* (London, 1958), respectively.

18. "The Function of General Laws in History," *op. cit.,* p. 350; "The Logic of Explanation," *op. cit.,* p. 350.

19. "Truisms as the Grounds for Historical Explanations," reprinted in *Theories of History,* p. 467.

20. *Op. cit.,* pp. 464 ff.

21. *Ibid.,* p. 464.

22. *Ibid.,* p. 466.

23. *Ibid.,* p. 464.

24. N. Rescher and O. Helmer, "On the Epistemology of the

Inexact Sciences," *Management Science* (October 1959), 25–40; R. Rescher and C. B. Joynt, "On Explanation in History," *Mind* (1959), 383–87; N. Rescher and C. B. Joynt, "The Problem of Uniqueness in History," *History and Theory,* I, 2 (1961), 150–62.

25. "On the Epistemology of the Inexact Sciences," *op. cit.,* pp. 27 and 29.

26. *Ibid.,* p. 28.

27. *Ibid.,* p. 38.

28. See Ryle, *op. cit.,* p. 268.

29. Review, *Philosophical Quarterly* (1960), 192.

30. "Explanation and Interpretation in History," reprinted in *Theories of History,* p. 412.

31. "Explanations in History and the Genetic Sciences," reprinted in *ibid.,* p. 387.

32. A. Montefiore, "Professor Gallie on 'Necessary and Sufficient Conditions,'" *Mind* (October 1956), 534 ff.

33. *Op. cit.,* pp. 72, 93–94.

34. "Explanation in History," *Mind* (1957), 153.

35. "Social Science and Historical Antinomianism," *Revue internationale de Philosophie* (1957), 448–49.

36. A statement which was made in the original paper, and which I have come to see misrepresents Professor Hempel's views, has been deleted at this point.

8

Comments on Historical Explanation

LEONARD KRIEGER
Yale University

SOME YEARS AGO, when the new criticism was all the rage in literary circles, I was present at an informal discussion of T. S. Eliot's poetry. When some of its meanings came into hot dispute, I asked mildly why they didn't ask Eliot what he meant, whereupon one of the new critics looked at me as if I were an idiot and coldly informed me that Eliot's feelings on the matter were completely irrelevant. As an historian in this assemblage I think I know how Eliot would have felt. But since I have wandered into the lions' den I intend to follow Machiavelli's counsel and make like a fox—I intend, that is, either to keep out of the way of the lions' internecine squabbles or at least to occupy myself in no position long enough to be caught in it. To judge by the personae in Professor Dray's little drama of academic conflict, in which nary an historian appears, the danger is great, since what philosophers seem to be interested in are the remains rather than the views of historians. It may be inferred that the philosophy of history remains much more philosophy than history.

As long as we have Mr. Dray, however, I am not at all sure that historians do have to get into the act. As much as any philosopher that I have read, he tries and succeeds in being faithful to the common assumptions of the working historian. It is not simply that Mr. Dray brings philosophical support and respectability to historians' visceral reaction against what he calls "the covering law theory"—a theory which, rightly or wrongly, historians view as supra- or transhistorical, and consequently as a species of academic imperialism by the mother country of all the sciences. We appreciate Mr. Dray rather for adopting two criteria which are fundamental to modern historians. He grasps, in the first place, an essential feature of what satisfies the historian in the way of explanation—that when an historian seeks to explain a particular action what he wants explained is precisely the particularity of the action: why it was produced by this man at this place at this time. If an historian understands that the relationship between his condition and his action is a case of a generic relationship between classes of such conditions and such actions, then he sees in this not an explanation but something to be explained—how his relationship differs from the others in the class, that is, what the specific identity of his action is in human history. Mr. Dray's second appeal to historians lies in his unabashed plurality. He is entirely candid in limiting his theory of "rational explanation" to the individual historical act undertaken for good reasons and in admitting that other kinds of explanations apply to other kinds of acts and events. Historians are confirmed pluralists, and again we salute Mr. Dray for making our predilections philosophically respectable. I would even call him the historian's philosopher if I did not suspect it would be the kiss of death.

It must be confessed, however, that Mr. Dray's caution, commendable as it is, does reduce his value for the modern historian. If I understand him aright, he would apply his theory of explanation only to agents who undertake actions for "valid" reasons and he would refuse its application to "defective" action. Now, fortunately or unfortunately, the great bulk of history which deals with rational actions has already been written. Most historians today find their problems precisely in the gaps or flaws of rationality perpetrated by historical agents. Now the errors of historical agents are of two kinds, both of which fall, for different reasons, outside Mr. Dray's model: there are errors of logic, where the cause and effect fall within the model but the process from cause to effect does not, and there are what Mr. Dray calls, in passing, errors of judgment, where presumably the cause itself is outside the model because it refers to the actual rather than the envisaged state of affairs—in historians' terms, to the event rather than to the action. What makes the "errors of judgment" classification so important for historians is that they put a broad species of errors of information into it. For between the situation as agents envisaged it, and the situation as it actually was, is the situation as the agents should have envisaged it. The defect or distortion in the agent's view of the situation, as measured by the information available to him, is for the historian a type of rational defect, distinguishable to be sure, but of the same order as errors committed within the circle of the agent's information, purposes, and action. Since these areas of inquiry frequently mean a shift of the *explanandum* from the action to the cause or the logic, it is clear that even within the realm of individual actions Mr. Dray's theory is of limited applicability today. I should welcome a theory of irrational explanation.

But all this, I admit, seems somewhat beside the point, since it covers what Mr. Dray intentionally does not cover. It does, however, contain a dimension that is relevant to his model. For on the one hand, Mr. Dray emphasizes the historical agent's view of the situation, his purposes, and his action, and he agrees that the reasons for the action must be not only "good" but also "actual." But on the other hand, he implies that the agent need not himself be conscious of such reasons since it is our formal ordering of his motives, beliefs, and action rather than his own recital of causal propositions that constitutes the explanation. What puzzles me here is the meaning of "actual." I take it that for Mr. Dray it refers to our claim that the agent not only might have but did have such reasons whether or not he was wholly aware of them. But the admission of "actuality," even in this restricted sense, raises the problem of the general relevance of extra-agential factors to rational explanation itself. Whatever the implications for Mr. Dray's logical calculation may be, as a matter of fact historians interpolate or reinterpret the agent's reasons to include information beyond the agent's ken, in the interests of actuality.

But we are still only nibbling around the edges of Mr. Dray's position, for he might well argue that the good and actual reasons, however arrived at, remain the criteria of explanation in the historical arena which he has marked out. Besides, I have attacked him from the rear, for he has not here made a *general* defense of these positions; he has argued them vis-à-vis variants of the covering law theory, and this is his main concern. Now much as I prefer his theory to his opponents', since it is more solidly supported by the empirical evidence of what historians not only do but try to do, I must confess that he has gone too far even for me, that he is, in this sense, more historically minded than I am. One of the reasons for the categorical differences between Mr. Dray and the covering law theorists is the difference in their starting points, in their respective notions about the function of the philosophy of history. For Mr. Dray, clearly, it is the explication of the fundamental internal relations that make up the distinctive field of historical reality; for the covering law theorists it is the external relations that integrate history into the other approaches to reality. Mr. Dray's constant tendency is to emphasize that his approach is one among many, that it is one particularly appropriate to the study of human agency and that it can be juxtaposed with other theories designed for other purposes. The burden of my argument so far has been to emphasize the permeability of Mr. Dray's distinctions, and I should argue now that however distinctive the end product of a particular rationality may be, the determination of that rationality involves a process which brings the historian not into juxtaposition but into conjunction with other approaches. Rather than distribute various approaches over various objects the historian brings various approaches to bear on the same object. He uses covering laws, absolute or modified; he uses periodic generalizations; he uses normic generalizations; he uses dispositional explanations; he uses whatever life and knowledge has taught him in the attempt to discover actual reasons—but he uses them as questions and not as canons. He asks always: does this fit? or this? or this? The historian, then, sees no disjunction in the application of a covering law and of rational explanation to the same action. They are successive rather than alternative. The problem obviously becomes the determination of fitness. How do we know when something fits, i.e., contributes to a rational explanation? With this question we come to the main point of my comment.

In the determination of the criteria of historical explanation a dimension that is equally neglected by Mr. Dray and his covering law opponents looms in my mind as more important than the dimension that separates them. The neglected dimension is time. I find nothing in his exposition that would distinguish between historical action and any action whatsoever, and his rational explanation of historical action works just as well for any action whatsoever. Now if Mr. Dray wishes to maintain that any and every action that has been consummated becomes, at the moment of consummation, an historical action, that is perfectly satisfactory to me but it will leave a lot of you unemployed. Two distinctions seem to me obvious: first, the distinction between the immediate past—that is, what an historian would loosely call the present—and the historical past; secondly, the distinction between the historical and the nonhistorical past within the remoter past. Ideally, what we require is a single definition of historicity which would apply to the latter case and a fortiori to the former. What we require is not an historical explanation of actions—and I have not the foggiest notion what this title of Mr. Dray's means—but an explanation of *historical* actions, and I am enough of a Diltheyan to believe that a rational explanation of historical actions must be an explanation in terms of a distinctively historical reason.

A mere historian cannot essay anything as rigorous as a definition, but let us try to approximate a characterization of historical action. An action becomes historical when it is viewed as the intermediate point of a temporal process in which it is produced, and then in turn helps to produce a subsequent action. Two features are to be remarked in this characterization. In the first place, the production of an action through a temporal sequence is not necessarily the same as the genesis of an action in the beliefs and motives of the agent. In the latter case, the action may be considered, as Mr. Dray considers it, as the product of formal reasons extending through an indefinite time span. In the former case, however, the action is seen as produced by no original reasons but rather by the changing career of these reasons from time point to time point in a definite span, until they crystallize out in the action. Historical explanations therefore are either narratives or characterizations of narratives; actions are not explained in themselves but only for their role in the narrative. The actions of individuals are explained in terms of reasons grounded in motives and beliefs only as shortcuts when such actions are contributory to social actions. When the actions of individuals are treated for themselves, then their explanation must also be subjected to the narration of their antecedents through time.

But not their antecedents alone. For the second vital point in our characterization of historical action is that it does not become historical until it has fed into another action. It is this attribute that distinguishes the immediate past from the historical, but it is this attribute too that distinguishes actions treated as absolute culminations anywhere in the past from the historical. They may be antiquarian but they are not historical. This attribute is not arbitrary; it is a postulate of an essential function of historical reason: the capacity to analyze backward as well as forward along the time dimension. The historian finds an action explained only when he understands what came out of it as well as what went into it. Why should this be so? Let us omit the angle of the historian himself. It is because the crystallization of tendencies into action creates a new truth, a truth manifested only subsequently. If this formulation seems to apply more to objectified actions than to the doing of actions, which is Mr. Dray's problem, then we may rephrase it in the following way: an action is as explicable by the direction it sponsors in a man's subsequent behavior as it is by the reasons for which he began to undertake it. And if this be a covering law, so be it. I shall apply it where it fits. And so we are back at the crucial question which we left in abeyance. If the historian uses all kinds of theories and generalizations and perceptions as hypotheses for understanding the actual reasons for actions, how should he judge which of them fit? From the above considerations we may conclude that the historian should use those hypotheses, either singly or in combination, which enable him to account for the antecedents of the action, the action, and its aftereffects in such a way as to constitute a sequential unity. Inevitably historians will put forth different versions of this unity, for explanations in history, whether narrative or conceptual, invariably violate or neglect some of the facts. The temperament and the predisposition of the historian determines in which selection and arrangement he will find his unity—dramatic, dialectic, evolutionary, or didactic—but in any case an explanation of explanation that does not provide for variety as well as consensus is a philosophy of utopian history.

We have come a long way from Mr. Dray, and I do not doubt that I have transgressed many times the boundary lines which he has so carefully laid out around his subject. As an historian I could not help but do so, for I have had little experience of his automatic rationality and once we open the search for criteria of rationality it is a Pandora's Box. But one conclusion emerges that may perhaps prove fruitful: the original reason for the divergence of philosophers and historians on the philosophy of history is that they do not mean the same thing by history. For the philosopher it would seem to comprehend all of past reality, and, with suitable modifications for its pastness, it is subject to the same kind of analysis as is reality per se. For the historian it comprehends only the visible surface of past reality and is subject to the special skill in tracing lateral connections up to that near point within which the eye can no longer focus. Clearly there is room for mutual understanding here—if we can only begin to agree about what it is we are disagreeing about.

9

Reasons and Covering Laws in Historical Explanation

CARL G. HEMPEL
Princeton University

1. DEDUCTIVE AND PROBABILISTIC EXPLANATION BY COVERING LAWS

As a background for the following discussion of historical explanation, which is prompted mainly by Professor Dray's substantial and stimulating paper, I propose to present first a brief sketch of, and some amplificatory comments on, the covering law analysis of explanation.

The suggestive term 'covering law model of explanation' was introduced by Professor Dray in his monograph, *Laws and Explanation in History,* in which, after a very fair-minded presentation of this conception of explanation, he develops a number of interesting arguments against its general adequacy, particularly in the field of historical inquiry.

In his book, Mr. Dray used the term 'covering law model' to refer to the construal of an explanation as a deductive subsumption under covering laws. In an explanation of this kind, a given empirical phenomenon—in this paper, I will normally take it to be a particular event—is accounted for by deducing the *explanandum* statement, which describes the event in question, from a set of other statements, called the *explanans.* This set consists of some general laws and of statements describing certain particular facts or conditions, which usually are antecedent to or simultaneous with the event to be explained. In a causal explanation, for example—to mention one important variety of deductive explanation by covering laws—an individual event (e.g., an increase in the volume of a particular body of gas at a particular place and time) is presented as the "effect" of certain other particular events and conditions (e.g., heating of that body of gas under conditions of constant pressure), from which it resulted (from whose realization its occurrence can be inferred) in accordance with certain general laws (e.g., gas laws).

In explanations of the deductive, or "deductive-nomological," kind the covering laws are all of strictly universal form; i.e., schematically speaking, they are statements to the effect that in *all* cases where a certain complex F of conditions is satisfied, an event or state of kind G will come about; in symbolic notation: $(x)(Fx \supset Gx)$.

But there is a second, logically quite different, kind of explanation, which plays an important role in various branches of empirical science, and which I will call "covering law explanation" as well. The distinctive feature of this second type, to which Mr. Dray briefly alludes in his paper, is that some of the covering laws are of probabilistic-statistical form. In the simplest case, a law of this form is a statement to the effect that under conditions of a more or less complex kind F, an event or "result" of kind G will occur with statistical probability—i.e., roughly: with long-run relative frequency—q; in symbolic notation: $p_s(G,F) = q$. If the probability q is close to 1, a law of this type may be invoked to explain the occurrence of G in a given particular case in which conditions F are realized. By way of a simple illustration, suppose that after one particular rolling of a given set of four dice, the total number of dots facing up is greater than 4. This might be explained by the following information (whose factual correctness is, of course, an empirical matter and subject to empirical test; it would not be true, for example, if one of the dice were loaded): (i) For every one of the dice, the statistical probability for any particular face to show up as a result of a rolling is the same as for any other face, and (ii) the results yielded by the individual dice, when rolled jointly, are statistically independent of each other; so that the statistical probability for a joint rolling (R) of all four dice to yield a total of more than four dots (M) is: $p_s(M,R) = 1295/1296 = .9992...$ This general probability statement, combined with the information that the particular occurrence under consideration, say i, was a case of joint rolling of the four dice (or briefly that Ri), does not logically imply that in the particular case i the total number of eyes facing up will be more than four (or that Mi, for short): but the two statements provide strong inductive grounds, or strong inductive support, or, as it is sometimes put, high inductive probability, for the assumption or expectation that Mi. The logical character of this explanatory argument may be represented by the following schema:

(*Explanans*)	$\left\{\begin{array}{l} p_s(M,R) = 1295/1296 \\ Ri \end{array}\right\}$	confers high inductive probability on
(*Explanandum*)	Mi	

The probability which the *explanans* is here said to confer upon the *explanandum* is clearly not of the statistical kind; it does not represent an empirically determined quantitative relation between two kinds of event, such as R and M; rather, it is a logical relation between two statements—in our case, between the conjunction of the *explanans* statement on one hand and the *explanandum* statement on the other. This relation of inductive-logical support or probability is the central concept of the logical theories of probability developed by Keynes and by Carnap, to mention two outstanding examples. Carnap's theory, which is applicable to formalized languages of certain kinds, in fact provides ways of giving an explicit definition of logical probability in quantitative terms. To what extent these systems of inductive logic are applicable to actual scientific contexts is still a subject of study and debate; but that does not affect the basic thesis that in an explanation by means of probabilistic-statistical laws, the "subsumption" of the *explanandum* statement under the "covering laws" rests, not on a deductive implication, but on a relation of inductive support between the *explanans* and the *explanandum* statement. I will therefore refer to this kind of explanation as *probabilistic or inductive explanation.* Explanations of this kind play an important role in several areas of scientific inquiry; for example, the irreversibility of certain macrophenomena, such as the mixing of coffee and cream, is probabilistically explained by the assumption of certain purely statistical uniformities at the level of the underlying microevents.

2. A NECESSARY CONDITION OF ADEQUACY FOR EXPLANATIONS

The two kinds of explanation by covering laws have this feature in common: they explain an event by showing that, in view of certain particular circumstances and general laws, its occurrence was to be expected (in a purely logical sense), either with deductive certainty or with inductive probability.[1] In virtue of this feature, the two modes of explanation clearly satisfy what is, I submit, a general *condition of adequacy* for any account that is to qualify as a rationally acceptable explanation of a given event. The condition is that any such explanation, i.e., any rationally acceptable answer to a question of the type 'Why did X occur?' must provide information which constitutes good grounds for the belief that X did in fact occur.[2] To state the point a little more fully: If the question 'Why did X occur?' is answered by 'Because Z is, or was, the case,' then the answer does not afford a rationally adequate explanation of X's occurrence unless the information that Z is, or was, the case constitutes good grounds for expecting or believing that X did occur: otherwise, the explanatory information would provide no adequate grounds for saying, as it were: "That explains it—that does show why X occurred!"

Two amplificatory remarks may be indicated. First: the condition of adequacy just stated is to be understood as a necessary condition for an adequate explanation, not as a sufficient one; certain kinds of information—such as the results of a scientific test—may provide excellent grounds for believing that X occurred without in the least explaining why.

Secondly, the covering law concepts of explanation, as schematically represented by the models, refer to the logic, not to the psychology, of explanation, just as metamathematical concepts of proof refer to the logic, not to the psychology, of proving mathematical theorems. Proofs and explanations that are adequate in the psychologic-pragmatic sense (which is of interest and importance in its own right) of making someone "understand" whatever is being proved or explained may well be achieved—and are in fact often achieved—by procedures that do not meet the formal standards for the concepts of proof or explanation construed in a nonpragmatic, metatheoretical sense. For example, it may be sufficient to call to a person's attention just one particular fact or just some general principle he had overlooked or forgotten or not known at all: taken in combination with other items in his background knowledge, this may make the puzzling item, X, fall into place for him: he will "understand why" X is the case. And since the proofs and explanations offered by mathematicians and empirical scientists in their writings, lectures, and informal conversations are normally formulated with some particular kind of audience in mind, they are accordingly elliptic in varying degrees. But this surely does not show that attempts to construct nonpragmatic, metatheoretical concepts of proof and explanation are either mistaken in principle or at any rate bound to be unilluminating and theoretically unprofitable. In the case of proof-theory, the contrary is well known to be the case. And while the logical theory of explanation cannot claim achievements comparable in depth and importance to those of recent proof-theory, it has led to some significant insights. For example, certain results by Ramsey and by Craig illuminate the role of "theoretical entities" in scientific theories and shed light on the possibility of avoiding reference to such entities in scientific theories without loss of explanatory import; and problems such as these clearly concern the logic, not the psychology, of explanation.

As I mentioned a moment ago, the explanatory accounts actually offered by investigators in various fields of empirical inquiry, ranging from physics to historical research, will often fail to meet the condition of adequacy set forth above, and yet those accounts might intuitively be quite satisfactory. Clearly, in appraising the logical adequacy of a proposed explanation we must in fairness take into account not only what it explicitly tells us in the *explanans,* but also what it omits as not requiring mention, as tacitly taken for granted and presumed to be understood. Of course, it is not the task of a logical theory of explanation to tell us how to carry out an appraisal of this kind—any more than it is the task of a logical theory of inference to tell us how to judge whether a proposed argument that falls short of the formal standards of deductive validity is to be qualified as invalid or as deductively valid but elliptically formulated. The parallel to the case of mathematical proof is clear.

The condition of adequacy here proposed conflicts with a claim that has been made particularly, but not exclusively, with respect to historical explanation, namely, that sometimes an event can be quite adequately explained by pointing out that such and such antecedent conditions which are necessary but not sufficient for its occurrence, were realized. As Mr. Dray mentions in his survey of various modifications that have been suggested for the covering law construal of explanation, this idea has been put forward by Frankel and by Gallie; it has also been strongly endorsed by Scriven, who offers this illustration in support of his view: [3] Paresis occurs only in persons who have previously suffered from syphilis; and the occurrence of paresis in a given patient can therefore be properly explained by antecedent syphilitic infection—and thus by reference to an antecedent which constitutes a necessary but far from sufficient condition: for in fact, only quite a small percentage of syphilitics develop paresis. This "explanation" clearly violates the condition of adequacy proposed above. Indeed, as Scriven is the first to point out, on the information that a person has had syphilis, "we must . . . predict that [paresis] will *not* occur." [4] But precisely because the statistical probability for syphilis to lead to paresis is so small, and because therefore on the given information we must rationally expect the given person *not* to have developed paresis, the information that the patient has had syphilis (and that only syphilitics can develop paresis) clearly no more explains the actual occurrence of paresis in this case than a man's winning the first prize in the Irish Sweepstakes is explained by the information that he had bought a ticket (and that only a person who has bought a ticket can win the first prize).

3. INDIVIDUAL EVENTS AND "COMPLETE" EXPLANATION

In his paper, Mr. Dray touches briefly upon a question that has received a good deal of attention in the recent literature, namely, whether any individual event admits of a *complete* explanation, and in particular, whether such an explanation could possibly be achieved by means of covering laws. I would like to comment briefly on this issue.

In any covering law explanation of an individual event, the event in question is always characterized by a *statement*, the *explanandum* statement. Thus, when we ask why a given body of gas, g, increased in volume between 5:00 and 5:01 PM, or why the particular rolling i of our four dice yielded a total of more than four dots facing up, the *explanandum* events are described by the statements 'the body of gas, g, increased in volume between 5:00 and 5:01 PM' and 'the particular rolling i of the four dice yielded a total of more than four dots facing up.' Clearly then, only individual events in this sense, as described by statements, can possibly be explained by means of covering laws. (This is not to say, of course, that every such event can actually be so explained: the covering law analysis of explanation presents a thesis about the logical structure of scientific explanation, but not about the extent to which individual occurrences in the world can be explained: that depends on what laws hold in the world and clearly cannot be determined just by logical analysis. In particular, therefore, the covering law analysis of explanation does not presuppose or imply universal determinism.)

Quite frequently, however, the notion of an individual event is understood in a very different way. An event in this second sense is typically characterized, not by a statement describing it, but by an individual name or by a definite description, such as 'the Children's Crusade,' 'the October Revolution,' 'the eruption of Mt. Vesuvius in 79 A.D.,' 'the assassination of Julius Caesar,' 'the first solar eclipse of the 1960's,' and the like. Individual occurrences thus understood cannot be explained by covering laws nor in any other way; indeed, it is unclear what could be meant by explaining such an event. For any event thus understood has infinitely many aspects and thus cannot be even fully described, let alone explained. For example, the various aspects of Julius Caesar's assassination include the fact that it was plotted by Brutus and Cassius; that Brutus and his fellow-conspirators were in such and such political positions and had such and such expectations and aspirations; that Caesar received such and such wounds; and—if I may trust an estimate I read some time ago, which may be quite well supported by physical theory—that with every breath we draw today, we inhale some of the molecules of oxygen and nitrogen that Caesar exhaled in his dying breath. Evidently, a complete characterization, let alone explanation, of an individual event in this sense is impossible.

For lack of a better expression, I will use the phrase '*concrete event*' to refer to individual events understood in this latter sense. Individual events of the only kind admitting in principle of explanation by covering laws, i.e., events describable by statement, might then be said to constitute particular *aspects of, or facts about, concrete events.*[5]

I need hardly add that concrete events are not limited to the domain of the historian. An event such as the first total solar eclipse of the 1960's also exhibits infinitely many physical, chemical, biological, sociological, and yet other aspects and thus resists complete description and, a fortiori, complete explanation. But certain particular aspects of it—e.g., that it is visible from such and such a region on the earth, that the duration of its totality is so many seconds, etc.—may well permit of explanation by covering laws.[6]

But it would be incorrect to say that an explanation by covering laws can explain only some *kind* of event rather than an individual event. For, first of all, a *kind* of event would be represented by a predicate-expression, such as 'total solar eclipse visible from Alaska'; and since such expressions, not being statements, cannot be the conclusions of any deductive or inductive argument, a kind of event cannot be explained in accordance with the covering law models. Secondly, what might be so explained is the *occurrence of an event of a certain kind in a particular space-time region;* for example, a lengthening of the mercury column in a particular thermometer at a particular place during a specified period of time, or a particular individual developing yellow fever after being exposed to mosquitoes of a certain type. But what is thus explained is very definitely an individual event, of the sort that can be described by a statement. On this point, therefore, I agree with Mandelbaum, who rejects Hayek's thesis that explanation and prediction never refer to an individual event but always to phenomena of a certain kind, with the comment: "One would think that the prediction of a specific solar eclipse, or the explanation of that eclipse, would count as referring to a particular event even if it does not refer to all aspects of the event, such as the temperature of the sun, or the effect of the eclipse on the temperature of the earth, and the like."[7]

I said earlier that a concrete event, having infinitely many aspects, cannot be completely described, let alone explained. But there is at least one other sense in which the possibility of a complete explanation has recently been discussed and questioned, even in regard to individual events described by statements. Mr. Dray raises the issue in his paper when he asks whether an event can be *completely* explained by subsuming it under statistical rather than strictly universal laws, and thus without showing that it "had to happen." And indeed, as was noted earlier, the *explanans* of a statistical explanation confers upon the *explanandum* only a more or less high inductive probability, but does not imply it with deductive necessity, as is the case in deductive-nomological explanations. The latter might be said, in this sense, to be complete; probabilistic explanations, incomplete.[8] If the terms are thus understood, however, it is important to bear in mind that a more complete explanation of an event is not one that explains more aspects of it; in fact, the idea of completeness here under consideration applies only to the explanation of events described by statements, whereas the notion of aspects of an event was introduced in specific reference to concrete events.

Finally, it is now possible to specify a sense in which one might speak of partial explanations of concrete events and in which some of those explanations might be called more complete—in a third sense of the term—than others. First, any set of deductive-nomological explanations, each of which explains some aspect of a concrete event, might be called a partial deductive-nomological explanation of that event; and if the aspects explained in one of the sets form a proper subset of those in the other, the former set might be said to provide a less complete explanation of the concrete event than the latter. These notions can be generalized so as to apply also to sets containing probabilistic explanations, but this is not the place to enter into further details.

4. EXPLAINING ACTIONS BY REASONS.

4.1 *Dray's construal.* I now turn to some comments on the central topic of Mr. Dray's paper, the concept of rational explanation. Dray holds that the method, widely used by historians among others, of explaining human actions in terms of underlying reasons cannot be construed as conforming to the covering law pattern: to do so, he says, would be to give the wrong kind of reconstruction, it would get the form of such explanations wrong. In my opinion, Dray's arguments in support of this verdict, and his own alternative construal of such explanations, form a substantial contribution toward the formulation and clarification of the perplexing issues here at stake.

According to Dray, the object of explaining an action by reference to the reasons for which it was done is "to show that what was done was the thing to have done for the reasons given, rather than merely the thing that is done on such occasions, perhaps in accordance with certain laws." [9] The explanatory reasons will include the objectives the agent sought to attain and his beliefs concerning relevant empirical matters, such as the alternative courses of action open to him and their likely consequences. The explanation, according to Dray, then provides "a reconstruction of the agent's *calculation* of means to be adopted toward his chosen end in the light of the circumstances in which he found himself," [10] and it shows that the agent's choice was appropriate, that it was the thing to do under the circumstances. The appraisal thus made of the appropriateness of what was done presupposes, not general laws, but instead what Dray calls a "principle of action," i.e., a normative or evaluative principle of the form 'When in a situation of type C, the thing to do is X.' [11]

4.2 *The problem of criteria of rationality.* Before considering the central question whether, or in what sense, principles of this kind can explain an action, I want to call attention to what seems to me a problematic assumption underlying Dray's concept of a principle of action. As is suggested by the phrase 'the thing to do,' Dray seems to assume (i) that, given a specification of the circumstances in which an agent finds himself (including, I take it, in particular his objectives and beliefs), there is a clear and unequivocal sense in which an action can be said to be appropriate, or reasonable, or rational under the circumstances; and (ii) that, at least in many cases, there is exactly one course of action that is appropriate in this sense. Indeed, Dray argues that on this score rational explanation is superior to statistical explanation because the question why an action had to be done often permits an answer that involves the rational ruling out of all possible alternatives—a result that cannot be achieved in a probabilistic explanation.

But the two assumptions just listed seem to be unwarranted or at least highly questionable. First of all, it is by no means clear by what criteria of rationality "the thing to do" in a given situation is to be characterized. While several recent writers assume that there is one clear notion of rationality in the sense here required,[12] they have proposed no explicit definitions; and doubts about the possibility of formulating adequate general criteria of rationality are enhanced by the mathematical theory of decisions, which shows that even for some rather simple types of decision-situation several different criteria of rational choice can be formulated, each of which is quite plausible and yet incompatible with its alternatives.[13] And if this is so in simple cases, then the notion of *the* thing to do under given circumstances must be regarded as even more problematic when applied to the kinds of decision and action the historian seeks to explain. I think, therefore, that the presuppositions underlying the idea of a principle of action require further elaboration and scrutiny.

However, in order not to complicate the remainder of my discussion, I will disregard this difficulty from here on and will assume, for the sake of the argument, that the intended meaning of the expression 'X is the appropriate, or rational, thing to do under circumstances of kind C' has been agreed upon and adequately specified by objective criteria.

4.3 *The explanatory import of citing reasons for an action.* The question we have to consider then is this: How can a principle of action serve in an explanatory capacity? Dray's account, both in his paper and in his book, would seem to suggest that a rational explanation of why agent A did X would take the following form:

Agent A was in a situation of kind C.
When in a situation of kind C, the thing to do is X.

Therefore, agent A did X.

The first statement in the *explanans* specifies certain antecedent conditions; the second is a principle of action taking the place which, in a covering law explanation, is held by a set of general laws.

Thus conceived, the logic of rational explanation does indeed differ decisively from that of covering law explanation. But precisely because of the feature that makes the difference it cannot, I submit, explain why A did X. For by the general condition of adequacy considered earlier, an adequate *explanans* for A's having done X must afford good reasons for the belief or the assertion that A did in fact do X. But while the *explanans* just formulated affords good grounds for asserting that the appropriate thing for A to do under the circumstances was X, it does not provide good reasons for asserting or believing that A did in fact do X. To justify this latter assertion, the *explanans* would have to include a further assumption, to the effect that at the time in question A was a rational agent, and was thus disposed to do what was appropriate in the given situation. When modified accordingly, our *explanans* takes on a form which may be schematized as follows:

Agent A was in a situation of kind C.
A was a rational agent at the time
Any rational agent, when in a situation of kind C,
  will invariably (or: with high probability) do X,

and it will then logically imply (or confer a high inductive probability on) the *explanandum:*

A did X

Thus modified, the account will indeed provide an explanation of why A did in fact do X. But its adequacy for this purpose has been achieved by replacing Dray's evaluative principle of action by a descriptive principle stating what rational agents will do in situations of kind C. The result is a covering law explanation, which will be deductive or inductive according as the general statement about the behavior of rational agents is of strictly universal or of probabilistic-statistical form. This construal of an explanation by reasons is evidently akin to Ryle's conception of an explanation by reference to dispositions; [14] for it presents A's action, as it were, as a manifestation of his general disposition to act in characteristic ways—in ways that qualify as appropriate or rational—when in certain situations.

It might be objected [15] to the broadly dispositional analysis here proposed that the "covering law" allegedly expressed by the third statement in the *explanans* is not really an empirical law about how rational agents do in fact behave, but an analytic statement of a definitional character, which expresses part of what is *meant* by a rational agent—so that the given action is not actually explained by subsumption under a general law. However, this objection does not, I think, do justice to the logical character of concepts such as that of a rational agent. The reason, stated very briefly, is that such concepts are governed by large clusters of general statements—they might be called symptom statements—which assign to the dispositional characteristic in question various typical manifestations or symptoms; each symptom being a particular manner in which a person who has the dispositional characteristic will "respond to," or "act under" certain specific ("stimulus-") conditions. The third statement in our *explanans* is then just one of many symptom statements for the concept of rational agent. But the totality of the symptom statements for a given broadly dispositional concept will normally have empirical implications, so that they cannot all be qualified as definitional or analytic; and it would be arbitrary to attribute to some of them—e.g., the one invoked in our *explanans*—the analytic character of partial definitions and to construe only the remaining ones as having empirical import.[16]

In sum, then, I think that Dray's very suggestively presented construal of explanations by reasons has a basic logical defect, which springs from the view that such explanations must be based on principles of action rather than on general laws. Dray explicitly makes a distinction between the two on the ground that the phrase 'the thing to do,' which characteristically occurs in a principle of action, "functions as a value-term," and that therefore there is a certain "element of *appraisal*" in a rational explanation, for it must tell us in what way an action "was *appropriate*."[17] But—and this seems to me the crux of the matter—to show that an action was the appropriate or rational thing to have done under the circumstances is not to explain why in fact it was done. Indeed, no normative or evaluative principle specifying what kind of action is appropriate in given circumstances can possibly serve to explain why a person acted in a particular way; and this is so no matter whether the action does or does not conform to the normative principle in question.

The basic point of the objection here raised has also been made by J. Passmore, who states it succinctly as follows: ". . . explanation by reference to a 'principle of action' or 'a good reason' is not, by itself, explanation at all. . . . For a reason may be a 'good reason'—in the sense of being a principle to which one *could* appeal in justification of one's action—without having in fact the slightest influence on us."[18]

It might perhaps be suspected that in arguing for a broadly dispositional analysis which presents explanations by reasons as having basically the logical structure of one or other of the covering law models, we are violating a maxim of which Mr. Dray rightly reminds us in his paper, namely, that a sound logical analysis must refrain from forcing historical explanation onto the Procrustean bed of some preconceived general schema, and that instead it must take careful account of the practice generally agreed to be acceptable within the discipline concerned; that it must show sensitivity to the concept of explanation historians normally employ. No doubt a historian who adduces an agent's presumptive reasons in order to explain his actions, may well conceive it to be his main task to show that in the light of those reasons, the action was the appropriate thing to have done. But in giving his account, the historian undoubtedly also intends to show why in fact the agent acted as he did—e.g., to take Dray's example, why Louis XIV in fact withdrew military pressure from Holland. And this question cannot be answered by showing that the action was a (or even "the") reasonable thing to do, given Louis' objectives and beliefs; for after all, many agents on many occasions do not actually do the rational thing. This observation seems akin to an objection raised by Strawson, to which Dray refers in his paper. Dray agrees there that human action can fall short of the ideal of rationality and he stresses that his claim is only that the criterion of rational appropriateness does function for actions that are not judged to be defective in various ways. But this seems to me the crucial point: If an explanation by reasons invokes standards of rationality then, to have the desired explanatory force, it must in addition make the empirical assumption that the action was not defective in relevant ways, i.e., that the agent was at the time disposed to act in accordance with the standards invoked, and that the external circumstances did not prevent him from doing so.

And it seems clear to me that a historian would simply see no point in displaying the appropriateness or rationality of an action if he did not assume that the agent, at the time in question, was disposed to act rationally (as he might not be under conditions of extreme fatigue, under severe emotional strain, under the influence of drugs, and the like). And since, in an explanation by reasons, this essential presupposition will normally be taken for granted, it will not, as a rule, be explicitly mentioned; it is rather when departures from rationality are considered that the need is felt explicitly to specify disturbing circumstances. But while an elliptic formulation that forgoes explicit mention of the assumption of rationality may be quite satisfactory for practical purposes, i.e., in the pragmatic-psychological context of explanation, it obscures the logic of the explanatory argument; and surely, an analysis that makes explicit this essential assumption underlying the historian's account does not thereby force the method of explanation by reasons upon a Procrustean bed.

I think the broadly dispositional analysis I have outlined applies also to the intriguing case, invoked by Mr. Dray, of explaining one's own actions by reference to the reasons for which they were done. To be sure, in an account of the form 'I did X for reasons R,' explanation and justification are almost inextricably fused, and yet, we do distinguish between a genuine explanation and a mere rationalization in such contexts; and an account of the form 'I did X for reasons R' would be suspected of being a rationalization if there were grounds to believe that I had not actually done X for the reasons given: e.g., that I had not in fact had the reasons and beliefs adduced in my account, or that I had been in a state in which I might well have tended not to take an action appropriate to my objectives and relevant empirical beliefs. Thus again, a statement given by me of the reasons for my action can have explanatory force only on the assumption of a disposition to act rationally in the given situation.

4.4 *The "rationality" of nondeliberate actions.* A dispositional construal of rational explanation can also resolve a difficulty inherent in a view that Mr. Dray expresses in his book, and to which he briefly adverts again in his paper. According to Dray, there are certain actions that qualify as rational although they are decided upon without the benefit of actual deliberation or calculation. Indeed, in his book he argues that insofar as an action is purposive at all—no matter at what level of conscious deliberation—it is capable of rational explanation because "there is a calculation which could be constructed for it," a calculation the agent might have performed had he had the time, and which he might produce if questioned later.[19] But since, by hypothesis, no such deliberation or calculation did take place, since considerations of rationality actually played no role in the agent's action, an explanation of the latter by reference to such calculations seems to me to be simply fictitious.

Responding to an objection by Nowell-Smith which appears to be aimed at this point, Mr. Dray states again in his paper that the reasons adduced in a rational explanation need not actually have been considered by the agent in adopting his course of action, and he adds that our understanding of that action may arise out of our perception of a rational connection between the action and the motives and beliefs the rational explanation ascribes to the agent. But again, our awareness of such a logical connection surely cannot show why the action was taken by the agent, who, by hypothesis, took no account of that connection at all.

But I think Mr. Dray has a point in regarding some of those actions that are decided upon "in a flash," without reflection, as being akin to those which are prompted by careful deliberation. And it is possible to do justice to this idea by giving it a different—and again broadly dispositional—construal. Under this construal, a "rational explanation" of such an action is effected by ascribing to the agent certain behavioral dispositions acquired through a learning process whose initial phases did involve conscious reflection and deliberation. Consider, for example, the various intricate maneuvers required in using a typewriter, in driving a car through heavy traffic, in drilling and filling a patient's teeth: all these are learned in training processes that involve more or less elaborate deliberation in the beginning; but eventually they become "second nature" and are performed routinely, with little or no conscious reflection.

A particular act of this kind might then be explained, not by a reconstructed calculation or deliberation which the agent in fact did not perform, nor by pointing out that his action was appropriate to his putative objectives, but by presenting it as a manifestation of a general behavior pattern that the agent had learned in the manner just alluded to.[20] And clearly, this derivative kind of rational explanation would again be broadly dispositional, and hence of the covering law variety.

To adopt the general conception I have presented here of explanation by reasons is by no means to deny that, as Mr. Dray rightly stresses, the historian adducing motivating reasons in explanation of an action normally does seek to show that the action "makes sense" when considered in the light of the purposes and the beliefs that presumably prompted it; nor is it to deny that perceiving an action as thus making sense can be a source of great intellectual satisfaction. What I have tried to argue is rather that—apart from the problematic status of the requisite concept of appropriateness—the presentation of an action as being appropriate to the given situation, as making sense, cannot, for purely logical reasons, serve to explain why in fact the action was taken.

NOTES

1. For a fuller account of the deductive-nomological model see, for example, C. G. Hempel, "The Function of General Laws in History," *The Journal of Philosophy*, 39 (1942), 35–48. Reprinted in *Theories of History*, ed. P. Gardiner (Glencoe, Ill.: Free Press, 1959), pp. 344–56. See also C. G. Hempel and P. Oppenheim, "Studies in the Logic of Explanation," *Philosophy of Science*, 15 (1948), 135–75. Secs. 1–7 of this article are reprinted in *Readings in the Philosophy of Science*, eds. H. Feigl and M. Brodbeck (New York: Appleton-Century-Crofts, 1953), pp. 319–52. The former of these articles also deals with the relevance of covering law explanation to historical inquiry. A more detailed logical analysis of inductive-probabilistic explanation has been attempted in C. G. Hempel, "Deductive-Nomological vs. Statistical Explanation," in *Minnesota Studies in the Philosophy of Science*, eds. H. Feigl and G. Maxwell, III (Minneapolis: University of Minnesota Press, 1962), 98–169.

2. The condition can readily be formulated so as to cover also explanations that are intended to account, not for an individual event or state of affairs, but for some general uniformity, such as that expressed by Kepler's second law, for example. But explanations of this latter kind—which are discussed, for example, in the second and third of the articles mentioned in n. 1—need not be considered in this paper.

3. M. Scriven, "Explanation and Prediction in Evolutionary Theory," *Science*, 130 (1959), 480.

4. *Ibid.* (Italics the author's.)

5. At the end of the present section, a derivative sense will

be suggested in which one might speak of more or less complete covering law explanations of concrete events.

6. The gist of what I have so far said here about individual events and their explanation was briefly, but quite explicitly, stated already in Hempel, "The Function of General Laws in History," *op. cit.*, sec. 2.2.

7. M. Mandelbaum, "Historical Explanation: The Problem of 'Covering Laws,'" *History and Theory,* 1 (1961), 233, fn. 6.

8. Completeness and incompleteness of explanation are obviously understood in this sense by J. Pitt, "Generalizations in Historical Explanation," *The Journal of Philosophy,* 56 (1959), 580–81.

9. W. Dray, *Laws and Explanation in History* (London: Oxford University Press, 1957), p. 124.

10. Dray, *op. cit.*, p. 122. (Italics the author's.)

11. Dray, *Ibid.*, p. 132.

12. For example, Q. Gibson, in his stimulating study, *The Logic of Social Enquiry* (London: Routledge and Kegan Paul; and New York: Humanities Press, 1960), asserts: "there may be various alternative ways of achieving an end. To act rationally . . . is to select what on the evidence is *the best* way of achieving it" (p. 160; italics the author's); and he refers to "an elementary logical point—namely, that, given certain evidence, there can only be one correct solution to the problem as to the best way of achieving a given end" (p. 162).

13. For a clear account and comparative analysis of such criteria, see, for example, R. D. Luce and H. Raiffa, *Games and Decisions* (New York: John Wiley & Sons, 1957), ch. 13.

14. G. Ryle, *The Concept of Mind* (London: Hutchinson's University Library, 1949). The construal here intended, which has been outlined only sketchily, differs, however, in certain respects from what I take to be Ryle's conception. To indicate this, I refer to the analysis here envisaged as "broadly dispositional." For a fuller account, see Hempel, "Rational Action," in *Proceedings and Addresses of the American Philosophical Association,* vol. XXXV (Yellow Springs, Ohio: Antioch Press, 1962); sec. 3.2 of that article, in particular, states and discusses the differences in question.

15. An objection to this effect was in fact raised in the discussion by Professor R. Brandt.

16. This idea is presented somewhat more fully in Hempel, "Explanation in Science and in History," in *Frontiers of Science*

and Philosophy, ed. R. G. Colodny (Pittsburgh: University of Pittsburgh Press, 1962), sec. 6; also sec. 3.2 of Hempel, "Rational Action," *op. cit.,* has a direct bearing on this issue.

17. Dray, *op. cit.,* p. 124. (Italics the author's.)

18. J. Passmore, "Review Article: Law and Explanation in History," *Australian Journal of Politics and History,* 4 (1958), 275. (Italics the author's.) Passmore then goes on to argue very briefly also that an explanation by reasons amounts to an explanation "by reference to a general statement," for to "take a 'reason' to be the actual explanation of anyone's conduct . . . is to assert, at least . . . the general statement: 'People of type X, in situation Y, act in such a way as to conserve the principle Z.' " (*Ibid.*)

19. Dray, *op. cit.,* p. 123.

20. In a similar vein, I. Scheffler, in "Thoughts on Teleology," *British Journal for the Philosophy of Science,* 9 (1959), 269–75, has suggested that an interpretation in terms of learning may shed light on some types of nonpurposive teleological behavior.

PART IV

Contributions by Other Participants

10

Cause and Reason in History

RAZIEL ABELSON
New York University

THE BIG, FAT, JUICY PHILOSOPHICAL QUESTION about history is: What *is* it? So fat and juicy is this question that when it was asked of a group of articulate people at the Institute, streams of answers came flooding out in all directions, as if someone had stepped on a ripe grapefruit. The question is *too* juicy, because history is lots of things and not just one thing. History is art and science, poetry and journalism, explanation, narration, and criticism; it is epochal and parochial, holistic and individualistic, materialistic and spiritualistic, objective and subjective, factual and normative, practical and theoretical. Attempts to define history in terms of one style, one purpose, or one methodology reveal only the special preoccupations of the writer. For history is mankind thinking about itself, remembering, reporting, appreciating, explaining, moralizing, and even, as Professor Meyer Schapiro pointed out, dreaming.

Professor Morton White's remarkably lucid effort to boil down history to a syntactical essence is therefore as misguided as was Hegel's conceptual blueprint. Professor White defines history as a chronicle (sequence of true statements of fact) plus an explanation (set of logically linked "because" statements). There seems to be no room in this syntactical bed of Procrustes for some of the best historical writing. In his *History of the Russian Revolution,* Trotsky writes that "the Revolution made its first steps toward victory under the belly of a Cossack's horse." This statement would be classified as part of a chronicle, on White's criterion, and thus as nonexplanatory, yet it is in fact brilliantly explanatory, for it provides the reader with a clear vision of an infinitely complex pattern of events, attitudes, and purposes. Trotsky's description is explanatory in the way that art, not science, is explanatory, in the way of illumination rather than of deductive inference. Aristotle's definition of art as the revelation of the universal in the particular applies as well to this kind of historical writing as it does to literature. And Trotsky's description of the young bolshevik who prevented a mob from breaking into the government's liquor supply, "Revolver in hand, he fought for a sober October," renders any neat distinction between poetry and historical truth glaringly inappropriate.

But if it is impossible to define just what history is, there is at least one thing we can definitely say history is not. It is not and cannot possibly be causal explanation. It is not and cannot be the natural science of human behavior. Although most people knew this intuitively all along, William Dray's illuminating study *Laws and Explanation in History* provided the first clear account of just why history cannnot be the deduction of events from laws and antecedent conditions. This is because voluntary human actions call for purposive explanations in terms of reasons, and not for causal theories. Dray has shown that the covering law model of historical explanation schematized by Professor Hempel and borrowed from natural science is irrelevant to what we want to know about history. We want to know the reasons why people did the things they did, and not how their actions could have been predicted in advance.

To me, the refreshing feature of Dray's analysis of historical explanation is that it supports our belief in human freedom, an implication that Dray (overcautiously, I believe) refuses to draw explicitly. In arguing that a historian's job is to find reasons rather than compelling causes, Dray nevertheless concedes to determinists that reasons *may* be a special subclass of causes (presumably "psychic" causes), and he professes not to be taking a stand in favor of indeterminism. Now, it is true that his analysis does not support indeterminism, but he is wrong in allowing reasons to be subsumed under causes. If reasons were causes, there would be nothing wrong with the covering law model. But the proper conclusion to draw from the distinction between reasons and causes is the one drawn by A. I. Melden in his book *Free Action:* to ascribe causes to human actions is to commit a category-mistake and to fail to make sense. To say that human actions are free does not entail that they have no causes, or that they have supernatural causes, but that the concept of cause and the concept of human action belong to different and incompatible modes of discourse.

But in arguing against the covering law model, both in his book and in his contribution to this symposium, Professor Dray goes too far in confining history to one particular historical concern, namely, that of tracing the rationale of human actions. History cannot be *exclusively* interested in finding the reasons for actions, because (a) not all rational actions are historically significant and not all historically significant actions are rational, and (b) part of the process of finding reasons involves considerations of another kind, including those emphasized by Professor Hempel. In what follows I shall try to justify these two claims.

(a) I take it as self-evident that not all rational actions are historically significant. In any case, it is not this statement, but its converse, that contradicts Dray's analysis of historical explanation. The decisions and actions of political leaders like Hitler and Stalin have undisputed historical significance, but it is doubtful if they are always rationally intelligible in accordance with Dray's criterion of intelligibility. According to Dray, the reasons cited by a historian to explain an action "must be *good* reasons . . . in the sense that *if* the situation had been as the agent envisaged it . . . then what was done would have been the thing to have done." (*Laws and Explanation in History,* p. 126.) Dray's criterion of adequate historical explanation is that the reason ascribed must be one that successfully justifies the action from the standpoint of the agent. But this criterion is either vacuous or clearly unsound. If what is meant is that the reason stated for the action of a man like Hitler must be one that Hitler *thinks* to be a good reason, then the claim is vacuously true because the criterion of what a man thinks to be a good reason is his willingness to act on it. There are many possible reasons for any given action. How do we know which of them was the agent's real or motivating reason? According to Dray, we know this when, on emphatically identifying ourselves with the agent, we see the reason cited as a good one. But first, there may be several good reasons from the standpoint of the agent. Which one is his motivating reason? And secondly, how do we know the agent's point of view? Doesn't the agent's "point of view" include the things the agent regards as good reasons for action? Thus we must identify his motives in terms of his point of view and his point of view in terms of his motives, and here we are in a vicious circle.

If, on the other hand, Dray's criterion of adequate historical explanation is to be interpreted in a nonvacuous way, we must make a distinction between the factual beliefs of the agent and his normative beliefs or values, since it is the latter that lead us into the circularity of identifying good reason by means of the agent's values and his values by what he takes to be good reasons. Perhaps, then, Dray means that the historian must find a reason for the agent's action that would be really (i.e., objectively) good if the agent's *factual* beliefs were true. This interpretation makes better sense of Dray's criterion, but it is not without difficulties of its own, for it entails that every historical personage is rational in the sense that, given the factual situation as he sees it, his actions are faultless. It follows that Plato was right in claiming that no one does evil voluntarily, and that all errors are intellectual rather than moral. We do not blame a person for mistaken beliefs about the circumstances under which he acts. If a man gives his wife poison in the sincere belief that he is giving her medicine, he cannot be accused of murder. The very important point of distinguishing between a person's factual beliefs and his ethical commitments is that we hold him morally responsible for the latter but we excuse him for the former. Thus on our second interpretation of Dray's criterion, all actions are either justifiable or excusable. But surely such a consequence is a *reductio ad absurdum* of the premisses from which it follows.

(b) There must, then, be more to historical explanation than justification in terms of the beliefs of the historical agent. Some actions, like Hitler's extermination of the Jews, cannot be rationally justified in terms of any set of beliefs. The motive for an action need not be a good reason. It might be a bad reason. But good or bad, the motive is a reason and not a cause. To this extent, Dray's criticism of the covering law model of historical explanation is sound. The difference between a motive and a cause should be clear from the fact that a motive cannot be identified until after the deed it is said to motivate, while a cause is, in principle, identifiable in advance of its effect. To say that X's motive for doing A was M, when X never did A, would be senseless, while saying that event C is the cause of event E, even if E has not occurred, makes perfectly good sense. It means that *if* C occurred, then it would be followed by E. Counterfactual conditionals are common parlance in natural science, but motivational counterfactuals are unintelligible.

Suppose a historian offers a reason why a historical personage acted as he did. How does the historian know that the reason he gives is the real or motivating reason for the action? For example, when Professor Gershoy claims that Bertrand Barère's reason for turning against Robespierre was to save the Revolution rather than to save his own neck, how does he substantiate his claim? He tries to trace a general pattern in Barère's behavior from which he can inductively infer that Barère had certain character traits. He then argues that, in the light of accepted psychological and sociological generalizations, it is probable that a person of Barère's character and background would be motivated by the one reason rather than by the other. In other words, probabilistic and deductive patterns of inference à la Hempel may be employed to prove that a given reason was, in fact, the agent's real reason, rather than to deduce his action from his alleged reason.

This brings me to my main objection to Professor Hempel's covering law model of historical explanation. Hempel suggests that Dray's notion of rational explanation is subsumable as a special case under the covering law model, because an agent's reason is part of the antecedent conditions from which his action may be deductively or probabilistically inferred, in accordance with the following schema:

From the premisses:

1. Anyone of the psychic makeup of person P who is in state R will (probably) do action A, and
2. P was in state R

We can derive:

3. P did (or was likely to do) A.

Disregarding the terribly misleading classification of reasons as psychic *states,* Hempel's model is vitiated by what might be dubbed the "fallacy of misplaced proof." In effect, Hempel has offered a schematic form for proving what doesn't need to be proved: the fact that P did A, which, *ex hypothesi,* the historian *already knows.* What needs to be proved is not the conclusion of Hempel's schema, but the *premiss* that P was, in fact, motivated by reason R. For if we already know that P was motivated to do A by reason R, then we must already know that P did A. Thus our historical deduction is, as Dray has remarked, perfectly trivial.

But Dray has overlooked an area where Hempel's deductive schema applies in a more illuminating way. The historian's work is hardly finished when he suggests a possible explanation of an agent's action in accordance with an alleged reason, as Professor Gershoy has demonstrated in his study of Barère. The historian must then *prove* (to some unspecifiable degree of conclusiveness) that the reason he alleges for the agent's action was the real or motivating reason. His proof may well involve accepted sociological, psychological, and biographical generalizations from which he can derive, by Hempel's schema, the likelihood that the agent acted for the reason alleged. Hempel's schema should therefore be read *backward:* Given that P did A, and that someone with P's character and historical circumstances usually does A for reason R, we can conclude that P was probably motivated by reason R.

I am not denying that deductive inference can be effectively employed in proving that human actions occurred, as well as in proving that they were motivated by certain reasons. I am merely claiming that deduction is a method of proof and not, in history, at least, a method of explanation. When a historian proves that an action occurred, he is not *explaining* the action, he is merely justifying his claim that the action took place. Again, when he proves that the action was performed for a certain reason, he is not explaining anything, but merely convincing us that the explanation he has already suggested is a true one. It is in the creative activity of describing the purposive pattern in which the action occupies an appropriate place that the work of explanation is performed, whereby a vision is evoked in the mind of the reader that illuminates the historical scene and makes sense out of chaos. While explanation and proof may have the same logical structure in natural science, they are quite distinct in structure where human action is concerned. This is because actions are done for motives, and motives are neither antecedent conditions nor events. Motives neither exist nor occur. They merely explain and, on occasion, they justify or excuse.

11

Rational Explanations in History

EVELYN BARKER
Columbus, Ohio

IN HIS SYMPOSIUM PAPER, "Laws and Explanations in History," Professor Dray maintains that what he terms "rational explanations" provide a logical analysis of the characteristic explanations of the actions of individual historical agents more in line with the practice of historians than the so-called covering law model. Furthermore, Professor Dray contends that even if the latter type of explanation were forthcoming in historical writing, the rational explanation of actions would still have the advantage of representing the kind of history which is "humanistically oriented," and to which the covering law model sets up a "conceptual barrier." Those who sense some artificiality in the application of the covering law type of explanation to history, as well as those who appreciate history as, in part at least, a humantistic discipline are naturally drawn to Mr. Dray's new model of analysis. Nevertheless I find myself dubious about several points in his account of rational explanations, and especially skeptical of his charge that covering law types of explanation are essentially nonhumanistic in character.

In order to elaborate these misgivings, I should like to review some polar oppositions between rational and covering law types of explanation described by Mr. Dray. On the covering law model, says Dray, an action is shown to be "routine," i.e., it is explained as the kind of action a certain type of individual would be expected to perform in given sorts of circumstances; but on the rational model, the action is seen to be "the thing to do," i.e., as the rational choice of an individual faced with a particular problem situation. According to the covering law model, explanation of the action is mediated by general laws of human behavior which the particular action instantiates, and from which it can be deduced. The historian employing the rational model of explanation, in contrast, explains the action by providing the "practical calculation" from which the choice of the particular course of action issues as a conclusion. Included in the practical calculation are the agent's goals, his principles of action, his beliefs concerning his own situation and the consequences of alternative courses of action. General laws of human conduct need not enter into such an explanation, either as necessary or sufficient conditions, Dray insists. The task of the historian is the ordering of the aforementioned ingredients of the calculation to show how they render the action adopted by the agent an "appropriate" one, from the agent's point of view. Thus rational explanation involves an empathic projection of the historian (and ultimately his reader) into the historical agent's situation, while the covering law type of explanation results in a species of spectatorism. Dray also suggests that rational explanations require an evaluative appraisal of the action by the historian, while the covering-law historian displays ethical neutrality.

These characteristic differences between the two types of explanation underlie Dray's claim that only explanations of a rational type can function in a humanistically-oriented history. At first blush his contention sounds plausible. The rational model furnishes the explanation of an action as the solution to an ethical problem. Since the ethical point of view is primarily, if not solely, a human viewpoint, we may readily assume that an explanation adopting such a standpoint could not fail to be humanistic in character; while the scientific viewpoint of the covering law theory which explains human action on the same model as nonhuman occurrences is dispassionate and inhumane. However, I shall argue that this assumption, plausible though it may be, is questionable. The polar differences between rational and covering law explanations stressed by Dray are either specious or exaggerated, in my opinion. Furthermore, I believe it to be the case that covering law types of explanation have a rightful place in humanistically-oriented history, and that the rational model of explanation suffers one defect that makes it inadequate to the task of supplying the kind of explanation of an action to be expected of such a history.

Dray concedes that not all individual historical actions are susceptible of explanation of a rational type; he merely maintains that in cases where such explanation is possible, it is preferable to a covering law type of explanation. However, I believe I can show that his model contains an essential limitation which severely impairs its adequacy (especially for a humanistically-oriented history) in many cases where it is applicable. It is the following: a rational explanation of an action is adequate only when the agent whose action is to be explained has a high degree of self-knowledge—about the order of that of the philosopher-kings in Plato's *Republic*, I should say. This condition, I submit, is not often satisfied by historical agents. What the humanistically-oriented historian often does is to provide his reader with the kind of knowledge about the agent and his situation which the agent did not himself possess, and which makes his action intelligible to the reader. Here is an example of such an explanation from W. H. Prescott's *The Conquest of Peru*. Pizarro, in desperate straits, conceived the bold plan of taking by force Atahuallpa, the Inca chief, and for that purpose, invited him to visit. Atahuallpa, after accepting the invitation, unexpectedly deferred his visit one day. Fearing that delay would undermine the flagging spirits of his small company, surrounded by an immense Peruvian force, Pizarro urged the Inca to come at once. Atahuallpa acceded to Pizarro's request, and going unarmed with a small retinue, was captured in a bloody massacre. Prescott explains Atahuallpa's conduct as follows:

> It is difficult to account for this wavering conduct of Atahuallpa, so different from the bold and decided character

which history ascribes to him. There is no doubt that he made his visit to the white men in perfect good faith; though Pizarro was probably right in conjecturing that this amiable disposition stood on a very precarious footing. There is as little reason to suppose that he distrusted the sincerity of the strangers, or he would not thus unnecessarily have proposed to visit them unarmed. His original purpose of coming with all his force was doubtless to display his royal state, and perhaps, also, to show greater respect for the Spaniards; but when he consented to accept their hospitality and pass the night in their quarters, he was willing to dispense with a great part of his armed soldiery and visit them in a manner that implied entire confidence in their good faith. *He was too absolute in his own empire easily to suspect; and he probably could not comprehend the audacity with which a few men, like those now assembled at Cajamarca, meditated an assault on a powerful monarch in the midst of his victorious army. He did not know the character of the Spaniard.*[1]

The italicized portion of this paragraph, which is essential to make Atahuallpa's action intelligible, is quite different in *kind* from a rational explanation. Atahuallpa could not have recognized these things about himself and his situation which Prescott reveals to us, and have acted as he in fact did. Thus such things could not be included in an explanation of the rational type—indeed, they are specifically debarred: a rational explanation only provides the reasons for acting of which the agent might conceivably be conscious and which could thus have entered into his practical calculation. Since the historian only "reworks the agent's calculation," his rational explanation cannot include things of which the agent was ignorant, and thus explain those actions where this ignorance was a crucial factor in the action, as in Atahuallpa's case. Explanations of the above kind are, however, not rare in history, and they represent the kind of explanation which more naturally fits into a covering law type of theory. The historian presents an analysis of the agent's character and circumstances which places his conduct within a recognizable pattern of human behavior which can be formulated in general terms. Such a procedure not only constitutes a genuine explanation, but also one which offers no conceptual barrier to a humanistically-oriented history.

In making such an accusation Dray is under a misapprehension concerning spectatorism in history. There is a species of spectatorism that genuinely belongs to history, and particularly, to humanistically-oriented history: that which we associate with the spectator of a drama. Such a spectator of course empathizes with the characters represented, but his understanding of the course of events comes from a recognition of the relations between character, circumstance, and action which transcends the empathic point of view, and can be expressed in general propositions about the causes and consequences of human actions. Michael Scriven, we may note, suggests the applicability of the notion of dramatic inevitability to historical narration.[2] Prescott, in his preface to *The Conquest of Peru* makes clear his efforts to mold his historical material into a dramatic form. Such an approach to history better represents the viewpoint of the humanistically-oriented historian than the empathic point of view. I should like to quote Prescott commenting that the historical spectator can achieve a better insight into historical events than the actors themselves or their contemporaries:

> Yet it must be admitted that the chronicler who records the events of an earlier age has some obvious advantages in the store of manuscript materials at his command—the statements of friends, rivals, and enemies furnishing a wholesome counterpoise to each other—and also in the general course of events, as they actually occurred, affording the best commentary on the true motives of the parties. The actor, engaged in the heat of the strife, finds his view bounded by the circle around him, and his vision blinded by the smoke and dust of conflict; while the spectator, whose eye ranges over the ground from a more distant and elevated point, though the individual objects may lose somewhat of their vividness, takes in at a glance all the operations of the field. Paradoxical as it may appear,

truth founded on contemporary testimony would seem, after all, as likely to be attained by the writer of a later day, as by contemporaries themselves.[3]

Not only is there nothing implicitly nonhumanistic in the spectator viewpoint of covering law explanations, but they are in fact necessary to produce the kind of insight into human affairs which Professor Dray describes as the motive for history, i.e., that knowledge of "past human activities which will allow us to cope with present problems." It is relevant in this connection to recall Aristotle's famous comparison between poetry and history in the *Poetics:*

> The difference between a poet and a historian is this: the historian relates what has happened, the poet, what could happen. Therefore, poetry is something more philosophic and of more serious import than history; for poetry tends to deal with the general, while history is concerned with delimited particular facts. An instance of "the general" [with which poetry undertakes to deal] is this: What are the sorts of things, which, according to the laws of probability and necessity, various types of individuals tend to do and say? This is what poetry aims to make evident when it attaches names to characters. An instance of "particular facts" [with which history deals] is: What did Alcibiades do, or what was done to him?

Obviously, what covering law theorists set up as the ideal for historical explanation of individual actions is the overcoming of the deficiency which Aristotle attributes to history in comparison with poetry; in Aristotle's terms, covering law theorists require that the function of history be united to the function of poetry. When the historian is able not only to describe the particular, but reveal the universal which it embodies, his history rises to the level of art. It would be difficult to maintain that a history which approached the ideal of poetry is not humanistically oriented.

Dray is both misleading and misled when he persists in saying that according to covering law theory an action is shown to be "routine." There is no reason why an action, explained on a covering law model, should therefore qualify as being routine. An example out of the domain of human action may suffice to show this: the famous Lisbon earthquake may unexceptionally by Dray be admitted to be explicable according to the covering law model, but would this kind of explanation show it to be a routine occurrence? Similarly, Atahuallpa's conduct is not shown to be routine, in any proper sense of the word, because of the kind of explanation given to it. Nor does Sophocles render routine Oedipus' murder of his father when he displays the irascibility, pride, and impetuousness which characterized Oedipus and which lead us to understand that Oedipus was just the sort of person who would act rashly when provoked into anger.

What Dray really intends by saying that a covering law explanation shows an action to be routine is that it shows an action to be *determined,* I suspect. He candidly admits his preference for the rational model over the covering law model because the former is compatible with libertarianism, while the latter implies determinism in human actions. In arguing against the covering law model of explanation in his book, he observes that in historical explanation, "unless we are prepared to hold the agent responsible for what happened, we cannot say that his action *was* the cause."[4] From the preceding, I gather that Dray is accepting the thesis that a deterministic view of human conduct is one according to which human beings are never properly held accountable for their conduct. Some philosophers have argued such a thesis, but it is by no means impregnable. Since I cannot properly go into this substantive question, I will just refer to George Pitcher's recent paper, "Necessitarianism," which exposes some fallacies of this position, and mention that there are a number of reputable philosophers—Spinoza, Hume, Mill—who have held that a deterministic viewpoint does not absolve an agent from moral accountability.[5] At any rate, this position is not sufficiently established to reject the propriety of covering law explanations of actions on such grounds.

Finally, I want to suggest that the rational model of explanation in Mr. Dray's account is compatible with a radical ethical relativism subversive of a humanistically-oriented history. This can be seen in his assumption that if a rationale can be provided for an action, then that action qualifies as a rational action. However, we are very reluctant to describe as rational an action which controverts well-established and generally accepted moral principles. Professor Tomas' example in discussion illustrates this well: even if there is a rationale for Nero's putting to death of his mother, we would not call this a *rational* action. To call an action rational, or to speak of the rationality of an action, connotes that at the least, it is a morally unexceptionable action. Thus we must distinguish between an action having a rationale, and a rational action. If one confounds the two, one falls into a thoroughgoing relativism which commits the historian who provides the rationale for Hitler's anti-Semitic actions or Stalin's purges to approving of them morally, or at least to *not* disapproving of them morally—but I, for one, would not feel that such a historian was humanistically oriented. That Dray is teetering toward such a position because of this confusion, can be seen in this passage from his book:

> The goal of [rational] explanation is to show that what was done was the thing to have done for the reasons given . . . the phrase 'thing to have done' betrays a crucially important feature of explanations in terms of agent calculations—a feature quite different from any we have noticed so far. For the infinitive 'to do' here functions as a value term. I wish to claim therefore that there is an element of *appraisal* of what was done in such explanations. . . . In the ordinary course of affairs, a demand for explanation is often recognized to be at the same time a challenge to the agent to produce either justification or excuse for what was done. In history, too, I want to argue, it will often be found impossible to bring out the point of what is offered as an explanation unless the overlapping of these notions, when it is human actions we are interested in, is explicitly recognized.[6]

But the historian who provides rational explanation of an action in Dray's sense does not engage in an appraisal in any genuinely ethical sense. The historian does not appraise the rationality of the act itself, he only displays the relation between the agent's beliefs, principles, and goals which made the action *seem* appropriate or "the thing to do" to the agent. Dray admits that the historian may realize that an agent's beliefs about his situation were mistaken, may not share the agent's purposes, or may consider his principles "peculiar" without thereby being incapacitated from giving a rational explanation of his action; but in any one of these cases, the historian would not be likely to consider the action "the thing to do," even from the agent's viewpoint, however "appropriate" it might *seem* from that viewpoint, given the agent's mistaken or misguided beliefs, goals or principles. Of course the historian, perhaps especially the humanistically-oriented one, may express his views about the propriety or rationality of the action, but that is an entirely separate undertaking, and one which is also open to a historian employing the covering law model.

In conclusion I should like to offer a defense of Dray's rational explanations from one objection, and in so doing indicate what I consider a respect in which it is superior to the covering law model, and perhaps more humanistically oriented. Dray reports and answers this objection made by Passmore in his paper: the historian giving a rational explanation of an action will be inclined to make of our behavior "something much more a matter of principle than it actually is." Dray replies that this difficulty does not affect the correctness of *form* of a rational explanation, but only indicates a way in which the explanation may go wrong. Drawing an analogy with covering law theory, he argues that as we may err in the formulation of the general law invoked to explain an action, so we may be mistaken in the particular reasons we ascribe to an agent performing a certain action. But this answer seems to me to miss the point: Passmore is raising the question whether it is proper to say that an agent was moved to act as he did because he held certain principles or goals, *whatever* these might be, and this question does bear on the *form* of rational explanations, as Dray describes them. It is not merely a question of mistaking the particular principle or goal, but of whether goals or principles can be invoked at all.

I would suggest the following defense to Passmore's objection: When we are dealing with an individual historical action, we are considering an action involving substantial interests, perhaps because of its consequences on the welfare of a nation or its significance in terms of some general policy, etc. In such cases usually, it is not too farfetched to assume that the agent took into consideration some kind of principle or goal. The crucial thing, it seems to me, is that an action of historical significance is being explained, and not one whose importance is entirely within some private or limited domain. Hence Passmore's observaton that the explanations an individual may give of his conduct are "hollow-sounding . . . as if they were constructed to satisfy our audiences rather than as explanations of our action" does not have so much force in relation to actions which have a place in history. The historical agent often undertakes action with an awareness that he may have to explain his conduct to some audience—his constituents, his countrymen, perhaps even the posterity the historian writes for.

Dray's model represents a demythologizing of Hegel's notion of the "cunning of Reason" through which universal aims, goals, and principles become melded into the world-historical individual's private aims and desires. Its merit is to stress the coherence of an action with the agent's beliefs, principles, and goals. The latter are of especial interest to us, not only as objects of "humane curiosity," but because they are determining factors in human action which are susceptible of change and control, to the detriment or betterment of mankind. Account of these factors can also be taken in a covering law type of analysis, but they do not stand out with such prominence among other factors and general laws. Dray's rational explanations thus isolate a salient characteristic of human action—its dependence upon thought. This characteristic, when present in actions to be explained, is always important and interesting; it is probably to be found to a greater or less degree in the greater part of the actions which the historian is concerned to explain. Thus Dray's model reminds us that history records the actions of at least fitfully rational beings making ill- or well-reasoned choices—in doing which, it does serve one purpose of a humanistically-oriented history.

NOTES

1. Mentor Books, pp. 248–49, italics mine.
2. "Truisms as the Grounds for Historical Explanations," reprinted in *Theories of History*, ed. P. Gardiner (Glencoe, Ill., 1959).
3. *Ibid.*, p. xxxiii.
4. *Laws and Explanations in History* (Oxford: Oxford University Press, 1957), p. 100.
5. *Philosophical Quarterly* (July 1961).
6. *Op. cit.*, p. 124.

12

Observations on History

LEE A. BELFORD
New York University

APPARENTLY INEVITABLISM IS DEAD. None of the distinguished philosophers and historians who participated in the Institute attempted to explain history as the product of some single determinant. There was no Marxian in evidence to illustrate the iron necessity with which historical tendencies work toward an inevitable goal, nor was there a Freudian to point out that subconscious psychological forces exercise a determining influence on human thought and action. The reductionist inevitablists have been relegated to the limbo of pseudoscientists where they rightfully belong because the fallacy in a reductionism that delimits the causative factors in history to a single force is apparent. For example, we read with amusement Freud's biography of Leonardo da Vinci in which he claimed to have reconstructed the "whole" unconscious life of his subject, to have "fully" explained his traits of character, all on the basis of psychoanalytic techniques applied to "all" available fragments of Leonardo's life and age.

It might be possible to maintain a posture of inevitablism by avoiding the reductionist fallacy and by claiming that there are many causes which, if sufficiently understood, could explain all events satisfactorily. But even those who might assume that there are fixed laws are confronted with the fact that they are so multiple and complex that inevitablism cannot be proved or, that due to the complexities of human nature, the laws are unknowable. Others conclude that there is an element of freedom in the constitution of man which excludes in principle any concept of inevitablism.

There is no way in which relativism can be escaped, so far as history is concerned. The historian works within a discipline which defines certain rules for significant research and narration, a logic of a sort, but these are no more than the framework within which he does his work and no more binding than the rules of proper syntax. The historian does acknowledge economic and other social factors with a degree of imputed causality. However, the degree of causality is related to the counterauthority ascribed to individual and corporate psychological forces. For example, every significant movement may either be viewed as the shadow of a great man or may be attributed to such powerful forces that it would have developed without reference to a particular individual or individuals, or, as is most generally the case, a position somewhere in between—that social forces and heroic figures must be taken into account in order to understand the particular movement.

The historian cannot confine himself to the methods of the natural scientist. As Jerome Frank has said on numerous occasions, the historian uses the methods of the law courts. The judge must ascertain the facts in a case dealing with past events. He listens to the witnesses, some of whom, in spite of the sanction of perjury, prevaricate. Others, with the intention of being truthful, are so influenced by prejudice and fright or some other emotion that their witness is unreliable. The judge, through his experience and the discipline of his profession, has been taught to ask certain questions in order to elicit the truth, but he also asks other questions which have their source in intuition. Upon weighing all the evidence, the judge can only hope that his decision has been correct.

The relativism implicit in history appears under several headings in the papers and comments given at the Institute.

1. *Selecting the topic.* Though the problem of why the historian becomes interested in a certain topic may be dismissed on the assumption that it is no more relevant to the

method of the historian than why a physicist becomes interested in one problem rather than another, there is a close relationship between why the historian chooses a certain topic and colligates his material as he does and the problem of the evaluation of his finished work.

2. *The hypothesis.* In order to have a focal point for the selection of his material, as Leo Gershoy made quite clear, the historian projects a hypothesis which he has not yet proved and then deals with the relevant data, reserving the right to reject his hypothesis if it cannot be substantiated. Obviously the type of hypothesis that is projected is affected by the viewpoint from which the historian has approached his task.

3. *Vicarious experience.* William Dray suggested this element. Were it not for the sharing of experiences as if we were "there," much less history would be read. It is not only in tragedy following the dicta of Aristotle that there is an identification and catharsis. We can put ourselves in the boots of others, living for a moment in their time and place, and, sharing their experiences, increase in our own experience and presumably grow and develop as persons. Questions of meaning and value arise, and problems of fate and freedom, good and evil, demand some sort of understanding and explanation. It is because everyone is something of a conciliator and mediator that we can identify ourselves with a figure like Barère, asking as we do so, how much cowardice, opportunism, and courage are implicit in our roles. However, the degree of vicarious experience is conditioned by the extent to which we can identify with an historical personage, or at least, with some aspects of his personality.

4. *The historian.* Gershoy tells us that he became interested in Barère initially because Lord Macaulay's appraisal of the Frenchman was "so intemperate in its expression." Gershoy in his statement tells us something about himself—that he is distrustful of intemperate expression, and we can assume that he would be distrustful of anyone who was inclined to divide categorically the sheep and the goats, to separate with an invincible barrier the children of the light and the children of

darkness. Value decisions affected Gershoy's initial interest in Barère and value decisions affected his treatment. It is impossible to speak of tyranny and chaos, slavery and license, without conveying something of one's own values. It is redundant to add that viewpoints and values are inseparable and that both are relative.

Morton White suggested the impossibility of writing true histories if the criterion for the selection is to be only "the most interesting facts," those that present the "smiling aspects of life," etc. yet acknowledges that the historian does include statements for reasons of curiosity, the beauty or ugliness of what they report, etc. In reference to choosing a feature of an historical subject that is central in an objective sense, around which data are to be colligated, there remains the problem of what material is to be included. In both situations, the personal predispositions of the historian are significant.

White admitted that he cannot supply a definition or a criterion for historical memorability. We suspect that no one else could without walking where angels fear to tread. How much more can be said than that one approves of a history "because the author seems to look at the evidence with one's eyes and one's heart?" Yet the way a person looks has been conditioned by a community of persons who look and feel in a similar, even though not identical, way.

On the basis of what has been said, it is apparent that the strictly logical and empirical aspects of philosophy are severely limited in the appraisal of history for two reasons: (1) History cannot be reduced to an exact science. (2) The historian and his critic are influenced in their judgment by their viewpoints. If philosophy is to serve the historian, then a clarification of viewpoints is in order. Such a suggestion may invoke the criticism that it is nothing more than a return to the pluralism of the "school philosophy" or to the phenomenology of Dilthey and others. To an extent this is true, but if the frames of reference may be reduced by a categorizing of viewpoints, then each may be criticized in terms of what it says about the nature and destiny of man. Perhaps the sharp knife of the logician, so well honed in the last generation, will be dulled in the process, but there is also the possibility that philosophy will be able to serve the humanities once again.

One viewpoint is the Greek-Oriental. To the extent that nature is viewed as a veil behind which is to be found the really real, to the extent that phenomena are *maya* or illusions, there is no concern with the particularities of history, and therefore history is dismissed as trivial. Certainly, dates and faces are irrelevant and so, too, is the concept of the self.

Another viewpoint is the naturalistic. To use B. A. G. Fuller's definition:

> Naturalism is the teaching that the universe needs no supernatural origin or explanation, but is self-explanatory or self-existent; that its behavior is not teleologically explicable by final causes and purposes; that human life and behavior are in no way exceptional and outside the course of natural events, and are to be explained by the same principles as obtain throughout the rest of nature; and that human values, moral ideals, and conduct are determined by the organic structure and needs characteristic of the human species.

If nature is the focal point of all ultimate sanctities, then nature is of primary concern. If man is viewed exclusively as a biological organism reacting to natural environmental stimuli, then obviously there is exclusive concern with organismic man and social forces.

Another viewpoint is the Biblical-Hebraic. Here nature is disenchanted, as Max Weber would express it, for man is viewed as both in nature and yet remaining out of it in his capacity for self-transcendence. Underlying all reality is a transcending God who is the ultimate, knowable only in part, who acts in history. There is no denial that man, as a part of nature, is conditioned by social forces, but human events are viewed as more than mere natural events for each novel happening is an occasion to which man reacts in his self-transcendence and in the domain of eternity. The concept of history is lineal—it is moving, heading somewhere, for it has a *telos.*

It is through the happenings of history that it is assumed that God speaks to man. The fatherhood attributed to God gives a dignity to human beings and establishes a special kind of relationship between human beings. Among the values asserted is the quest for truth, for, strictly speaking, truth must be pursued regardless of where it leads.

Difficulties emerge the moment religious language is used. It must be acknowledged that God's existence and activity cannot be rationally proved or empirically demonstrated. But, it cannot be denied that the Biblical-Hebraic viewpoint is one from which some historians approach their task. It cannot be denied that the viewpoint has a relationship to choosing a topic, establishing hypotheses, the whole matter of vicarious experience, and the values expressed by the historian at his task.

We may dismiss the Greek-Oriental viewpoint as irrelevant to history. This leaves only two viewpoints—the naturalistic and the Biblical-Hebraic. However, the line of demarcation cannot be drawn too finely. On the basis of a limited knowledge, it would seem that many historians, though placing themselves in the camp of the naturalists, follow a secularized version of the Biblical-Hebraic approach to history. They presuppose certain values which cannot be demonstrated. They act out of a situation of faith.

The domain of philosophy has been reduced from a *weltanschauung* which encompasses all areas of man's experience to little bits and pieces of knowledge. Analysts avoid anything like a philosophy of life as if such a philosophy were a plague, and indeed it is, if philosophy is to concern itself only with the language and methods of the natural scientists. Yet human beings do have philosophies of life, human beings do write histories, and human beings read histories. Human thinking is conditioned by aims, conduct, and the will. Does philosophy have nothing to say to the ordinary man in clarifying his viewpoint? Does it have nothing to say about the truth-transcending areas of life?

Philosophers would serve a valuable purpose if they used

ontological principles as statements to clarify the viewpoints from which the world is seen, if they used speculative arguments to indicate that when certain principles are accepted, the consequences must also be accepted. Collingwood is right in suggesting that this would not be a radical departure from the metaphysical tradition but a development of it.

13

Personality Traits as Causal Explanations in Biography

R. B. BRANDT
Swarthmore College

I. THE LOGIC OF TRAIT-EXPLANATIONS IN BIOGRAPHY

Professor Gershoy remarks in his paper that the historian could not function without postulating that human behavior is determined by ascertainable causes. What does this postulate amount to, in biography?

It is agreed that the biographer should not simply chronicle the overt actions of his subject; part of his job is to depict his subject's actions as the understandable behavior of an intelligent human being—to enable his readers to understand them as they can understand the actions of a close friend. But what is involved in this?

One thing that is required is an account of the leading personality traits of his subject. An example of this is the accounts of Barère which Gershoy summarizes in saying that they characterized Barère as a "cowardly opportunist and a trimmer." While Gershoy was suspicious of such characterizations, doubtless because they depicted Barère as simple and less humane than most intelligent people are, they were doing part of the biographer's job in drawing the lines of a consistent picture of a man: of one without principles, who would sacrifice any principle or cause or person to save his own skin, whose personal advancement was second in importance only to his own safety. A person *could* be like this, and the picture does explain actions.

How does any picture of a person's traits explain his actions? One way in which they do this is through implying—this is part of what some trait-names *mean*—something about the person's values. For instance, if we learn that the dominant feature of a man's character is cowardice, we have learned that—certain abnormal frames of mind excepted—he puts the safety of his skin first and foremost. And, through implying something about his values, a trait-ascription may enable prediction of behavior; for to set a certain value on a certain kind of situation is for a person to be disposed, to a corresponding degree, to adopt a line of action which he thinks will lead to that kind of situation. Not that knowledge of a person's values *alone* enables prediction: we also must know how an individual sees his situation, the courses of conduct he thinks open to him, and where he thinks these courses of action will lead. If we have all these things, we can—except for abnormal frames of mind, and for cases of conflict of traits or values—predict behavior. Thus if we know that Mr. X is a coward, and that doing *A* seems to him the only really safe course of action, then—special exceptions aside—we can safely predict he will do *A*, or, if he has already done *A*, we properly feel we have explained his action.

Not all traits of personality imply something about one's values. Cowardice, ambition, and generosity do; but impulsiveness, ignorance, and slow-wittedness do not. The latter traits therefore help us understand behavior in a way somewhat different from the former; they play a different role in the reconstruction of the "field" of a person, relevant to a given action. If we know that a person is impulsive, we know he is liable not to be guided by all his knowledge and values relevant to a given choice, but by a small segment of them that happens to dominate his attention at moments of decision. Much the same for ignorance, and so on.

Names of traits of personality are sometimes viewed as mere terms of classification, which explain behavior only in the way in which "dormitive capacity" explains sleep. Trait-ascriptions are thought to explain behavior at most by setting it in a broader pattern of more of the same—illuminating much in the way in which the fact that all crows are black illuminates the fact that this crow is black, but not more so.

Such a view of trait-explanations is at best one-sided. They can just as fairly be compared with the physicist's explanation of a curving line on a photograph by appeal to the mass, charge, and probable velocity of an alpha-particle, and the intensity of a certain magnetic field. Take for instance Barère's ballot for the guillotining of the king. If we account for this by saying that Barère was a coward, we are not merely classifying, for obviously it often takes much courage to vote for someone's death. Indeed, we must begin by analyzing the situation as Barère saw it, in order to determine what a coward's values would lead a man to do. Moreover, a cowardly man does not always do cowardly things. The coward may be in an abnormal frame of mind: emotional stress primitivizes cognition and reaction, so that the coward, say, when burning with anger, may momentarily forget his safety. There may also be conflicting traits: if the coward happens to be an impulsive man, he may commit himself to risking his skin before he thinks. To ascribe a set of traits to a person is to assign a set of forces which, like the forces assigned an alpha-particle or a magnetic field, will operate in various situations when he is in a normal frame of mind, and from knowledge of which predictions of probable behavior can often be drawn—of course, without the power which comes with quantitative measures.

There are other facts about human traits which repel labeling trait-names as mere classifications: laws relating them to learning processes, and to each other.

How can the biographer show that one theory of a man's personality is better justified than another? Obviously, by showing that it explains all the facts better than its rival, or that it fits in better with other knowledge. What the "facts" are, of course, may not be obvious. As Professor Gershoy points out, one theory may lead us to see subtle points in the data which we should otherwise have overlooked. Again, the raw evidence must be assessed. Is a person's jotting in his diary good ground for conclusions about what he thought then, or earlier? In answering this question we properly bring to bear our knowledge of the prevalence of simplifications in recall and of concessions to one's ego.

Much behavior cannot be explained by any set of trait-ascriptions, and its occurrence therefore cannot logically support the set of trait-ascriptions. One reason for this is that some behavior requires explanation by temporary conditions of the self. Food-seeking behavior is not explained by personality traits alone; it requires the assumption of a state of hunger. Again, Barère might be a fundamentally courageous and principled man, but do a cowardly thing because he had just had an unnerving interview with his wife, who was terrified by certain prospects. People sometimes panic. Another reason is that some traits are probabilistic only. When we say a man is impulsive, we do not mean that every decision is impulsive, but only that he has a tendency in that direction. Impulsiveness does not exclude acting, on frequent occasions, in a cautious and prudent manner. Furthermore, people have traits which imply values that are conflicting for a given situation. Often it is impossible to know which of the values is the stronger; indeed, an agent himself will often not wish to lay a bet on how his choice will go when the time for decision comes. Indeed, a biographer may have to adopt a conception of an agent's traits, supported by strong evidence, even in the face of what seems incompatible evidence of conduct, if in the total situation it is not unreasonable to suppose there *could* have been special circumstances which render the conduct compatible with his hypothesis.

Despite all these complications, I suggest that one implication of Professor Gershoy's remark that the historian can function only by postulating that human behavior is determined by ascertainable causes is this: that the biographer's theory of his subject's traits of personality, which he necessarily uses in explanation of his behavior, must itself be chosen on the basis of its relative capacity to explain the facts (in the total context, including available theoretical psychological knowledge), and that one such conception must get the palm if it incorporates a larger body of the facts than do the others.

If so, what room then is left for Gershoy's view that the biographer's methods leave "room for the contingent, the unforeseen, and the accidental"? Agents, he says, are free to do what they don't do. Gershoy does not explain what he means by this. I suggest that part of what he may mean is the sort of fact just adverted to: that some traits are probabilistic, that our knowledge of traits is imprecise and nonquantitative, that temporary states of the self such as states of bodily need or emotional conditions are often important for behavior. Often, then, our knowledge—necessarily based primarily on other specimens of behavior—of a man's traits will not enable prediction or explanation of what he does; we must content ourselves with saying that the decision was compatible with our conception of his traits, and with using the episode to make our conception of them more definite.

II. TRAIT-EXPLANATIONS, CAUSES, AND CAUSAL EXPLANATIONS

If the foregoing account of the logic of biography is correct, then Professor Dray is misleading in giving pride of place to "explanation" in the sense of showing what it was rational for the biographer's subject to have done in the circumstances.[1] The "covering law theory," or something very like it, is theoretically more adequate, although Dray's preferred kind of explanation may often, or even usually, be the best the historian can do to give an explanation of conduct or events, given the evidence at hand. However, in another respect the "covering law theory" may be less adequate as an account of biography: if trait-explanations do not, at least normally, contain any *law* in the sense of the theory. I wish now to explore this matter briefly. I shall do so as part of an inquiry into a slightly more general question: whether traits of personality can be said to be *causes of conduct* at all, and if so, whether it must be in a slightly different sense from that in which we can talk about causes in natural science; and whether trait-explanations can be said to be causal explanations in the sense of the natural sciences, or only in some special sense. Evidently our questions raise the issue how "cause" and "causal explanation" should be explicated, for the case of the natural sciences.

First a preliminary point. The terms "cause" and "causal explanation" are properly used, in English, in connection with trait-explanations. Suppose a child gives aid to a wounded bird: takes it to the veterinarian, feeds it, and cares for it until it is able to fly again. It is perfectly natural to say that such behavior is *explained* by the fact that the child is sympathetic. Again, a historian may say that the basic *cause* of some catastrophe was the king's ignorance, or his wife's ambition. (Traits are here not being appealed to, however, as causes of the same person's actions.) We say these things naturally, and it is therefore correct to say them.

A very influential contemporary explication of these terms is as follows. The term *explanandum* is used to refer to a state of affairs at some time which is to be explained. Now consider a set of true laws, some of whose variables can take as specific values the features of the *explanandum.* Moreover, let us conceive these laws to be universal, and also general in the sense that statement of them (or an explanation of their meaning) does not require reference to any particular event or continuant. Now let us suppose that the assertion of these laws will, when combined with assertion of certain true singular statements about states of affairs prior to the time of the *explanandum,* entail singular statements descriptive of features of the *explanandum.* When the total *explanandum* is entailed by the conjunction of a set of laws and singular statements in this way, we shall say that we have a "causal explanation" of it. And we can say that the states of affairs at earlier times, statement of which was essential in the deduction of the *explanandum,* are "part-causes" of the *explanandum.*

Can we say that traits are causes, or somehow provide causal explanations, of *actions,* in this sense?

In order to get the logical situation clear, let us consider a sketch of a possible explanation of the event of Barère's voting for the guillotining of the king. The premises might run something like this:

Premise 1: At t_1 Barère thought that the only safe course of action for himself would be to vote for the guillotining of the king.

Premise 2a: At t_1 Barère was a cowardly man, and therefore, by definition,

Premise 2b: At t_1 Barère would be motivated to do any action *A*, which he regarded as the only one which would provide reasonable security for his personal safety, more strongly than to do any conflicting action non-*A*, provided he were in a normal frame of mind.

Premise 3: Barère was in a normal frame of mind at t_1.

Conclusion: Therefore, immediately after t_1, assuming nothing intervened, Barère voted, or decided to vote, for the guillotining of the king.

The first thing to notice about this sketch is that it contains no *strictly general* law, at least as formulated. Premise 2b is a universal conditional, but it is a conditional statement about the individual Barère, and hence, following Ryle's terminology, can at most be called "law*like*." The sketch therefore does not qualify as a causal explanation, given the above explication of "causal explanation." The status of Premise 2b is especially clear when we notice that, at least as represented above, it is a partial explanation of the meaning of Premise 2a.

If we ignore the fact that the sketch does not contain a law but only a lawlike conditional, and if we ignore some possible puzzles about the time-references, we could then say that the fact cited in Premise 1 (and possibly that in Premise 3) is at least a part-*cause* of the *explanandum.* But we could *not* say this of the fact stated in Premise 2a: for in effect this premise is the law involved in the explanation, and in any case there is no variable in the law which could take this fact as a value. The consequence is that a trait cannot be cited as a cause of the action which manifests it, at least if we adopt the foregoing explication of "cause." A decision on this point, however, need not commit us to deplore, or applaud, the historian's talk of the queen's ambition being the cause, say, of a rebellion. For here the trait is not being said to be a cause of the behavior which manifests it. What is meant by such a statement has to be explained; but I think it can be explained in a clear and consistent way, and there is no need to repudiate the historian's mode of speech.

One question is whether we wish to retain, in our explication of "causal explanation," the requirement of a strictly general law, with the effect that trait-explanations are ruled out of the class of causal explanations.

Some philosophers would wish to rule out anyway, on other grounds, the idea that a trait-ascription could function in a causal explanation. Some philosophers would wish to do so on the ground that trait-ascriptions are only summaries of behavior or behavior-trends, and do not entail subjunctive conditionals. This is a large issue which cannot be discussed here. Some philosophers would wish to rule out the idea that traits can function in causal explanations on a different ground: that trait-names are vague, and that no conditional statement derivable from them can cite specific reactions which will occur in specifiable conditions. In this respect, they say, trait-explanations are very different from causal explanations in natural science. But to this two replies can be made. First, while it is true that trait-*names* are vague, a specific trait, as we can know it to be in an individual,[2] is much more definite. Second, vagueness in greater or less degree is characteristic of many dispositional concepts used in natural science outside physics and physical chemistry.

On the central question whether "causal explanation" should be so explicated as to require a strictly general law, there are several views one might take, on the issue of central interest to us, that of the status of trait-explanations. First, one might say that general laws are required and hence traits cannot function in causal explanations. This view might please some indeterminists. Second, one might say that strictly general laws are required, but argue that trait-explanations qualify after all, since a more careful examination of trait-explanations reveals that after all strictly general laws do occur in them, first appearances to the contrary notwithstanding. In other words, the above sketch of the logic of a trait-explanation must be deemed inaccurate. This view, I believe, is one toward which Professor Hempel inclines. Third, one might prefer to relax the requirement of a *strictly general* law in one's explication, thus permitting trait-explanations as a species of causal explanation.

The third of these views seems to me most plausible. I shall conclude by discussing some ways in which the second may be defended, and some objections to these ways—as a device for recommending the third view.

How might one argue that there are after all strictly general laws in trait-explanations?

(a) One might argue that every trait has a brain-correlate. For instance, in the case of the trait *cowardice*, let us suppose there is a brain-correlate *B*. We might then argue that we know the following strictly general law: "For all persons with the property *B*, if they perceive something as being the only course of action which will secure their personal safety, they will be very strongly motivated to adopt that course of action." This statement is strictly general.

Unfortunately, this general statement does not give us what we want. For it is not involved in *trait*-explanations. What it shows is that if we were to give a neurophysiological explanation of behavior, a strictly general law would be involved. There is a further difficulty at the present time: that the only way we can describe the brain-correlate is by saying it is the property one has when one is cowardly, viz., when the subjunctive conditional mentioned above applies. If we substitute such an expression for "with the property *B*," we are left with a tautology.

(b) A second possibility is to assert that a strictly general law of the following form can always properly be affirmed when a trait-explanation is being used: that *any* person who in the past had behaved in the manner which is the reason for attributing the trait to some person in question, would behave in a certain way in the future—the way characteristic of the trait.[3] But this proposal blurs the distinction between the evidence for a law, and the law itself—a distinction we do wish to preserve. It is quite clear in the particular case of psychological dispositions that there is a difference between the *meaning* of the judgment which functions in the explanation (e.g., "is cowardly") and *evidence* the speaker may have for making the trait-ascription. Notice that we think the evidence renders the trait-ascription only probable, not certain. In the case of the natural sciences it is familiar ground that we see the force of a proposed explanation without being told the evidence for the subjunctive conditional (in this case strictly general) involved, although, as in the case of trait-explanations, we recognize that the explanation is a sound one only if the subjunctive conditional (the law) is true and if there is good reason for thinking that it is. If we are to preserve the parallel with the natural sciences, the role of general laws, in the case of trait-explanations, is played by the nongeneral subjunctive conditional; and the role of the evidence for the law is played by the behavior of the person which constitutes the ground for ascribing to him the trait in question.

(c) The third possibility, favored by Professor Hempel and others, is to construe trait-names, not as names of dispositions definable by subjunctive conditionals, but as theoretical constructs, undefined predicates in the language of psychology which receive "partial interpretation" through the laws and correspondence rules which connect them with other theoretical constructs and with observables. On this view, "A cowardly person will be motivated more strongly to do *A* than any conflicting non-*A*, provided he is in a normal frame of mind, if he thinks that doing *A* is the only way of providing reasonable security for his personal safety" can be regarded as a universal and general *law,* and not just as a definition of "cowardly" or as an analytic truth. Hence, the advocate of this view would insist on the following changes in my sketch of an explanation of Barère's action. Premises 1 and 3, and the Conclusion, would be unchanged. Premise 2a would read simply: "At t_1 Barère was a cowardly man." Premise 2b would be eliminated in favor of the universal and general law about cowardly people, as just stated above. In this way a close parallel between trait-explanations and explanations in the natural sciences would be preserved, and a trait-explanation would be a causal explanation by the standard explication of "causal explanation."

My chief objection to this view is that it portrays trait-names as not being understandable outside a whole system of laws and correspondence rules. This portrayal seems to me not to square with the facts. We have a quite definite understanding of terms like "cowardly" by themselves; and this understanding seems accurately represented, in part, by the subjunctive conditional I have sketched. (I am discussing this analysis more in detail elsewhere.) If one happens not to like subjunctive conditionals, there are substitutes which will do fairly well in their stead. Furthermore, there are advantages in avoiding all talk of "partial interpretations."

Is there any positive and independent reason for construing trait-names in this way? It has been argued that psychological concepts of this sort, as applied to other persons, cannot be defined—even by use of subjunctive conditionals—in terms of *publicly observable* events or properties.[4] This is true. But the assumption that such terms must either be explicitly definable in terms of publicly observable events or properties, or else be viewed as theoretical constructs, is a vestige of logical behaviorism which some philosophers find it difficult to shake off, but which need not be adopted. I agree that it would be unwise to insist on renouncing the theoretical construct view of trait-names, if we were already compelled, for some reason other than one which is a part of the metaphysics of dogmatic logical behaviorism, to view as theoretical primitives the very predicates we need to use for the subjunctive-conditional analysis of trait-names—terms like "motivated," "fear-feeling," "perceives that . . . ," and so on. Some philosophers, including Professor Hempel, appear to think that we are constrained to adopt this very view. It is conceivable that they are right in this, but the matter—and it raises the question how intentional language should be construed—seems to me far from settled. At present the option of a subjunctive-conditional construction of trait-names seems to me to have solid merits.

My conclusion about the matters discussed in the first paragraph of the present section, then, is that "causal explanation" should not be construed so as to require strictly general laws, and hence that the "covering law" theory of explanations in biography is not quite accurate, since trait-explanations are best viewed as causal explanations although they do not contain any strictly general law. Trait-explanations, furthermore, *are* causal explanations in the sense of the natural sciences, if we relax the general explication of "causal explanation" so as not to require strictly general laws. (It is of course still true that the natural sciences do have general laws in their explanations, whereas the subjunctive conditionals which occur in trait-explanations contain reference to individuals.) Finally, traits of personality *cannot* be said to be part-causes of the conduct which manifests them—although this conclusion leaves open the question whether they may be part-causes of other events or states of affairs.

It is worth notice that Professor Hempel's example, in his contribution to the present volume, need not be construed as utilizing a general law. It employs an ostensibly general law, about what rational persons will do. But this statement can be regarded as analytic, and therefore not a law in the sense of the natural sciences. We can so regard it, because we can take it to be true by definition that a rational person will do what he takes to be the course of action which will probably maximize utility in his situation. If his situation is described in such a way that we know that a given agent thinks an action *A* will maximize expectable utility in the circumstances, we need no further premise to tell us that a rational agent will perform *A*. If I am correct in this, then a relaxed explication of "causal explanation" is necessary in order to accommodate Professor Hempel's own example—construed as it perfectly well can be construed.[5]

NOTES

1. See his paper in this volume, and *Laws and Explanation in History* (Oxford: Oxford University Press, 1957), pp. 137–55.

2. See, for instance, Gordon Allport, *Pattern and Growth in Personality* (New York, 1961), chap. XV.

3. A somewhat similar point is made by Jonathan Cohen in *Philosophical Quarterly,* X (1960), 191. He says that if the historian wishes to explain Disraeli's attack on Peel by appeal to ambition, he must assume that any person who had behaved ambitiously in the particular ways Disraeli had done in the past would be disposed to behave ambitiously in this particular way as well. Hence he assumes a general law. But I believe this view takes "trait-explanations" far too atomistically. What is involved in this explanation is simply the supposition that Disraeli was motivated very strongly by considerations of ambition; given his "field" of values, and his understanding of the situation, we need no more to see the necessity of his attack on Peel. Whether there is good reason for attributing this degree of motivation to him, without reference to the fact of his attack on Peel, is another question.

4. See, for instance, H. Feigl, "Principles and Problems of Theory Construction in Psychology," in *Current Trends in Psychological Theory,* ed. W. Dennis (Pittsburgh: University of Pittsburgh Press, 1951).

5. The foregoing remarks have had the benefit of critical comments by my colleague, Dr. Jaegwon Kim. Furthermore, Professor Hempel kindly sent me a copy of "Rational Action," his presidential address to the American Philosophical Association, Eastern Division, to be printed in *Proceedings and Addresses of the American Philosophical Association,* 1961–62. I have had this before me while writing the above.

14

Do Historians Use Covering Laws?

CARL N. DEGLER
Vassar College

AS A PRACTICING HISTORIAN I have long been fascinated by the question which philosophers of history have been grappling with ever since the appearance of Carl Hempel's well-known article on the place of "general" or "covering" laws in historical explanation. For a long time Hempel's position has been dominant, but with the appearance in 1957 of William Dray's *Laws and Explanation in History* some serious doubts have been raised as to the applicability of the covering law model to history. Indeed, since then, the philosophical literature on the subject has burgeoned, as the papers in this symposium make clear. Nevertheless, even with all this philosophical interest, no historian has attempted to apply the theory of the covering law to the actual practices of historians. A number of historians, it is true, have written extensively about the process of history writing, but, to my knowledge, no historian, even those at this symposium, has addressed himself directly to the specific question of covering laws.

Since philosophers of history are interested in analyzing what in fact the historian does, rather than in prescribing rules for his activities, it seems to me that the time has come for some historian to try to assess the covering law model for historical writing. That is the task which I should like to attempt here. Undoubtedly there are historians better equipped, philosophically, than I for this job, but since no other historian seems to be undertaking it, I'll make my effort.

A "covering law," as I understand the term, is an assertion

of regularity in which, when event C occurs at a certain time and place, event E will also occur. According to Hempel and other covering law theorists, only when there is such an empirically derived general proposition about the relationship between an event and its cause can one speak of a valid historical explanation. Explanation in history, then, in the Hempel view, takes the same form as explanation in science. Let me illustrate the covering law view as it would operate in history. When an historian says that a particular revolt took place because the people were heavily taxed, the explanation carries credibility, conviction, or force—both to the historian himself and his readers, because such an explanation for a revolt agrees with the general proposition, which most people carry around in their heads, that taxes are truly reasons why people revolt. As Patrick Gardiner has pointed out, these general propositions lying behind any historical explanation may be quite numerous, but they are there, nonetheless.

One point is clear: no one supposes that historians explain revolutions or any other large historical event by reference to a general law of revolutions. Historians do indeed compare different revolutions, different governmental systems, different societies. But in no case does the historian make these comparisons in order to draw up covering laws about causes for revolutions or for any other social changes. The use of the so-called general or covering laws is in connection with the much more minor and numerous actions which together go to make up a revolution, lead to the outbreak of a war, or decide an election.

The question then remains: does the historian use covering laws even in this narrow sense? An excursion through the process of history writing itself may be helpful in answering this question. Certainly it does no good to ask historians, for, by and large, they do not use such language and few of them even know that the conception exists. Let us, then, try to follow the steps an historian would take in establishing an acceptable explanation for an historical event—say a revolution. The first step, an unphilosophically-minded, working historian would say, is "to go through the evidence." This process would entail reading and taking notes on everything related to the event under investigation: newspapers, official and unofficial documents, letters, diaries, and so forth. After examination and interpretation by the historian, some of the evidence he examined would suggest possible causes for the event. Tax records, for example, which showed a rise in taxes in the two years before the revolt would certainly suggest to the historian that high taxes might be a cause for the rebellion.

Several times among his materials the historian would come across bald statements of causes for the revolution by participants. To this kind of evidence the historian would certainly give weight, though not before he had checked carefully as to whether such statements were to be discounted or even discarded because they might be rationalizations of actions, efforts to confuse contemporaries, etc. From these statements of motives in the contemporary evidence, the historian would also begin to form possible explanations for the coming of the revolution.

In interpreting both kinds of materials (self-conscious ascriptions of causes, and indirect or "mute" ones), though, the historian would have in the back of his mind a number of acceptable explanations for revolt. He might think that the increase in taxes was a plausible reason for revolt, because, as we have noted, everyone knows that high taxes can bring revolution. But suppose he then turns to his newspapers, diaries, letters, and other sources of the period and finds no mention of taxes as a cause for the revolution. A good historian, at that juncture, would certainly be given pause in calling high taxes one of the causes of the revolution. What he thought was a cause was just not borne out by his participant-sources, as I shall call the evidence from those who were there at the time of the event.

One actual case illustrates this aspect of the historian's way of operating. For many years one of the standard causes cited for the American Revolution was the English Navigation Laws. If one examined those laws with their severe restrictions on colonial trade, it seemed plausible, especially to men of an age of freer trade, that Americans in the eighteenth century would revolt to break out of the system. So it seemed to George Bancroft in the nineteenth century, and to Louis Hacker in the twentieth, who, though he had different reasons for thinking so, agreed in substance with Bancroft. Then in 1951, O. M. Dickerson in *The Navigation Acts and the American Revolution* showed, among other things, that in the voluminous colonial literature of complaint between 1765 and 1776 there were virtually no objections to the Navigation Laws. Indeed, Benjamin Franklin offered to have the colonial legislatures endorse the laws as an earnest of colonial loyalty to England. Since then it has been very difficult, though not impossible—historians being as loath to give up cherished views as the next man—to adhere to the old view, however plausible it may seem.

From this example several observations can be made about the way in which an historian explains the past, but I shall postpone making them until we have considered one further example. The historian's attention to his evidence may force him not only to abandon an otherwise plausible explanation, as in the illustration just given, but also suggest one for which he has no covering law. Let us take a simplified, hypothetical example. Suppose our historian, in an effort to explain a riot, is examining letters and diaries written by participants in that riot. From what he knows of the event he may consider it a simple bread riot because times were hard and a flour warehouse was looted. (The general proposition that hungry, unemployed men sometimes storm food stores is an old chestnut among covering laws.) But as he goes through his sources he finds that a number of them speak of the writers as hating the proprietor of the store because of his red hair, which, in fact, he has. Some of the letters even give the color of the store owner's hair as the reason for participation in the riot.

No historian, I venture to say, has any covering law, probabilistic or otherwise, which explains riots or violence by reference to the color of the hair of the victim. In fact, just because of this lack he would be careful to examine his sources closely as to their authenticity, and the statements as to their reliability as expressions of motivation. For example, a statement of motive found in a newspaper would receive less weight in his mind than one found in a private letter written to a close friend. Yet, if after all this careful probing and analysis the participant-sources are authenticated, the historian would certainly begin to think he had come upon an explanation which he had not anticipated and for which nothing in his previous experience or knowledge prepared him.

Nor should this use of participant-sources be thought naïve. It is true that since Marx and Freud we are more wary of men's explications of their own actions than ever before, but that does not mean we cannot use them, if proper care is exercised. After all, the whole field of public opinion polling rests on the assumption that men do know and will articulate their motives. And though opinion polling has its admitted weaknesses, its predictive successes have been impressive. The historian by judicious, canny, and careful use of documents from the past also can and does derive valid statements of motivation. Certainly the use of private papers of historical persons has been one of the mainstays of historical research for just this reason.

Let us now look at some of the implications in our two examples for the place of covering laws in historical explanation. First of all, it is evident from both examples that the historian does, at times, employ covering laws in trying to explain events. At those times, the historian is as much a follower of Hume in his conception of cause as the next man. But the example of the redheaded store owner suggests that the historian will also explain historical changes without reference to a covering law if his evidence seems to warrant it. The most obvious way in which he will be drawn into such explanations is through the testimony of participants in the historical events. The important point, of course, is that unlike the natural scientist, the historian has a way of getting at the cause of an event from the actors themselves, simply because his "subjects" can and often do leave records of their motives. Moreover, these statements of motives are often, though of course not always, taken as valid explanations of why the participants in a particular historical event acted as they did. Finally, from the example of the American Revolution it is evident that participant-sources (or the lack of them) can invalidate an otherwise quite plausible covering law. Nor should this fact be put down as simply a case of inaccurate or insufficient evidence as might occur in an explanation in the natural sciences. The covering law in this instance was rejected because the participants in the event "informed" the historian that his covering law could not apply, though other evidence he possessed supported the law.

It might be objected that the number of participants who testified to the same motive constituted a kind of empirical verification of a general law. But this seems rather farfetched. Not only is the verification not of the "if a, then b" variety, but its application is narrowly restricted to a particular time and place. Few historians, it seems to me, even if their participant-sources convinced them that hatred of redheads caused this particular riot, would generalize therefrom to say that hatred of carrot tops is often or even sometimes a cause for riots. Most important, these several examples are not occurrences in the empirical sense of testing the generalization. They are simply the testimony of participants, of the subjects of the historian's investigation.

In my effort to clear away distracting elements, my example of the redheaded storekeeper is obviously extreme. But, though the testimony of participants would not be as clear-cut as I have said it was or the cause quite as implausible as I have made it, the example does make clear that in actual historical writing it would be quite possible for an historian to explain an event without reference to any covering laws.

In fact, something like the process described above must happen whenever an historian investigates a society or culture sharply different from his own and in which some of the covering laws of human behavior derived from his own cultural experience do not hold. Too often, it is true the historian is not careful to recognize this requirement and blithely applies, inappropriately, covering laws derived from his own and therefore alien culture. For generations, for example, historians of economic thought have been sneering at Aristotle's views on money, trade, and economics in general, because they seemed irrational and unlearned. But as Karl Polanyi, in chapter V of his *Trade and Market in the Early Empires* (Glencoe, Ill., 1957), has shown, Aristotle was not irrational or ignorant in his writings on economics; he was simply resisting the market economy which was then only beginning to spread through Greek society. Unlike the historians who have belabored him, Aristotle rejected the values and assumptions of a market society. Thus the historians, in applying the covering laws of human behavior of their nineteenth century to an age in which such "laws" were foreign, misread Aristotle's purposes. The careful historian, though, like the careful anthropologist, tries to think as his subjects did, and within their system of values.

In summary, the historian in explaining an event undoubtedly relies upon some form of covering laws, however loosely they may be formulated. But covering laws are only one way in which the historian establishes a connection between an event and its cause. Unlike the natural scientist, the historian can and does take the words of his participant-sources and thus arrives at an historical explanation without benefit of a covering law. To that extent, it seems to me, Mr. Dray's conclusion that covering laws are not the only form of historical explanation agrees with the way I understand the historian goes about his work.

15

History as Factualized Fiction

ERNEST VAN DEN HAAG
New York University

I. HISTORY AND HISTORIOGRAPHY

In one respect, history scarcely differs from life: if we ask what, if any, is the meaning of history and what, if any, are its laws, we will perforce receive the same answer we receive when asking about the meaning and the laws of life; for history is but life past. Historiography is *sui generis* nonetheless. For one thing, historians must write as though those questions about the meaning and the laws of history had been answered—and positively, too.

Of course, the protagonists of history need pay no more heed to questions about meaning or about historical laws than people do currently. Anyone may live unaware of the laws (causes) that shape his life. Yet, a scientific description presumes such laws. And a biography (or a novel) seeks and finds meaning—else there is no way of discriminating between the significant and the insignificant event in the career to be described. Life, past or present, can ignore questions about itself; but the contemplation of it cannot. And historiography does not reproduce history (or a novel life) but simultaneously recalls and contemplates it.

To drag the past forward into the present, to re-present it, as historians must, is to select the significant events, *res gestae,* among countless happenings. Thus historiography, unlike history, implies criteria of meaning and theories of causality which allow us to include the significant events, and those causally relevant to them, and to exclude the rest.[1] The criteria of selection are moral, aesthetic, and causal. In espousing and applying them, the historian makes judgments and avails himself of the skills of art and science. Yet his craft cannot be reduced to either and his task differs from both. For, unlike novelists or philosophers, historians cannot altogether invent meaningful patterns and ideas. They must draw their interpretative patterns from what actually happened at specified places and times; at least the patterns must fit demonstrable actualities. (These raw happenings may appear as inchoate as Rorschach blots or, sometimes, as tightly structured as syllogisms.) Yet, though more bound to their material than artists, historians, unlike scientists, must use moral and aesthetic judgments to work their material. Though consistent with demonstrable universal laws, the historian's interpretations are not drawn from these laws and go beyond.

II. THE NOMINALISM OF HISTORIOGRAPHY

Scientists establish universal laws but historians string together particular events. History and life, of course, stress neither one nor the other. The emphasis of (nomothetic) scientists on universal regularities and of (idiomorphic) historians on unique particulars, distinguishes the task and method of each; their material is the same and lends itself equally to both treatments: [2] the uniqueness of historical events emerges from historiography, just as the universality or recurrence of events emerges from science. If "history" is often confused with "historiography," and takes on its particularities, whereas science is not confused with its object, it is because history can be experienced only through historiography, while science can be experienced separately from its object, which is also in the present.

By sufficient abstraction sociology or political science can view revolutions or wars as classes of events, persons as bearers of status, or as members of social classes (or castes or estates), just as, by sufficient abstraction, economists view men as profit maximizers, theologians as souls, psychologists as personalities, physiologists as bodies, physicists as masses, etc. On the other hand, by sufficient concretization, and stress on its roots and ramifications, and on the situation which produces the event, historiography reveals the unique aspects of every happening, though remaining abstract enough to make it intelligible. The very class names—conquest, religion, ambition, poverty—indicate that the particulars have enough common properties to form classes, that there are regularities and recurrences, which permit us to say "the battle," while singularities are indicated by saying "of Waterloo." Thus the proper names, dates, and places of historiography draw attention to the singularities of the events which constitute the classes scientists are concerned with.

III. HISTORIANS AS CONSUMERS OF SCIENCE

Since historians do not try to establish universal laws, they do not view events as instances or counterinstances of such laws. Thus, to the scientist, historical facts are evidence for (or against) his laws; to the historian, these laws are part of the evidence for (or against) the events actually having happened. The historian, in the first place, is interested in proving the facts; the scientist is interested in what the facts prove.

Yet, in stressing particulars, historians do not renounce science. They use it, as a court of law does when investigating the past actions of an individual. Only the rules of science permit us to infer from present evidence—all the court and the historians have—any past events whatever. And, however the historian's interest in specific events be awakened or justified, he must ascertain whether they occurred. In examining the genuineness, credibility, and sufficiency of the evidence for the occurrence of past events, historians apply the same empirical and logical rules which characterize science. Finally, the historian could not perceive or "explain" the relationships among his data without relying on the regularities which science observes, articulates, and refines. And it is only when he conceives of relationships that he can tell his tale, or even look for the events to be strung together.

Historians thus are certainly consumers of science. But they are not producers: they do not use their materials to construct or confirm scientific laws, they merely use the latter to test and to help make sense of their materials. And scientific laws, though necessary, are not sufficient to make sense of the past. Historians holding the scientific searchlight in their hands turn it whichever way they want to go. They must account for the array of facts thrown into relief. Yet, they retain a wide range of choice; within this range they find their way by means of nonscientific judgments.

In the application of science, the selection of goals is analogously nonscientific. Yet the progress of historiography does not resemble that of engineering: the science applied in historiography plays a lesser role. Historiography is neither as testable as applied science is, nor as directly and specifically instrumental. And though the past offers a range of choice to the historian, it is not the type of range offered to the applied scientist. Above all, when we apply, e.g., a law of physiology to "cure" a sick person, we utilize the law to achieve our desire. But we do not feel that our criteria for the selection of events from the past should merely reflect desire, *ad majorem gloriam nesciocuius;* we expect them to be inherent in history or, at least, justifiable by more than desire.

The idea that historians "retrodict" by essentially the same methods by which scientists "predict" covers a necessary part but is not a sufficient description of their task. They draw the past from present evidence, as the scientists draw the future from it, but (1) they apply but do not test or establish laws, (2) they draw not the past but an image of it that fits present evidence but is put together also, (3) by extrascientific (valuational) judgments of significance. Scientists may be motivated as historians are, but the truth of prediction is independent from motivation, whereas historiography cannot be separated from the criterion of significance of the historian: the truth of the image of the past is not exclusively dependent on fitting present evidence. In applied science, the science can be easily separated from the applied goal; but historiography does not exist independently of such goals.

IV. HISTORICAL SELECTION AND MEANING

The historian's task is akin to that of an individual memory: remembering and recalling the past. But rich and poor, intellectuals and the illiterates, artists and athletes, stockbrokers, steelworkers, generals, housewives, diplomats, and chorus girls remember different events. Historiography, the institutionalized memory of a society, may be no less idiosyncratic; but historians must justify their selective memorializations by more than mere personal involvement; and their justification hinges on their value judgment. (Certainly today's French historian of Babylon or of Charlemagne "remembers" neither. However, the documents or ruins he studies indicate events because they recall things within his experience, however indirect, and he recalls them to us.) The scientific question: did the events actually take place? arises only once the events have been selected as significant. Thus, Ranke's *wie es eigentlich gewesen* is the problem and not the solution: we cannot reproduce, we must interpret, and our interpretations depend largely on the value judgments Ranke thought avoidable.

Now, to some, life (and thus history) has meaning; to others: "it is a tale/Told by an idiot, full of sound and fury/ Signifying nothing." (Did Macbeth become a murderer because he thought so? Or did he think so because he became a murderer? Or because he miscalculated?) Although "life" possibly can afford to be "an idiot" and tell a tale "signifying nothing," the historian cannot. He must give some meaning to his tale: the seamless series of numberless events which is history becomes intelligible only if the historian sees a pattern which permits him to select and relate events. Yet history does not determine its own interpretation; it only sets limits and suggests possibilities.

The meanings found in history are of different kinds though, ultimately, they always rest on value judgments. The historian may decide that those events of the past are important that led to a subsequent past situation—those seventeenth century happenings are significant that caused the eighteenth century to become what it did become (as the historian sees it); or the historian may give importance to those past events which most influenced what seems most important to him in the current situation; or, perhaps in a future situation he envisages or desires. However, since neither the present nor the future is self-defining any more than the past, the historian, to decide what is significant in the past has to decide what is important in the present or future. And this decision depends less on the facts than on their evaluation.

To some extent the criterion of present or future importance is always applied in interpreting the past which, therefore, is never wholly the past. Nor could it be for us: we necessarily look at it with present and not with past eyes. Even if the past could be altogether reproduced, we could not be. Applied incautiously, the criterion of present importance leads to anachronisms. Events which may seem important only in retrospect are given a meaning quite different from what was experienced by contemporaries who did not have our experience to direct their perception. (Karl Popper's *The Open Society and Its Enemies* is a fine example of anachronism elevated to a method.) Yet, though anachronistic selection can never be wholly avoided, the historian can try to confront it with the contemporary reaction to contemporary events. Above all, he need not compound the hazards of interpretation by deriving significance for the past from a future that is still unknown, or worse, from one that he desires more than predicts. The evaluative element is unavoidable. But that certainly is no reason to enlarge its scope beyond necessity. (I believe that E. H. Carr gratuitously advocates doing so in his *What Is History?* [New York: A. A. Knopf, 1962].)

Instead of selecting the events that have affected what seems to him important later, the historian may vest subjects with importance by undisguised fiat. This decision is more candid though not less problematic. One might write the history of an idea or institution (e.g., progress, liberty, democracy, the church, dogma, religion, the family, drama). Or, one may select an individual—Napoleon, a thing—the bathtub, or the cotton gin; an event—the World War, or a complex of activities, ideas, institutions, feelings, and things—fashion, the economy, philosophy, love, music, science, Uruguay, Elizabethan England. (Unlike Toynbee, I cannot see that the units of history are more than conveniences and conventions for historians. Which is not to say that his delimitations may not be as useful, though as arbitrary, as others.)

The selection of a subject by fiat does not end the historian's evaluative tasks. He must still decide what belongs to the history of the drama, of Napoleon, of Uruguay, or of philosophy; and, finally, what is most important in it. The initial choice is but a first step. Nevertheless, the more the historian limits his subject, the fewer his problems of selection afterward. Thus, a history of Brooklyn may avoid questions that would occur in the history of the United States; a history of American fashion may avoid even more questions and a history of American eyeglasses, 1850–1900, still more. A history confined to one object, over one short span, avoids further problems of selection altogether, though at the cost of scarcely deserving to be called history.

However, narrowing the limits of the subject only relocates the problem of selection. The problem appears to a lesser extent within the narrowed limits of the subject only because it has been confined *ante portas*. When the significance of the narrow subject within the broader context of history is assessed, the problem returns. Certainly historiography needs specialized monographs concerning narrow subjects. But fashioning and carrying bricks becomes absurd, if those who do it pretend that their work solves the problems of architecture, or takes the place of that of the architect. Except to plumbers, the history of the bathtub is important only as part of the history of our civilization.

V. CAUSALITY, EXPLANATION, AND MORAL JUDGMENT

Having decided, no matter how, what subject is important enough to write about, the historian must decide what is important to the subject. Events, if not defined as part of the subject, become relevant only because of their causal relation to it. To determine what to relate, and how to relate it, historians implicitly rely on causal laws usually borrowed from elementary social science and common experience. (There are some exceptions. Marxist historical theory is explicit and hard to reconcile with common experience. This is true also of Toynbee or Spengler. But their causal interpretations are, if anything, less scientific than those here considered. These theories, as well as those of Plato, Hegel, or the Scholastics, might be called metahistorical: they use historiography rather than being used by it.)

Is the selection of causal theory a matter of evaluation, too? Aren't causal theories testable by the usual scientific criteria? They are, but not when they serve as principles of historical explanation and selection. Although we can often test the general correctness of the causal relation used, we can hardly ever test its correctness qua explanation: the historian has many correct causal relations, or sets of causal relations, to choose from and selects the one he uses as explanation by means of a largely moral or aesthetic judgment. I think that this is perceived, but too vaguely, by those who hold science inapplicable to history. Science is insufficient, but not inapplicable. Confusion of historical causality with historical explanation further generates the frequent but demonstrably mistaken claim that causal relations somehow do not hold in history, or differ from those found by the sciences.

Causal theories may explain on numerous levels. Even as seen by a single social science, an action may be "overdetermined"—several factors, each known to be sufficient to cause the action may be present. Further, each social science abstracts from all aspects of its subject that do not fall within its jurisdiction. Economics is concerned with economic causation, psychology with psychological causation. But the jurisdiction of the historian is not confined to one or the other; he explains the event, not merely its psychological or economic aspects. In practice, the historian can choose between, e.g., psychological and economic explanation by implying a *ceteris paribus* cause. We may say there was an "economic cause" for the Opium War against China in 1839, if we presume that the British psychological disposition to respond to the sudden Chinese prohibition of opium imports (to threatened economic deprivation) with violence is a constant. But if the British psychological disposition were regarded as a variable and the Chinese action as a datum, the causes of the war would be regarded as psychological. If the causes of all wars are presumed economic, the response of all noneconomic factors to economic change is presumed constant. But actually, in most situations both the known psychological and economic factors permit alternative decisions and neither can be regarded unquestionably as a constant. Marx, confusing the—sometimes—necessary with the sufficient was led astray here. His view can be "defended" only by making it meaningless. Yet his error is instructive: in his period the noneconomic was constant, relative to the fast moving economic variables which he, therefore, regarded as decisive. Many other factors may be regarded as "causal" since they too are variable: the domestic factors that led to the Chinese enforcement of the prohibition of opium imports at that moment may be "causes" as well as the Chinese military weakness, the European missionary spirit, rivalry among European powers, etc.

The historian is likely to find the (explanatory) "cause" of an event in what he regards as the most decisive variable and/or the variable within the power of his protagonists to control. To some extent his choice will depend on his level of analysis: is he interested in basic causes (what caused the inflammable condition?), in precipitating ones (who threw the match?), in general ones (why were no extinguishers provided?), or specific ones (why did some protagonist act as he did?); in necessary or in sufficient causes; in motives, intentions, or effects; in the responsibilities of persons, or in circumstances that brought these persons into responsible positions (would Hitler have come to power without the depression of the 1930's); or in surrounding conditions that made it possible for them to act as they did, to foresee or not to foresee, etc.

Certainly the historical judgment has unavoidable moral components. Hitler caused the World War by making demands that he could not hope to see fulfilled without war. Here we assume the constancy of the factors that resisted his demands, and by implication we feel that the resistance was morally more right than the demands. The World War, on a different level, was caused by the Stalin-Hitler pact; or by the refusal of England and France to rearm in time; or by their tolerance of the reoccupation of the Rhineland, and of German rearmament; or by the partial yielding to German demands which encouraged others; or by their unwillingness to satisfy the latter. Obviously, we need not underestimate these factors to consider Hitler guilty of causing the war. This verdict implies that his responsibility (interpreted as *mens rea* and effective autonomy; or as unforeseen effect of his action, without *mens rea,* and with, more or less culpable, neglect) in taking the initiative was greater than the responsibility of those who failed to prevent him. It is a moral judgment.

Thus, causal explanations in historiography contain a necessary scientific element (the causal relation) and a moral one (the explanatory use to which it is put) which makes them sufficient. If we reflect that science has long given up the essentially moral notion of cause used in historiography, our conclusion is reinforced. For science only indicates correlations: there is a relationhip "y" between "a" and "b" under circumstances "c," "d," "e," "f," *ceteris paribus.* Historians, however, need explanations. Just as they select actual events to relate, though the criterion of selection is moral or aesthetic evaluation, so they select actual causal relationships, though the criterion of explanatory use (selection) is moral or aesthetic evaluation.

It is possible to accept a rule for moral judgments which leaves only the facts to be investigated. For instance, the law attempts to take the moral judgment out of the court's hands, leaving the investigation of the facts and, even there, providing rules of relevance. But historians are their own legislators. Still, we may call "aggressor" whoever uses violence first. If "aggressor" is used as a term of total blame, we imply the moral judgment that no grievance justifies attack. This judgment still would leave many questions of interpretation, e.g., about preemptive and simultaneous attack, internal subversion and external support thereof, etc. (A questionable judgment, though in an age of hydrogen bombs, perhaps a correct one.) However, we do not often use such general rules as "the attacker is always wrong." Rather we ask: what are the causes of the conflict that ended in violence?

Certainly we do not say the workers are wrong because—as aggressors—they went on strike. We do not even think it decisive if the strike occurred in defiance of law or contract. Perhaps the workers had grievances that "caused" the strike; or the union acted because it was led by militant socialists; or racketeers; or by leaders afraid of not being reelected without a strike; or the union had reason to believe it would win easily (e.g., its judgment of the economic situation of the employers); or the union had government support, etc. On the other hand, we can say the strike was "caused" by the employers' refusal to satisfy the workers' grievances; by government support for this refusal; by the employers' expectation to win (their judgment of the economic situation); by differences in contract interpretation, etc.

Thus the decision on the "causes" of the last World War or the Korean War or the hypothetical strike is largely moral: in the historian's view, those are morally responsible, or "caused" the event, who made unreasonable demands, or refused unreasonably to satisfy reasonable demands, or used unreasonable means to enforce their demands, or their refusal, or unreasonably failed to take timely measures to avoid the conflict. The historian may assess responsibility in, say, the

Korean War further in terms of Russian misjudgment of American intentions and abilities; and of American failure to indicate these to the Russians. And similarly in the World Wars. But whatever the level, "cause" as an explanatory category represents a moral judgment not only because we may mean "responsibility" by "cause" but also because the selection of causal acts as explanatory depends on their moral evaluation.

VI. AESTHETIC JUDGMENT IN HISTORIOGRAPHY

Historiography, I have concluded, is facts and interpretations requiring judicious inquiry, reliance on scientific laws, moral, and finally, aesthetic judgments.

"Aesthetic" here refers to two related matters. First, unlike scientists, historians do not merely inform us of what can be experienced under certain conditions. Historiography itself is our experience of history. Though with a cognitive content a novel need not have, and factual about dates, places, and events, as a novel need not be, historiography is like the novel in being itself our experience of what it narrates—whereas science and scientific writing contain but information and rules for obtaining experiences. The experience of the past re-presented thus depends, in part, on the presentational skill of the historian and on his aesthetic judgment. He must convey a sense of the uniqueness of past events, and yet cast them into an intelligible pattern held together by recurrent threads. Indeed, if he fails to make sense out of events—however senseless they seem—the historian commits the equivalent of the novelist's pathetic fallacy.

The aesthetic judgments of the historian also influence the selection of events to be re-presented. Some events enter historiography not because judged intrinsically important, or relevant to what is, but because they serve as symbols, metaphors, or synecdoches of events judged to be important. Other insignificant and irrelevant events are selected because they serve as symbols of the human predicament in general. This (aesthetic) use of symbols occurs in historiography, is characteristic of art, and is uncharacteristic of science. (Scientists may occasionally communicate by these means, but, unlike historians, they can do without.) Of course, unlike the novelist, who uses potentialities, the historian uses (past) actualities. His symbols are actual events—not imaginary ones. But this does not make the use to which he puts these events less metaphoric. And, the utilization and selection of events as symbols requires an aesthetic judgment.

Novelists as do historians try to reveal a pattern of reality by using events selectively. Proust's Marcel, Thomas Mann's Adrian Leverkuhn—the protagonists of fiction and all that ever befalls them are, above all, patterns of events shorn of the irrelevant to reveal the significant. So are those of historiography. To be sure, the novelist has more freedom. He need not peruse present evidence to locate his events in space and time. His tale only need be possible, convincing, and revealing, whereas the historian must find out what actually happened and fit his pattern to it.[3]

But good fiction is fiction only in the invention of events, not in the revelation of meaning; and even events and characters are not so much invented as observed, selected, and shaped. Good historiography observes, selects, and shapes as well, though the events used must remain verifiable. Factual accuracy, completeness, consistency, and plausibility, etc. are necessary but not sufficient tests to determine whether a work of history be true. The significance of the historiographic work is tested as well (and that of the work of fiction is tested exclusively) by asking: does it ring true? does it make things intelligible? does it tell what is the meaning, what are the causes of events?

Like novelists, historians explore the possibilities of human experience even though confining themselves to experiences which have become actualities. Fiction, if it be truly art, interprets and organizes experience. The fiction of the novelist organizes and reveals potential experience. The factualized fiction of historiography uses actualities. Both, however, reveal the potentialities of the human career on earth and present a meaningful image of it.

NOTES

1. History scarcely could have meaning without having laws (regularities), at most teleological, at least correlative. Conversely, however, history might have (correlative) laws without having a meaning—unless one defines "laws" and "meaning" as synonyms which would be odd and useless. For by "meaning" surely a purpose or goal—which may include, but is not exhausted by the totality of laws—is meant. The difficulties of establishing such a "meaning," e.g., infinite regress or nondemonstrability, would not affect its psychological or historiographical (selective) function.

2. It is sometimes argued that human behavior is distinctive because less "determined" or because influenced by predictions about it, and that not science, therefore, but historiography, dwelling on particulars, is the appropriate method for doing justice to human behavior. Though human behavior may be indeed distinctive, I doubt that there is an "indeterminateness"—in the sense of nonpredictability in principle—which could be a proper basis for distinction. Certainly the influence of predictions on behavior is not distinctive at all. Prediction may affect human behavior. (There is a psychological influence even though there be no logical reason.) Mere description may do as well: a rather crude young man may tell the girl he is attempting to seduce, "All the other girls do it," and he may persuade her. Yet the influence of prediction or description on human behavior does not differ—except for sometimes being unintended—from the influence of commands or generally of communications and conditioning on animals. Prediction can condition the human mind quite predictably just as communications may condition an animal, or for that matter, a machine.

3. The daily newspaper fails to be contemporary historiography (though it can be an occasional source) because editors select among events according to whether they are "newsworthy." Whatever people want to read about is "news." (Newspapers do not try to form people's taste, they try to cater to it and pursue no

other object.) Thus a mixture of significant and insignificant events, pronouncements, interviews, observations, etc. is offered; a mixture so chaotic that all events lose significance and singularity and become diversion. (This effectively simplifies the world and protects readers from experiencing it fully, while assuring them of participation in commonness if not community.) Historians, too, select events. However, their purpose is not to divert; they attempt to trace the pattern that relates events and to reveal the singularity and the meaning of what happened. It is the difference between reporting the loudest and most sensational sounds within one's hearing and composing a symphony.

16

The Philosophy in History

ALBERT HOFSTADTER
Columbia University

HISTORY AND PHILOSOPHY are related in more ways than one. In the first place, philosophy itself is an historical phenomenon. Whether its history can be written independently of that of other phases of culture or whether it can be understood only in the context of a larger cultural process is a question that calls for determination; but in either event philosophy, in its form and content and as a living activity, participates in historical existence, is subject to historical conditions, and thus forms part of the historian's subject matter. Secondly, as philosophy enters history so history enters philosophy. It becomes that part of the philosopher's subject matter that is dealt with in philosophy of history. The shape taken by philosophy of history depends on the kind of philosophizing that is at work. It is sometimes thought that certain philosophies—such as the Aristotelian and, in general, classical philosophy—do not even permit the possibility of a genuine philosophy of history because of their failure to give due weight to the ontological significance of the uniqueness and unrepeatability of historical events, whereas other philosophies are essentially philosophies of the historical—as, for instance, the philosophies of Hegel, Marx, Dilthey, Bergson, Dewey, Whitehead, and Heidegger—since in them (in different ways, to be sure) temporality is featured as a constitutive phase of being, existence, or reality. This, however, is a moot question and one which I do not wish to pursue here. The topic to which I address myself lies in a different direction. It should, however, be noted that since the historical *is* a mode of being, *some* philosophy of history is required, and if one kind of philosophy does not provide it another that does must be sought for.[1]

History of philosophy and philosophy of history are different, if not entirely distinct, enterprises. Thus in Hegel's writings the two occupy different works, and in his thought itself their subject matters occur at different stages in the dialectical evolution of mind: history is the last stage of objective mind whereas philosophy (which is identical with the history of philosophy) is the culmination of absolute mind. No one wishing to think clearly about the matter will confuse the two. Nevertheless there are shadings that must be observed. Thus philosophy itself is historical not only in the sense that it participates in history and thus has a history, but in the more pregnant sense that its participation in history is genuinely historical; that is, philosophical thinking is bound to its time, its categories are formulated in the language of its time, its perennial problems are defined and conceived in the light of the vision of its time, and its changes—even if they exhibit some forms of progress—are not entirely progressive but rather qualitative, partly like religion and partly like art. This historical nature of philosophy as a living mode of thinking requires treatment on its own account. I overlook it entirely in what follows. (This introduces a certain schematic inaccuracy into the account, which, however, is unavoidable.) On the other hand, as philosophy is historical in nature so history is philosophical in nature, and this—the philosophy *in* history—is the theme of the present discussion. Because history is concerned with the realization of human life in time, and because the fundamental drive of human life is toward its own existential validity, and because the concern of philosophy is with this validity, history, in its ultimate intention and therefore in its most basic and originative thinking, is inescapably philosophical. That is what I now try to make out.

I

What is it that has a history? Does the earth, for instance, have a history? In a sense it does. Its history is studied, in certain aspects, in so-called historical geology (stratigraphical geology). In terms of the order of the various systems of rocks it is possible to distinguish for a given region a succession of periods connected with a succession of earth movements. As a result the surface of the earth can be envisioned as going through a sequence of changes from the past to the present. Yet the sense of "history" applied here is not of interest to the philosophy of history. The reason is that the earth, which is supposed to have a history, is not itself an historical being.

To be an historical being is to be one into the structure of whose existence historicity enters essentially. It is to be one about which (whom) the truth can be told only in the form of historical narrative. In a secondary, though perfectly correct, sense, *things* may be historical, but only insofar as they are implicated in human existence. Thus a stone block by itself, as a physical thing, though subject to time, is not itself an historical entity. The truth about it, as such, does not take the form of historical narrative. One can of course raise questions like: How did this block happen to be at this place at this time? How did it happen to have the shape and size it has? Where did it come from? What will happen to it? And in answering them one can write a continuous narrative. But such a narrative is not yet an historical one. If, however, the block happens to be a statue, and one asks analogous questions about this statue, the narrative becomes definitely historical; for the being of a statue, which is an entity richer and more determinate in its being than a physical block of stone, lies within the ontic region of an historical world. A statue is in a sense a thing, but it gets its historicity of being not through being a thing merely but through being a work—as a work of man it participates in historical being.

If a statue gets its historicity through being the work of man, man has historicity, or better *is historically*, simply by being man. To be historical(ly) is to have the capacity to distinguish time as past, present, future, and to be under the necessity of acting in the light of that distinction. This is characteristic of a finite being whose mode of existence is describable in terms of purpose and intention, that is, man. A being that fulfills these conditions is a being that perceives, remembers, plans, forecasts, strives, fails, succeeds. Only for such a being does time exist *as* time, being distinguishable according to present, past, and future. The incessant change of what merely exists becomes historical only as it enters the context of life of this kind of entity. Thus to be an historical being is to be in this particular way. Historicity and temporality enter into the structure of existence of an entity of this nature; it is an historical being because its being is qualified by historicity. The earth is not an historical being and, consequently, is not taken by the historian or the philosopher of history as a genuine subject of history.

In a similar way, although we speak of the "history" of life in the world as a subject studied by palaeontology and the science of organic evolution, and even though the origin and history of man ultimately falls within that whole, the whole itself is not historical in the prime sense that interests history and philosophy of history. For we cannot rightly think of life as itself an historical being, remembering, perceiving, forecasting, planning, striving, failing, succeeding.

On the other hand we speak of the history of an institution (banking in the United States), a group (the Mormons), or an art (music), as well as the history of a person (Frederick the Great). And indeed, although the human person, as the being that perceives, remembers, forecasts, plans, strives, fails, succeeds, is the historical being in a very central sense of the term, we tend less to think of him than of the groups, associations, institutions, and practices to which he belongs and which belong to him, as having a history. Biography is undoubtedly a form of historical thinking and writing; yet in the thinking of the historian and philosopher of history it is neither the most characteristic nor the supreme form. The reason is that the life of the individual human person is not one that can be or be understood independently of those of other persons. Man, though he exists as an individual person, is a person and has a personal history only within the group and in the context of the institutions and practices of the group, even when the most signal feature of his life is his revolt against the group and its practices.

The primary subject of history is not the individual historical being—the human individual—but the superindividual group, with its associations, institutions, and practices. Now a group does not literally perceive, forecast, plan, strive, fail, succeed; at least it does not do so in the comparatively direct and uncomplicated sense in which the individual person does. Yet it is because such functions have their parallels in group life that we conceive of it as being historical, and of the group as having a history. Particularly, it is because the group can take note or fail to take note of an occurrence, remember or fail to remember what has already happened in its experience, and so forth, that it becomes of interest to the historian. It should hardly be necessary to add that this does not mean that the historian is compelled to view the group as having a group-soul or group-mind in the sense of a large-scale metaphysically individuated entity, like an individual mind but of a higher order, such as the Absolute or Zeitgeist of idealist philosophy; nor does it mean that the historian must view the group as having a biological life-principle of its own, with its own quasi-physiological mode of birth, life, and death, as in the speculative vision of Spengler. It does, however, mean that group life is more than the sum of individual lives and that there is a determinate sense in which it can be sensibly said, for example, that a group has attempted the planning and execution of a certain project—e.g., the construction of a canal across a given isthmus—and has failed or succeeded.

Moreover, it is not only what a group does that is of central interest to the historian, but also and equally what it undergoes. History is an account that illuminates not only the actions and achievements of a people, but also its sufferings and its fate—ultimately its whole struggle to be. The historian sees the group within a larger context, namely, within the group's world, and sees it enacting and undergoing its life within that context. His concern is with the group's life itself, not as a mere instance of a class or as a mere illustration of alleged sociological or other laws, but as an individual course of life, single, unrepeatable, in the concrete meaning-fulness of its poignant temporal passage. For this the historian has a passion.

II

Let us return provisionally to the individual person as historical being—most of what has to be said may be said in that less complex connection. The historian as biographer wishes to give an account of the person and his life. He could treat the life not for its own sake but as an illustration of trends, circumstances, or other general features of the period, but so far he would be giving only a derivative historical significance to the individual. Suppose, rather, his concern is with the individual in his own proper historical being, so that the individual is accorded an original, underivative historical significance. What kind of thinking must the historian perform in the shaping of his account?

The form of the biographer's account must be such as to make intelligible, so far as this is possible, the subject and (in) his life. He must tell, as truly as he can, what the person is and how he exists as such, what he strives for and why, what he succeeds or fails in doing and how; and in all this, taking into account accidents and contingencies as well as intentional acts, he must show the subject's doings and undergoings in their place and significance within the whole of the life, so far as the life exhibits wholeness.

What mode of thinking does the biographer have available as a way of ordering his account? This is tantamount to asking what is the principle of the form of the life of an individual person so far as that life exhibits form, and it is obviously one of the most difficult questions facing human knowledge, if we expect as an answer to it a concrete and particularized account of the principle of life-form. Hence the temptation is to escape from the challenge of dealing with it by handing it over to the psychologist as the putative expert in understanding the forms of life. Unfortunately, psychology today is hardly in a position to get very far with this question, for in order to answer it the psychologist would have to have mastered the dynamic principles involved in all the forms of human activity, e.g., sexual, economic, social, political, legal, artistic, cognitive, religious, philosophical. Does any form of contemporary psychology even begin to approach the beginnings of a scientific treatment of this subject?

Moreover, there is an obstacle of principle in the way of any attempt to derive the form of historical thinking from science alone. As soon as we reach the sphere of mind and spirit, normative elements begin to enter into factual matters, in such a way that it becomes not only impossible, but also undesirable to try to keep them separate or, in the name of an historical objectivity patterned after scientific neutrality, to eliminate valuation altogether. Writing of the naval battle at Syracuse (413 B.C.) and the retreat and annihilation of the Athenians, Thucydides says:

> Of all the Hellenic actions which took place in this war, or indeed, as I think of all Hellenic actions which are on record, this was the greatest—the most glorious to the victors, the most ruinous to the vanquished; for they were utterly and at all points defeated, and their sufferings were prodigious. Fleet and army perished from the face of the earth; nothing was saved, and of the many who went forth, few returned home.
>
> Thus ended the Sicilian expedition. (VII, 87)

Here the Athenian historian estimates the defeat of the Athenians as the greatest Hellenic military action on record—thus manifesting an objectivity regarding a matter of value attained not by eliminating the normative element of judgment but by attempting to set aside personal partisanship in reaching the judgment. How could an historian give his reader a realization of what happened without imparting a realization of the magnitude of the event and, therefore, without a judgment of this sort? How dispense with the estimative expressions—greatest, most glorious, most ruinous, utterly and at all points, prodigious—or, indeed, the evaluational implications of the tone and the structure itself, with the masterful touch of its simple declarative ending, without abandoning the most essential features of the picture? For to see the event in these value-colors is part of seeing the event truly—provided the estimations are just—and to see it deprived of these colors is to see it incompletely and falsely. History is written by men, about men, for men. Its mode of thought and truth is contained within that context.

So it is too with biography. In describing the debate concerning the Sicilian expedition, Thucydides offers a brief glimpse of Alcibiades.

> The most enthusiastic supporter of the expedition was Alcibiades the son of Cleinias; he was determined to oppose Nicias, who was always his political enemy and had just now spoken of him in disparaging terms; but the desire to command was even a stronger motive with him. He was hoping that he might be the conqueror of Sicily and Carthage, and that success would repair his private fortunes, and gain him money as well as glory. He had a great position among the citizens and was devoted to horse-racing and other pleasures which outran his means. And in the end his wild courses went far to ruin the Athenian state. For the people feared the extremes to which he carried the lawlessness of his personal habits, and the far-reaching purposes which invariably animated him in all his actions. They thought that he was aiming at a tyranny and set themselves against him. And therefore, although his talents as a military commander were unrivaled, they entrusted the administration of the war to others, because they personally objected to his private habits; and so they speedily shipwrecked the state.

It surely needs little reflection to bring to awareness the degree to which this picture is pervaded by a consciousness impregnated with civilization, so that to understand what it says the reader must himself enter into that mode of vision. Take as example what is apparently the least valuational of the sentences: "He was hoping that he might be the conquerer of Sicily and Carthage, and that success would repair his private fortunes, and gain him money as well as glory." Without a word of explicit judgment, the historian places Alcibiades perfectly for the reader, in whom he presupposes an understanding of men, values, and motivations. In this brief and superficially value-neutral statement the reader already detects the soil in which treason grows. Unless this were the case Thucydides would not have been writing history nor would we now read what he wrote so long ago. What we wish to know in history is the story of human life understood as human and therefore understood in human terms. This presupposes an understanding of values, meanings, purposes, and validities that qualify human life, and history can be conceived and written only in the terms and spirit of such an understanding. One of the most fundamental problems of historical method is that concerning the nature of objectivity and truth when these have to do with the kind of understanding required of the historian.

If we look to the forms of life, we note that there are many varieties of unity of doing-undergoing, from the relatively uncomplicated response to a physical stimulus, through the varied modes of daily and secular behavior, to the highest forms of integrative experience, aesthetic, religious, philosphical. In all of these the individual realizes life-form in lesser or greater degree; each of them is a case of a meaningful unity of doing-undergoing. Some are less and others more comprehensive, and the latter become so by building on the former, making them ingredients in their self-formation. In developing his skill in the use of the plow the agricultural worker makes use of the simpler mechanisms of response to physical stimuli, building them into the kind of capacity called a skill. The employment of this skill is, further, made a constituent in a more inclusive form of life, namely, the maintenance of home and family; and this domestic life is in its turn contained within more comprehensive forms, legal, political, ethical, social, and ultimately the integral forms of the religious, aesthetic, and philosophical. The existence of this stratification, in which lower forms of life-unity are comprehended within higher forms while being transformed and enriched by being given a deeper meaning—*aufgehoben* in the sense of being uplifted rather than canceled—makes possible the answer to our question. Whatever the degree of form and unity actually realized by an individual in the course of his life, the principles by which the individual life can be understood as a particular human life, and in reference to which an historical narrative may be written which will view that life as a human life, must be drawn from this stratification, ultimately from its highest, most inclusive level. The horizontal course of an historical life in time can be understood as such a life only if viewed in relation to the vertical structure of forms of integration possible to the historical subject. This structure provides, as it were, the ordinate by which the shape of the life-curve can be plotted along the abscissa of time. It provides at one and the same time the means of estimating what is happening in the life—the substantive form of the individual's history—and the criterion of meaningfulness and validity of what is realized or unrealized in it.

Accordingly, the historian has two basic tasks to fulfill in reaching an account of the individual life. He must, on the one hand, uncover in the life of the subject the striving, failing, succeeding through which the life achieves whatever form it does, and on the other hand, he must reveal the degree of meaningfulness and validity that is therein realized. And these —though I separate them by the device of "on the one hand—on the other hand"—are not in themselves separate; the process of showing the form achieved in a life *is* a process of revealing its degree of meaningfulness and validity and conversely. I distinguish them because in accomplishing the concrete task itself the historian is obliged to look in two directions at once and bring together the threads of his account from two sources, namely: (1) the facts of the life and (2) an ultimately philosophical understanding of the stratified phases of human life-form.

(1) *The facts of the life*

I do not mean by this the data that the historian (biographer) can gather from whatever sources are accessible to him. I mean rather the facts about the life-form that takes shape in the life. It is a fundamental *hypothesis* of the view I am here putting forward—a hypothesis about the facts of life—that the individual human person is motivated in everything he does by the basic aim of attaining what to him is a valid structure of life, that is, a valid mode of carrying on the dynamic interchange between himself and his world that constitutes the process of his living. The hypothesis is that the basic aim is single, and that it is an aim at an ultimate singleness or unity of the life-process that I designate under the heading of "valid life-process" or "valid mode of interaction of self and world." On this hypothesis the life of the individual is essentially a project in which he endeavors to shape within himself the plan, the concrete form of will, of such a valid life-form while simultaneously striving to realize it in his actual interplay with his world, the two processes going on hand in hand, each contributing to the determination of the other. He experiences a life-form as valid when he finds, in his own experience, that he can will and continue to will the form of life he has attained to, that he can say yea to what comes into the scope of his doings and undergoings, that whatever happens enters as an element contributing its own share to the fuller meaning of the life. (Naturally such a life in fully realized form is either beyond human power or extremely rare, although there are moments of validity—the essential moments, those that have the value of eternity—that occur in many lives.)

The story of a man's life, seen from this angle, is ultimately the account of the form this striving takes. It is the story of the degree to which the man develops for himself a recognizably human shape, actualizing it in the time span contained between the dates of his birth and death. In it the protagonist engages in a single fundamental agon, the prize of which is his own validity of being. This striving interplay of man and world is the theme of life, and the historian is the narrator of it.

(2) *A philosophical understanding*

A consequence of our observations thus far is that the language, thought, and categories of history lie at a level above that of value-free science. In order to be adequate to his subject matter, the historian must be in a position to make use of a mode of thinking that comprises within itself an understanding of everything pertaining to the life, from the physical up to the highest spiritual plane. Not only must he be able to handle matters of special interest, such as the economic, social, legal, technical phases of the life, but he must also come finally to the fundamental striving of the man and the form this striving takes in the nature and quality of his life. Now since human life is characterized at this root level by qualities of such a nature as are the objects of religion, art, and philosophical reflection, the historian is compelled to come to an understanding of these qualities in order to be able to place the contents of the life in terms of them. Further, since it is the language and categories of philosophy by which religion and art, as well as philosophy itself, are grasped in thought, it follows that the historian is compelled in the end to make use of philosophy not merely as something to describe from the outside, but as something at the core of his own historical thinking about his subject. And still further, philosophy is not only more than value-free scientific thought; it is also more than value-estimating thought, i.e., it is more than any moral or other value judgment of things human. It is, rather, thought set free to engage with what *is* in regard to its ultimate intelligibility and meaning and, in particular, with the possibility, in relation to one's own being and what is other than oneself, of the establishment of valid life, valid human existence in the light of that meaning. Accordingly, not only must the historian attain to an adequate mode of value judgment of his subject matter (the level of "pragmatic" history); he must ultimately come to a philosophical assessment of it, and develop his narrative in terms of this assessment. Philosophy in the form of *his* philosophizing lies at the very heart of the historian's thinking, so far as that thinking is commensurate with the historical reality itself.

Thus, reaching out toward his understanding of the nature of the human individual and the possibilities of his valid existence, the historian must bring this understanding to bear on the facts of the life. The struggle of the individual subject to realize a life must be seen in the light of an understanding of the nature and possibilities of valid human existence. Indeed, only in this light can the struggle be seen as the kind of struggle it is; that is, only by means of the categories provided by a philosophical understanding of life can one grasp an individual life as a life, in its own inexpugnable meaning as a life.[2]

III

I have been maintaining that the historian is compelled to make use of his own philosophical understanding of human life in order to be able to think adequately and truthfully about the actual substance of the life that is his subject. The reason is that the object of philosophical understanding is rooted in life itself. Philosophy, I have said, is thought freely engaging with what exists in regard to its ultimate significance; and, in particular, this thinking occurs in the process by which the thinker seeks to determine life as valid human existence. Life occurs in the context of a medium, as music occurs in the context of tone or poetry in speech. The medium of life is that of the events, qualities, quantities, relations, and entities belonging to existence or actuality. Within this medium the human being finds himself alive, i.e., inextricably involved in the enterprise of achieving and maintaining a form of life, a form of striving interplay with the world of the life-medium. His basic impulse is the endeavor to attain to a valid mode of interplay with the forces in this world. Valid here means: his interplay is a manifestation of the psychical forces belonging to himself in their meeting with the forces of existence, and in this interplay the total structure of forces comes to a balance of rightness, the rightness being determined in terms of the individual's own experience of it. When he attains to this, his mode of being is a being right with oneself and what exists; and the balance is not static but as dynamic as the person's nature demands. In this being-right, or ultimate adjustment of self and world, lies the ultimate condition aimed at by human life as such. "Adjustment" is, of course, a misleading word because of its connotation of yielding to external pressure. But if we take it in its literal sense—to adjust is to render things right, to relate them rightly to one another, to arrange them fitly into a whole—it carries the proper implication of the composing of the wild elements of existence, the wild forces of the self and the not-self, into an inwardly meaningful life-activity.[3]

If the historian is to penetrate to the roots of the life he is trying to understand, he has to make his way through the data toward the specific nature of the ultimate adjustment characteristic of the historical subject he is studying. That is, he has to try to understand finally the person's individual temperament, the fundamental direction of his basic drives, the peculiar tonality, emphasis, mode of composition, in short, the style that life assumes in this concrete individual form. As in art a style is "a development, a coherent grouping of forms united by a reciprocal fitness, whose essential harmony is nevertheless in many ways testing itself, building itself, and annihilating itself," [4] so in life. Life is an art (though no longer a merely aesthetic art) at which most of us are the merest bunglers; but bungler or not, each achieves more or less of a style, more or less of a self-definition or life-composition in time, in which the forces of self and world reach some degree of reciprocal fitness, under the constant challenge of the possibility of disintegration. And like art too, the composition of life takes place largely without self-conscious regulation, especially where fresh creative forces appear. In the process of integrating perception, memory, foresight, planning, and striving, the integrating agency, the "genius" of life, is largely something which the individual may feel but of which he has virtually no explicit knowledge and which in his mythologizing about it he may call his deeper self, or the god in him, or the creative unconscious.

Now the ultimate life-validity determined in this way is what philosophizing aims to bring to explicit thought, conscious, critical, and constructive; philosophy is the critical self-consciousness of man in the course of the composition of life. It is the theory that the creative spirit in the process of life-composition develops for itself as its own explicit mode of self-definition, self-interpretation, self-criticism, and self-guidance. In this respect it is like the indigenous aesthetic (e.g., cubist, classicist, romantic, expressionist, surrealist) that a style of art develops for itself as its own explicit mode of self-definition; but it is more comprehensive and deeper than any aesthetic because its jurisdiction is the fullness of life as compared with the enclosure of art.

If philosophy is concerned with ultimate life-validity then, conversely, the struggle for life-validity, while not an explicit philosophy, is the philosophical aspect or dimension of life. (That it is also the religious dimension, or at least the soil in which the religious dimension grows, is not a complication but, rather, an indication of the close relationship between philosophy and religion.) The kind of shape that the historical life tends to take, the kind of basic indwelling aim and life-interest the historical individual tends to display, the fundamental style "testing itself, building itself, annihilating itself" in the life-process, is the content whose self-definition is life seeking its validity and whose intellectual self-expression (also a self-definitory process) is philosophy as explicit thought. It follows that the task of the historian, in dealing with the self-determinative process (the "freedom") by which the individual develops (and fails to develop) a life-validity in time, is dealing with content of the nature of essentially philosophical subject matter. This is why the historian is forced finally to come to philosophical categories in the pursuit of the historical as historical.

IV

Turning now from the individual person to the group as historical entity and its career as historical process in the chief sense of "history," the foregoing discussion of the individual life makes it possible to be brief. Certain groups—e.g., associations—exist for limited purposes, and their story is one of origination for such purposes, steadiness or metamorphosis of purpose, realization of or failure to realize purpose, etc. in the course of their existence. There are, on the other hand, groups whose being is not reducible to any limited set of purposes, unless the purpose be that of life itself. Such groups—family, tribe, nation, people, humankind—develop their own purposes. Purposes, together with the associative and other mechanisms needed to pursue them, originate and grow within the life-course of these concretest of groups, and are intelligible only inside this setting. Hence the fundamental object of the historian's concern, even when he is dealing with an association, is the career of the concrete group, whose life-course is the whole within which the life-courses of individuals and their associations occur.

As in the case of the individual, the hypothesis is that the basic life-aim is single, that it is an aim at valid life-process of the concrete group. Insofar as the group has a history at all, hence insofar as it has a life-course or career at all, the process is one of the self-definition of a way of life, a striving to reach and maintain a form of life-validity at a communal level, which contains and makes possible that of the individuals belonging to the group. Its culture is the work by which the group endeavors to give shape to this form of life-validity. Culture, therefore, is not a mere means or tool toward predestined ends, but a vehicle in and through which the life of the group forms and defines itself. Through the diverse functions and institutions of culture—the gathering and distribution of information, the production and distribution of means of subsistence, education and the transmission of the heritage, the organization of common public enterprise, government, law, art, the church—the group arrives at some degree of doing and undergoing as a group, by which its life-course is constituted.

Again like the individual, the concrete group has to make an adjustment between itself and its world. Arising within the medium of existence, it exists and works only so long as it takes upon itself the burden of developing and maintaining an arrangement within the structure of which the energies of its members and, indeed, its communal spirit can find suitable expression. The group functions as though it also has a basic drive toward a valid mode of interplay within itself and between itself and its world, a being-right within itself and in relation to its world in which the forces it contains find an outward form of being and working that they themselves find appropriate for themselves. When a group loses this drive, this creative impulse toward the shaping of a valid life-form for itself, it begins to degenerate and die.

The fundamental quality of the group's life, defined in its culture, is intelligible only in terms of categories that show themselves in religion, art, and philosophy. This quality is manifested in the style of the form of life developed by the group. As in art, the forms of life grow in accordance with conventions which are themselves determined in the growth of the forms. These conventions afford the skeletal frame around which the group creates the body of its life. They penetrate into every area of life: language, work, law, politics, war, as well as art, religion, and philosophy. The life of the group is composed in terms of the harmony they permit. But, as the forms that define the group's characteristic mode of life-validity, they are intelligible only to a mode of thinking that is ultimately philosophical in its categories. The eternity of the old Egyptian life-form, the measure of the classical Greek life-form, the tensional power of becoming of the Western baroque life-form—these are concepts that only philosophy, pursuing its proper aim as the interpretation of the meaning of being and the foundations of life-validity, can grapple with. Now as in the individual so in the group—the striving and the failure or success of the group as the concrete subject in human history, the scope and degree of its realization of validity in communal life in time, is the ultimate and inclusive problem of the historian. To deal with this problem he needs to have accessible categories rich and deep enough to be congruent with the historical reality. These can be found only in philosophy, for only in philosophy does the concept of life-validity (together with the concepts to which it essentially relates itself—true, good, right, beautiful, sacred, holy) receive treatment on its own account.

Thus the historian has no alternative. Philosophical thinking about human life, as realized in time, is built into the demand for historical understanding of man because man, as individual and as social, is himself essentially a quest for life-validity, an experimental attempt to explicate and realize in concrete existence a meaning of being. This is the fundamental impulse in virtue of which human striving becomes fully intelligible as human, and the understanding of this impulse entails philosophical explication of its direction and content.

NOTES

1. There is a sense of "philosophy" in which history is part of philosophy's subject matter in a somewhat derivative manner. This is philosophy conceived as exclusively or primarily analytical, its task in regard to history being viewed as the analysis of meanings, usages, and procedures in the language of history and in the execution of historical inquiry. The contributions of Professors Dray, Hempel, and Nagel, and in part that of Professor White to the present conference are instances of this kind of philosophizing about history. As one may observe from them, as well as from the interest that prompts them, their subject matter is rather history as the historian's thought and language than history as the reality re-

ferred to by that thought and language. One cannot make an absolutely clean separation of the two. Nevertheless, on the whole, analytical philosophizing about history tends to concern itself with logical, linguistic, and methodological rather than substantive issues. Interest in this latter subject belongs to constructive philosophy. I take this opportunity to mention also a further point regarding Professor White's paper. His concern with the problem of the choice of a history "better than" other competing histories of the same subject leads him (or should have led him) into substantive issues, but in fact the substantive question was settled by him a priori in his definition of a history as a logical conjunction of explanatory assertions ("because" statements) regarding a chronicle associated with it. On this definition, a history consists essentially of a sequence of explanations of a sequence of events. In other words, the basic category of historical thought is assumed by Professor White to be that of causality. Apparently, according to him, the historian attempts to relate causally the "empirical" facts as they are placed in temporal sequence. But such a theory of the category-structure of historical thinking is too limited to do justice to the matter. For instance, Breasted begins his chapter on the religious revolution of Ikhnaton with the following observation:

> No nation ever stood in direr need of a strong and practical ruler than did Egypt at the death of Amenhotep III. Yet she chanced to be ruled at this fatal crisis by a young dreamer, who, in spite of unprecedented greatness in the world of ideas, was not fitted to cope with a situation demanding an aggressive man of affairs and a skilled military leader—in fine such a man as Thutmose III. Amenhotep IV, the young and inexperienced son of Amenhotep III and the queen Tiy, was indeed strong and fearless in certain directions, but he failed utterly to understand the practical needs of his empire. He had inherited a difficult situation. The conflict of new forces with tradition, was . . . already felt by his father. The task before him was such manipulation of these conflicting forces as might eventually give reasonable play to the new and modern tendency, but at the same time to conserve enough of the old to prevent a catastrophe. It was a problem of practical statesmanship, but Amenhotep IV saw it chiefly in its ideal aspects. His mother, Tiy, and his queen, Nofretete, perhaps a woman

> of Asiatic birth, and a favorite priest, Eye, the husband of his childhood nurse, formed his immediate circle. The first two probably exercised a powerful influence over him, and were given a prominent share in the government, at least as far as its public manifestations were concerned, for in a manner quite surpassing his father's similar tendency, he constantly appeared in public with both his mother and his wife. The lofty and impractical aims which he had in view must have found a ready response in these his two most influential counsellors. Thus, while Egypt was in sore need of a vigorous and skilled administrator, the young king was in close counsel with a priest and two perhaps gifted women, who, however able, were not of the fibre to show the new Pharaoh what the empire really demanded. Instead of gathering the army so sadly needed in Naharin, Amenhotep IV immersed himself heart and soul in the thought of the time, and the philosophizing theology of the priests was of more importance to him than all the provinces of Asia. In such contemplations he gradually developed ideals and purposes which make him the most remarkable of all the Pharaohs, and the first *individual* in human history. (James Henry Breasted, *A History of Egypt* [2 ed., London, 1909], pp. 355–56.)

The central thought of this paragraph cannot be expressed in any logical conjunction of explanations, despite the fact that the paragraph contains an important explanatory strand. In addition, it is questionable whether the notions of empirical statements and empirical facts can take care of a number of the constituent propositions. What Breasted is in fact doing here is to present an irony, to give the reader a view of the situation of Egypt at this time in terms of a contrast between its governmental needs and the new king's picture of them. This ironic contrast is itself a mode of *comprehension* which is not in the form of a "because," although it makes use of because-thinking in its formulation. The "thus" in the sentence beginning "Thus, while Egypt," is not the "therefore" of causality. Its function is to indicate that what follows sums up and presents as a whole what went before. The important formative word is the one that begins the second sentence, namely "yet." That word expresses the fundamental form of the passage, and perhaps it is unnecessary to say that "yet" cannot be reduced to "and" and "because," not even with the addition of "not." Moreover, a statement like the very first, and like others in the passage, can hardly be viewed as "empirical" in any simple, straightforward sense of the term. It is an estimate of need, and involves the implicit assumption of a schedule of values in terms of which the need can be assessed: it is itself an assessment. Similarly, characterizations such as "fatal crisis," "unprecedented greatness in the world of ideas," and "lofty and impractical aims" are hardly empirical predicates, but serve rather to give content and accent to the ironic picture being composed. The historian disposes of more than empirical statements and causal implications, and his task is more comprehensive than the provision of a logical conjunction of explanations regarding an associated chronicle. Thus Professor White's presupposed concept of history prevents his paper from being of use in the present context. I may add that in speaking of irony as a mode of comprehension I use the latter word intentionally in the sense of com-prehension, seizing together, for mind operates in understanding by way of more than one kind of seizing together, and historical thinking participates in mind.

2. An obvious implication is that it is a mistake to think of history as a mere combination of chronicle and causal explanation of the details of the chronicle, as mentioned in the previous note. This mistake stems from thinking of history as belonging to the same genus of knowledge as natural science. But the aim is different. Causal explanations are only part of the contexture of historical thinking and writing, ingredients rather than goals. History aims at giving a view of its subject in which one understands, comprehends, the life as a life. There are elements of appreciation, valuation, and —our language is deficient here—the grasp of ultimate validities such as is striven for in art, religion, and philosophy. These cannot be understood in merely causal terms. They have their own intrinsic modes of intelligibility, which must equally be given in historical accounts. And since these latter validities are comprehensive in scope, it is they, rather than the causal relation, that qualify and give meaning to the temporal historical slab of being. (Professor Dray's attempt to describe historical explanation as showing the rationality of an act in terms of the principles of rationality belonging to the *historian,* while it tries to escape in this way from the neighborhood of natural science to that of the humanities, is too artificial and thin in its concept of historical existence and under-

standing to be taken seriously. It eliminates actions from being historically intelligible on the absurd ground that they do not fall within the historian's own sense of fitness or appropriateness in the context. It thus substitutes for the real need of the historian—the need to master the different levels of meaningful human doing and undergoing, and to bring this to bear on understanding not only actions but thoughts, visions, sufferings, products, and finally the life-form and its realization as a life—an uncritically accepted sense of propriety that happens to belong to the individual historian or his circle. (Professor Dray's procedure here, in philosophy of history, is like that of present-day Oxford thinking about ethics, and it contains about the same amount of the sap of life.) The difference between causal explanation and historical understanding is reflected in the structure of the two modes of thinking. Causal explanation takes a deductive form, in which a conclusion (the statement of the event to be explained) follows from premisses (laws and circumstantial statements), as Professor Hempel maintains. But genuine historical comprehension is not such a logical progression. It is not a deduction, but a composition and an explication. In it thought seeks to apprehend the historical individual or group in its whole being, so far as that is whole, the life as life, and each constituent event or phase as what it is in the life. Hence historical thought is more like artistic comprehension: it seeks to grasp its object as an intelligible whole in a single act of comprehension, in an ultimately single imaginative (i.e., whole-forming) intuition. Unlike art, it is bound to the strictest faithfulness to the particular facts; and also its categories of interpretation are those belonging to the element of thought. But like art it is a form of synthetic rather than linear apprehension, and it aims at understanding the historical subject as a concrete entity and its life as a unique, unrepeatable process, rather than breaking it up into a step-by-step sequence of illustrations of general laws.

3. It is in this sense, in part at least, that Dewey used the concept of adjustment to define the religious attitude (*A Common Faith* [New Haven: Yale University Press, 1934], pp. 13 ff.). He speaks of the deepest kind of change of ourselves in relation to our world, changes that relate:

> not to this and that want in relation to this and that condition of our surroundings, but pertain to our being in its entirety.

> Because of their scope, this modification of ourselves is enduring. It lasts through any amount of vicissitude of circumstances, internal and external. There is a composing and harmonizing of the various elements of our being such that, in spite of changes in the special conditions that surround us, these conditions are also arranged, settled, in relation to us. This attitude includes a note of submission. But it is voluntary, not externally imposed. . . . It is a change *of* will conceived as the organic plenitude of our being, rather than any special change in will.

This deep-lying change in attitude, which Dewey uses to define the religious attitude, is chiefly subjective—a change in attitude rather than in the world. But religion is not merely subjective. In the individual as in the culture it is also an active process of creatively shaping the environment and the activities of men. Because it is an ultimate process of "adjustment," it impresses into its service all elements of existence and tries to compose them into a meaningful and valid whole.

4. Henri Focillon, *The Life of Forms in Art* (2nd English ed., New York: George Wittenborn, Inc., 1948), p. 7.

17

Objectivity and Reconstruction in History

SIDNEY HOOK
New York University

I

No matter what the upshot of our theoretical analysis of history turns out to be, historical judgment will continue to serve as a mainstay of our daily life. For our experience would be an incoherent extravaganza, without confidence in our memory; and memory is a primal form of historical judgment. Even when our memory turns out to be false, what we imagine the past to have been is a ground of belief as well as a cause of expectation. In this sense our very reliance upon natural events and regularities depends upon some historical memory. Nor can we plan for the future intelligently without assuming that we are in possession of some knowledge about the past.

The nature and grounds of historical knowledge is therefore not the special and exclusive concern of the historian or the philosopher of history. Every human being may be touched by its issues in that at some moment in his career the truth or falsity of some historical judgment may profoundly affect him. Sometimes his very life may be at stake. For once the law is clear and relevant, the fate of a man who finds himself in the dock depends solely upon the judgment by the jury of the historical facts: Did the defendant act as charged? Was the action premeditated? Were there extenuating circumstances? Every controversy which has raged over the justice or injustice of a judicial decision has assumed that the concept of historical truth is as meaningful as the concept of scientific truth, and that historical judgment, although often more difficult to establish than a judgment in science and daily life, can be as objective, even if not so firmly warranted. This generalization is not negatived by cases like the Dreyfus Trial. The anti-Dreyfusards consisted of two factions. One believed that the evidence actually established Dreyfus' guilt; the other believed that even if the evidence was tainted and Dreyfus innocent, the verdict should be permitted to stand because the honor of the French Army was involved. Neither faction challenged the concept or possibility of objective historical truth. What is true of the Dreyfus Trial is true of every other disputed legal process. The Moscow Trials are no exception. The more elaborate the frame-up, the more aware are those responsible for it of the facts in the case, in the same way as a person who deliberately lies must know, or believe he knows, the truth.

The fact that the reliability of historical judgment is presupposed by all human beings in the business of living does not justify, of course, the claims made for the study of history as a discipline in education. Indeed, it was exaggerated claims made for the consequences of such study which was in part responsible for the growth of historical skepticism among some leading American historians, and the formulation of a theoretical position about the nature of historical judgment which logically implied a relativistic subjectivism that hardly squared with their specific historical interpretations. Typical of the claims made for the study of history is the following passage from Thomas Jefferson's *Notes on Virginia* in which he outlines his scheme for public education.

> But of the views of this law none is more important, none more legitimate, than that of rendering the people the safe, as they are the ultimate guardians of their own liberty. For this purpose the reading in the first stage when they will receive their whole education, is proposed, as has been said, to be chiefly historical: History, by apprising them of the past, will enable them to judge of the future; it will avail them of the experi-

> ence of other times and other nations; it will qualify them as judges of the actions and designs of men; it will enable them to know ambition under every disguise it may assume; and knowing it, to defeat its views. In every government on earth is some trace of human weakness, some germ of corruption and degeneracy, which cunning will discover, and wickedness insensibly open, cultivate and improve. Every government degenerates when trusted to the rulers of the people alone. The people themselves therefore are the only safe depositories. And to render them safe, their minds must be improved to a certain degree.[1]

One may legitimately question Jefferson's simple faith that the study of history, by itself or in conjunction with other studies, is the best means of retaining freedom. It presupposes that teachers of history do not consider their interests identical with their rulers.[1] But the study of history is certainly not a sufficient safeguard of freedom; and there is no convincing evidence that it is even necessary. It was this common notion that history could be used to justify public policy and serve in some way to guide public affairs which led Charles Beard to a strong reaction against efforts to "historicize" arguments for good causes, from which he slid gradually into a naïve skepticism concerning historical objectivity, even as he called for a high level of intellectual performance by historians in their quest for "true and workable statements." Beard was wont to say that no aggregate of facts, including historical facts, determined a policy. If one means by determines here "logically implies" or "entails," this is an incontestable truism. As a truism, it is altogether irrelevant to the question of the existence and nature of historical fact. One could subscribe to an objectivism as extreme as that of Ranke's and still agree with Beard's truism that no aggregate of facts by themselves entails or logically necessitates a given policy. But if by "determines" one means not "entails" but "makes reasonable" or "sensible," then, unless the end or value goals of policies are themselves in dispute, it is difficult to see what else can determine a choice of a specific policy except the aggregate of relevant facts in context—*if* they are facts. Even when values presupposed by policies are themselves in dispute, and alternatives of action are beginning to shape up, the sensible choice among values must take notice of the probable consequences of acting on them. These consequences may be more clearly observed in the light of what has taken place in the past. History, as a close study of the past, may be extremely helpful in discerning the future consequences of alternative proposals of action. Anyone who defends a policy in a specific historical context, no matter what its consequences, is either a fanatic or a fool.

The nature of historical objectivity is therefore every man's concern. In my own experience I have found that the conception of objectivity has been made more problematic by historians reflecting upon their craft than by philosophers reflecting on the nature of historical knowledge. There is evidence that what inspired historians to question, if not challenge, the notion of scientific objectivity in history is familiarity with the writings of some European philosophers, notably Croce. If I may introduce a personal reference, when I was asked twenty years ago by the Committee on Historiography of the Social Science Research Council to serve as a philosophical consultant on the terms in use in historical writing, I found the Committee very much under the influence of Charles Beard, although with some misgivings which became progressively stronger as our deliberations went on. Beard, on the strength of his misunderstanding of what he conceived pragmatism to be, expected me to endorse and support his views about the historical process, causation, and the "comprehensive knowledge of history-as-actuality." This last was the standard by which he proposed judging the adequacy of historical events about the past, despite the fact that on his own view such "comprehensive knowledge" was unattainable, so much so that the use of statements attributing causal influence in history seemed to him impermissible. With great generosity of spirit, Beard accepted my analyses of terms like "cause" and "understanding," even though their plain implications were incompatible with the extreme relativism of some of his own formulations and of the underlying Crocean philosophy.

It has always seemed to me that Beard's own historical practice, as well as that of Becker's, and of the historians influenced by them could hardly be squared with their account of historical knowledge or even with the more careful and detailed accounts of writers sympathetic to their point of view. An extraordinary significance is attached to the fact that every historical explanation involves a threefold selection—a selection of a theme or problem to be explained, the selection of data considered relevant to the theme or problem, and the selection of an explanatory hypothesis or interpretation—as if these selective discriminations were unique to historical understanding. The commonplace fact, already stated by F. J. Turner that "*each age writes* [or rewrites] *the history of the past anew with reference to the conditions uppermost in its own time*" [2] has been made the basis of a puzzling view that "the meaning and significance" of any past event is "continually changing," and that these changes are "cumulative and progressive," and that they give us "increasingly adequate schemes of scientific explanation." Although I have characterized the statement that each age rewrites the past as a commonplace fact, it must be qualified by the even more commonplace observation that not the age but individual historians rewrite the past, often differing with each other as profoundly as their several views differ with the dominant interpretations of earlier ages about the past. If we are to take the reference to the cumulative and progressive changes in the meaning and significance of the past literally, we must be in a position to determine when the historians of an age are rewriting the past in such a way as to add to our reliable knowledge of it and when they are distorting the truth about it. It is rather difficult to make sense of the claim that the upshot of the process of reinterpretation results in an increasingly adequate scientific explanation of the past in the absence of a clear indication of *what* the explanation is adequate to—the available evidence of the past or the need or purposes of the historian in the present, and of criteria which guide us in deciding whether the interpretation of any given age is increasingly or decreasingly adequate. Without some such indications the result is not so much an objective relativism as objective confusion.

For example, suppose in a religious age, the age of Augustine or Aquinas, historians explain a pattern of events in the past by invoking the hand of God. In subsequent ages the same pattern is explained by reference to the magic of great personalities, or to psychological forces in individuals and in the mass, or to economic necessities, or the pressure of population and physical environment, or what not. If the successive hypotheses offered are incompatible with each other what sense would it have to say that the meaning and significance of the past is "cumulative" and "progressive," or apply these terms to the conclusions reached in any age? If God does not exist, then it is false to say that anything in history is explained by the finger of Providence *both* in a religious and irreligious age. If the underlying hypotheses of psychoanalysis are dubious or false, no historical explanations based on them are adequate—no less "increasingly" adequate—to anything. And this is so even if the consensus of historians in one age inclines to religious belief and in another to belief in psychoanalysis. Granted that new *questions* arise with new generations. This does not entail that the *answers* to the old questions necessarily become inadequate. Granted that knowing the past is not reconstituting or reconstructing or reliving the *past* as it actually happened. The historian, as distinct from the propagandist, wants to know the truth about the *past* even if such knowledge requires "experimental" redetermination of the situation in the present out of which his problem arises. There is a difference between using our knowledge of the history of the past in order to influence the future, to help bring about events we regard desirable and to forestall those which are undesirable, and making or manufacturing a history of the past solely with an eye to achieve our aims.

It is this failure to distinguish more clearly, on the one

hand, between the history of the past written in the present to influence the future and which necessarily reflects contemporaneous judgment of what is important in the present, and, on the other hand, the history of the past made by agents with *their* judgment of what was important, which is the source of the needless confusion that departs from a truism about the contemporary facts of selection and ends in the absurd belief that our criteria of importance must have prevailed in the past. This confusion is intensified when another fact about written history is misconstrued. It is true that history will be rewritten whenever new perspectives arise that enable us to see the significance of some past events which escaped their contemporaries. These events fall into patterns of continuity which embrace events that were future to those who lived in the past. But this does not necessarily affect the truth of the causal explanations of the behavior of those who lived in the past. The Luddites who wrecked the machines which deprived them of their livelihood were oblivious of the fact that the changes they set themselves against marked the onset of the industrial revolution that doomed their efforts to resist technological advance to failure. We can now see, as they did not, that no matter how many victories were won against the introduction of machinery, it was a lost war from the start. But this does not bear on any causal explanation of the behavior of those who acted as they did. Similarly, those who live after us in some ways will understand our age better than we do ourselves because they will be in a position to see what came out of events which we presently ignore and which are unsuspected beginnings of important trends that will reach fruition after we are gone. But the truths thus learned will as a rule supplement, not contradict, the answers we legitimately give to the more restricted questions: What happened in our age, how did it happen, and why?

Turner's commonplace tells us no more than that history is written and has been written by the survivors. The blunt but crucial point, however, is whether the survivors write or have written true history or false, whether their historical judgments are valid or invalid, adequate or inadequate in the light of the undoctored evidence. Were Stalin alive and triumphant today in the Soviet Union, would the charges made against the defendants at the Moscow Trial still be historically valid? If Khrushchev succeeds in burying the West and the universal history of mankind is prepared by the Institute of Red Professors or by the Communist Academy, will it be true that South Korea invaded North Korea, and that the United States used germ warfare during the Korean War? The question concerning the nature and possibility of historical objectivity is not only of theoretical importance. To the extent that dignity and honesty in the conduct of human affairs rest on the belief in such objectivity, reflection upon it goes to the very heart of the question concerning the nature and possibility of liberal civilization.

II

It has sometimes been charged by historians impatient with philosophers that problems which arise in the understanding of history, and in the methodology of historiography, have been artfully imposed on historians by philosophers who speak highhandedly either about the limits of historical knowledge or about its ideal scientific goal, and in both cases without any firsthand acquaintance with the materials of history and the specific tasks of the historian. To the extent that a philosopher is interested in the history of ideas, even if it is restricted to the history of philosophy, he is writing history of a sort. But I am not concerned to deny the impeachment of his status as a professional historian. I am concerned to deny that the philosopher has imposed his own concerns upon the historian. For the record clearly shows that particularly in America, philosophers until recently on the whole have not been interested in the logic, methodology, or philosophy of history. It has been the historians themselves, when they have taken distance to the details of their work, who have placed these problems on the doorstep of the philosophers.

I vividly recall the publication of a series of articles by Professor Swain [3] who under the title of *What Is History?* gave a brief account of the different interpretations which had been offered by historians of the fall of Rome, the French Revolution, and some other outstanding historical events. Although his account was far from exhaustive, no sign could be found of any "cumulative and progressive" pattern in the amazing variety of interpretations presented by historians of the same events. He concluded with the summary observation that historians are more likely to reflect the age in which they live than the age of which they write. This goes beyond Turner's commonplace, and places a time bomb in the very foundations of historical inquiry. Under the same title, *What Is History?*, E. H. Carr makes the same observation,[4] together with a number of other claims difficult to reconcile with it. With explicit reference to Gibbon he tells us that the point of view of an historian, his basic values and explanatory categories are more likely "to reflect the period in which he lives than the period about which he writes." The realization of this "truth" is supposed to make us more sophisticated about history than the *simpliste* approach which would take Ranke as a model, as he is commonly understood in the Anglo-American historical tradition.

Nonetheless the dictum breeds unacceptable paradoxes. One would hardly say of an historian that "he reflects the period in which he lives more than the period about which he writes" unless one believed that the historian has in some significant way *distorted* the truth concerning the period about which he writes. There would be no point whatsoever in pronouncing this judgment on an historian if one believed he was giving an adequate or truthful account of the past. It is only when we have good reason or evidence to justify the belief that the truth about the period he writes is *different* from the historian's account of it that the dictum becomes relevant. In the specific situation in which we utter it, we must be in a position to say that either there exists some account which does not distort the past but truly describes it or that there could very well be one. In other words the maxim cannot be generalized without inconsistency.

When Carr says of Gibbon that he reflects the eighteenth century rather than the centuries of the Roman Empire, how does he know this? Is he not clearly implying that he knows truly what the thoughts, sentiments, and judgments of the eighteenth century are? But if one were to apply his own maxim to his observations on Gibbon would not one be justified in saying that what Carr believes about the eighteenth century reflects the twentieth century more than the eighteenth? And if this is so how can Carr confidently assert that Gibbon is giving us an inadequate account of Rome or one less adequate than of the eighteenth century? To make sense of his observation in this particular case, Carr must claim that he knows the relevant truth about Rome and the relevant truth about Gibbon's England, and that Gibbon couldn't see the truth about Rome because he wrote with the blinders of the eighteenth century—something which is apparent to Carr because *he* writes without the blinders of the twentieth century.

It seems to me that the conclusion is inescapable that what makes an historical account, not *the* truth about what it describes but *truer* than another, once the historical problem under consideration has been selected, is whether it does justice to the available evidence by means of a method and criteria of relevance, which do not differ fundamentally from the way in which conclusions are confirmed in other fields like medicine or geology, in which hardly anyone raises the question about the possibility of warranted assertions or advocates a position of wholesale skepticism about objective knowledge. Truths in history may be more difficult to obtain than in other areas of experience: they are not more relative. (I shall have more to say about the question of the selection of historical problems later.)

Failure to see this on the part of some historians reflecting on their craft seems to me to be a consequence of some implicit assumptions which crop up in their writings even when on occasions they take positions that are tantamount to repudiating them. Any one of these assumptions, if seriously believed, would make history as written perhaps one of the fine arts but not a scientific discipline. These assumptions are: (1) Anything short of the whole truth about a subject lacks objectivity, that because selection is inescapable, subjectivity is inescapable; (2) that because every conclusion is modifiable in the light of further evidence and no judgment can be considered final or certain, no historical assertions are warranted; (3) that any passion or concern except to tell the truth is incompatible with the discovery of truth; (4) that the personal involvement of the historian in the subject matter of his inquiry makes historical knowledge different from scientific knowledge and the meaning of truth in history different from the meaning of truth in natural science; (5) that the fact that the historian's leading principles and principles of selection are influenced by his knowledge of the present commits him to a bet or faith in one kind of future rather than another, where the future refers not to the *evidence* to be discovered in the course of testing his hypothesis (something true for any assertion of fact) but to a commitment about the future of society or mankind; (6) that unless an historical account establishes some contact with the minds of those who lived in the past, the motives and purposes of men, their reasons and rationalizations, it cannot be a faithful rendering of what happened.

All of these assumptions—and I have made no attempt at exhaustiveness—seem to me to be either false or ambiguous, and when the ambiguity is cleared up, in no way prejudicial to the possibility of reliable objective accounts of the past. Take, for example, the notion that the personal involvement of the historian in the subject matter of his inquiry makes historical knowledge different from scientific knowledge. What is the nature of the involvement? That human beings—historians—are trying to understand human beings? So are we all. A whole branch of psychology is devoted to this. That as distinct from academic psychology, the historian is concerned with the social ideals, the good causes of the historical protagonists to which he cannot remain indifferent? What of it? Unless we assume that a man's bias necessarily makes the discovery of a truth not merely more difficult but in principle impossible, there is no difference except in degree between the operation of passions in history and in science. An individual's passion and zeal to liberate mankind from the curse of cancer may give him the drive necessary to make a significant discovery just as it may lead him to promulgate an announcement of a cure prematurely. A consuming rage to injure others, alas! has sometimes led to genuine discoveries about the properties of poisons and other lethal agents. I am far from endorsing the view of Professor Michael Polanyi who argues that "scientific passions are no mere psychological byplay but have a *logical function* which contributes an indispensable element in science," and that "In a clash of intellectual passions each side must inevitably attack the opponent's person." [5] But no one can contest the fact that Kepler sought the laws of planetary motion with a passionate religious bias, in a spirit of sacred fury. It is just as incontestable that the same bias which Kepler showed can lead and has led to false doctrine. In the presence of partisan bias therefore, there is wisdom in being on guard against possible errors to which passion and wish-thinking blind the investigator even when he himself seeks to discount their influence by candidly confessing his *parti pris.*

Aside from situations of this sort, it is hard to see in what way an historian is more personally involved when he studies the causes say, which led to an increase in the population of Rome, than his colleague who is studying the historical geology of the Tiber. Both are committed or personally involved to an hypothesis of sorts, and to a willingness to test it. Any other sort of involvement is extrinsic or peripheral to the concern of the historian. Suppose he holds that it was the exhaustion of the soil in Italy which led to the influx of bankrupt farmers into Rome and not a desire for the fleshpots and circuses. Let us assume further that as a result of new discoveries in chemistry or physics we are able to show that during the relevant periods the soil of Italian farmlands had become arid, unable to produce life-sustaining crops. Surely this would make the hypothesis more probable for all investigators of the subject, both those who inclined toward belief in its truth and those who were skeptical. Would there be any sense in saying that the historian had become personally involved with the laws of chemistry?

Or consider the view that we cannot understand what has happened in the past without reference to the future. This may mean several things: some obviously true, some dubious, and some obviously false. It may mean that the explanatory hypothesis applied to the past is one which we assume will also hold for the future because it seems to obtain in the present as well as in the past. On such a view if we select the spirit of nationalism, or the spread of technology, or the changes in the mode of economic production, or the growth of democratic institutions as "basic" in history, it is because we expect this factor to be of the greatest significance in the future. But this is simply false. One may believe, and have excellent evidence for believing, that differences in religious faith will have very little influence on events in the future and still maintain that the Thirty Years' War or the Crusades were predominantly religious phenomena. One may believe that the most fruitful hypothesis in explaining the major social and political developments in western Europe and the United States from the eighteenth century to 1914 is the expansion of the capitalist mode of production and the economic class conflicts to which it gave rise, and maintain on the weight of the evidence that today, and in the historical period ahead, not the mode of economic production is and will be of the greatest determining weight, but the mode of political decision.

The proposition about reference to the future may be construed as E. H. Carr seems to do as a value judgment concerning what the future should be, as a faith in that force among conflicting social movements which is likely to triumph, and in the light of which historical tendencies may be regarded as "progressive" or "reactionary."[6] According to this notion the objectivity of the historian who offers us a history of some past event is not measured alone by his faithfulness to relevant data, his scrupulous evaluation of his sources, his fairness in presenting the cases of struggling protagonists, the carefulness of his inferences, the nicety of his probable judgments, the support he musters for any hypotheticals contrary to fact. "The historian of the past can make an approach towards objectivity only as he approaches towards the understanding of the future."[7] The historian must choose the "right facts" by applying the "right standards of significance" and these are determined by his guess of what the future holds in store, by a value judgment that what has no future is obviously not progressive. In a remarkable sentence Carr asserts: "History is, by and large, a record of what people did, not of what they failed to do: to this extent it is inevitably a success story."[8] The objective historian is the one who writes more "durable" history, more durable because he foresees, explains, and justifies the movements on the way to future success.

To the extent that this is a description of the historian's activity it is surely inadequate. There are histories of "lost causes" from Josephus to the present, and these histories of what people failed to do are good, bad, and indifferent, independently of what the future turned out to be and whether the historian sympathized with the cause or not. What future is relevant in judging a "History of the Paris Commune"—the future of the Commune—it had none—or the future of the age in which the historian writes? If the historian writes in 1881, 1911, 1921, 1981—does the age and its values, typified, say, by the year 1911, justify the history written in 1881? And if the age and its values typified by the year 1981 differ, as it assuredly will from 1911, is the history written in 1881 therefore undone, deficient in objectivity? It is false to say that an objective history is a record of what people did, not of what they failed to do. What people failed to do, as well as what they did unsuccessfully, may be the most important key to what happened. What Kerensky *failed* to do after the Russian

Revolution of February 1917, and what he now acknowledges he could and should have done after Kornilov's insurrection, viz., to take Russia out of the war,[9] is of the first importance in understanding how the Bolsheviks were able to come to power despite the setbacks of the July days. Cannot a history written from the standpoint of the victims of the medieval Inquisition who had no future, be objective? The leaders of the Warsaw ghetto who perished in the uprising against the Nazis left moving accounts behind them of the last days of the struggle. Is their objectivity affected by the fact that the Nazis' triumph proved ephemeral? Would it be less objective if the Nazis had won the war? Some of the leaders of the uprising, like so many before them in similar circumstances, thought that their destruction would be followed by the universal triumph of the forces of evil. Mistaken about this they nonetheless wrote truly about the facts and causes of their destruction. The Hungarian revolution of 1956 was a failure but any historian who denied that the Russian Communists betrayed their promises to Nagy and Paleter would be guilty of simple invention, independently of whether Communism triumphs over the world or not.

To the extent that this view of history as a success story expresses a moral position, despite Carr's disclaimer, it is a brutalitarian attitude toward the past, coarser than Hegel's who at least deluded himself into the belief that there were no objective alternatives in history, and that the future, taken in the large, was necessarily better and more rational than the past. Gibbon, obviously, did not have "the future in his bones," which Carr regards as the sign of a good historian—certainly not the future of the twentieth century. But his interpretation of the chief causes of the fall of the Roman Empire can significantly be assessed without reference to the current strife between freedom and totalitarianism. Carr may have "the future in his bones." Since the late thirties he has been tolling the bells announcing the death of the open, democratic society. But even if he proves to be right—by itself this would have no bearing on whether or not his *History of the Russian*

Revolution is an objective and truthful account of how and why the Bolsheviks came to power, and how and why they used their power as they did.

Finally we may interpret the view which makes reference to the future an integral aspect of understanding the past as calling attention to the confirmatory role of future evidence. An hypothesis about the route Hannibal took in crossing the Alps or about the causes of his defeat commits us to the belief that it can be confirmed by some future experience. Statements about what happened in the past can be tested only by evidence which will come to light if we perform certain operations. What is discovered in the future may confirm our hypothesis about what actually transpired in the past or suggest new hypotheses. What occurred in the past cannot, of course, be the events in the future which we take as evidence of what occurred in the past. But a statement about the past implies many other statements about the future which if shown to be false invalidate the former. This is true on a scientific theory of meaning for any statement of fact and not merely statements about the past. There are certain epistemological difficulties which such a view must face that need not be explored here. To counter, however, with the retort that the attribution of causes in historical inquiry involves a value judgment about the present and future is to present us with another ambiguity. That one kind of causal attribution is better than, or superior to, another, in the sense that it is more fruitful, more consonant with what is known, simpler, etc. is to express a value judgment of sorts but it has no more to do with moral judgment, no less with specific epithets like "progressive" or "reactionary," than the ascription of superiority to one hypothesis over another in geology or medicine. The truth about historical events may be as bitter and distasteful as truths about anything else. The only value judgment about an historian qua historian which is relevant is whether or not he respects evidence. It may even be that his primary purpose is not quest of the truth. No matter *if* he finds it *and* tells it, even though we have good historical warrant for believing that few people find the truth unless they are in quest of it. This is not to deny that historians may on the strength of the evidence legitimately make value judgments. There are saints and scoundrels in history, admit as we must that they rarely play consequential roles. It does deny Professor Dray's startling thesis [10] that causal judgments are *logically* dependent upon judgments of moral value. Presumably, if Mr. Dray entertains an hypothesis about an event and either holds an attitude of moral approval toward it or expresses a judgment of moral approval with respect to it, he should be prepared to show that someone else who agreed that his hypothesis was sound but differed in moral attitude or judgment was guilty of a logical contradiction. This would be a tall order. The existence of anti-Dreyfusards who acknowledged that Dreyfus was innocent but who approved the verdict is an indication that there is no inherent logical connection between causal and moral judgment. Or to use one of Dray's own illustrations: It is possible to believe that the institution of slavery was the chief cause of the Civil War and morally either approve or disapprove of slavery without contradiction. Surely we must judge in history. Those who, like Professor Butterfield, tell us to leave judgment to God owe us a proof of his existence and of the validity of his moral judgment. But understanding must precede judgment. To reply that we judge in order to understand is to conceal the fact that we have been guilty of prejudgment in its most pejorative sense.

III

That historians are notoriously at odds with each other about the chief causes of great historical events—when it does not lead to despair—is the starting point of many critical inquiries into the nature of historical judgment and objectivity. Only yesterday, A. J. P. Taylor, not a German but an Englishman, not a reactionary but a liberal-minded socialist, broke the solid phalanx of professional historians, who have until now agreed about the predominant causal role of Hitler in precipitating the Second World War.[11] Taylor asserts that with respect to the war Hitler was more sinned against than sinning, that in 1939, "Hitler was not contemplating general war," and that the catastrophe was a consequence of grave blunders for which not Hitler but the statesmen of the West were chiefly responsible. There is hardly one great event in history concerning whose chief causes professional historians are agreed. The historical accounts do not merely supplement each other. They often contradict each other. And when they do they are usually written by historians whose *bona fides* cannot be justifiably impugned. Unless we are to yield to despair, and relegate the conception of objective historical truth to the limbo of unattainable ideals, I see nothing for it but dogged persistence in tracking down the data on which historical hypotheses are based, and trying to discover new data which will make one or the other or both of two conflicting hypotheses false.[12] Lord Macaulay and Professor Leo Gershoy cannot both be right about Barère.

One of the great merits of Professor Morton White's paper is his straightforward defense of the possibility not merely of objectively true chronicle but objectively true history which contains causal judgments. He draws the line on what he calls the quality of "memorability" of a history. This is a "truth-transcending" quality in the sense that it expresses an irreducible judgment of preference or value concerning what appears important to the historian, out of an indefinitely large number of possible characterizations, all true, that may be offered of any series of events. I go further than he in believing that to the degree that the judgments of memorability are serious enough to provoke question and controversy among historians, they are answerable by reference to the same general criteria which are used to differentiate between an "important," "far-reaching," "highly significant" scientific theory or discovery, and one that is not. To the extent that judgments of memorability express what an individual finds personally important, *his* tastes, then I agree with Mr. White—it is "truth transcending" but no more so in history than in any other inquiry including science. Had Mr. White considered specific illustrations of histories which he regarded as more memorable or less memorable than others, I believe we could differentiate more clearly between these two senses of "interestingness" or "memorability."

"What were the causes of the early military defeats of the Union armies in the American Civil War?"; "Why did certain Indian tribes accept the white man's domination while others resisted?"; "What were the causes of the Prohibition Movement?" are questions that interest some historians rather than others. What makes them interesting or important to the individual historian is a personal matter just as much as one scientist's interest in sound or another's in snails. But once a problem is formulated, the question whether or not a particular piece of information or causal insight is important is objectively controlled by its bearing on the problem, its generality, fruitfulness, etc. White asks us to indicate what we mean when we say that one history of a given subject is superior or "better than any other when all the competing histories are true in the sense of being composed exclusively of true statements." This question cannot be answered properly unless we are confronted with two such histories. It may be that one account contains more relevant truths than another where relevance is determined by what the consensus of practicing historians believe has a bearing on the theme. (I am assuming that the consensus of relevance has been established because of the past fruitfulness of such judgments in establishing historical facts.) It may be that the set of truths each contains is differently organized so that the truths in one account lie side by side in infertile conjunction with each other whereas the second establishes a plausible and fruitful causal connection between them. A true history of the migrations of a people would obviously be inferior to a true history of the migrations which explained the changes in the physical economy and political climate that influenced the migrations. A history contains not only judgments of causal connection but judgments that assign varied weights to some causal connections over against others. Where histories are supplementary to each other, the question of choosing one as superior to another does not arise. Because they are concerned with different problems or different aspects of problems, they are usually considered incommensurable, unless some working tradition among historians clearly gives one explanatory priority.

When histories are concerned with the same problems, or the same aspect of problems, and we cannot differentiate between them on grounds of relevance, comprehensiveness, consistency, fruitfulness, etc., then, judging by the way we assess oral histories, we tend to regard them as substantially the same history, telling the same story, and offering the same explanation. Whatever differences of style, detail, and color still exist are treated as peripheral to the truthfulness or validity of the history. The readability or vividness of written history may be compared to the eloquence of oral history. They are truth-transcending qualities because their presence does not make an historical account truer or their absence less true.

Does the quality of truth-transcending memorability arise from the fact that the true statements in a history record features of the subject that "are worth recording"? And does the fact that "different people find different things worth recording" or "what it is to be worth recording" make each person's judgment of what is worth recording sovereign and unassailable?

The great historical controversies are not about whether what is recorded is worth recording but about whether what an historian has believed worth recording is relevant or true. If we repudiate the claims to truth made for a certain statement about something alleged to be worth recording, we may also deny that in this particular account it is worth recording. But if we can show that in the past this type of phenomenon has been regarded as worth recording because of its proven usefulness in the search for truth, we are under an intellectual obligation to consider its claim to be worth recording. When an historian maintains that a hitherto neglected and therefore unrecorded series of facts is worthy of inclusion in an historical account (e.g., facts about the early childhood of historical figures) he must be prepared to show that it has a revelant bearing on other facts concerning which there is agreement among historians that they are worth recording. If one writes a history of trolley-car transfers or matchbox covers no one would take it seriously unless it were related to themes of larger concern. The very existence of an historical tradition already presupposes some types of facts are worth recording. The stock of such types of facts grows with the acceptance of true explanations of new facts. There was a time when the existence of rats and lice in history would have been regarded as not worth recording in an historical account but once a case, or even plausible claim, has been made out for their influence on the course of empire, a working historian is professionally bound to consider them.

Suppose we set out to evaluate several different biographies of Marx. One of them may be more concerned with Marx's carbuncles, his Jewish origins, his felicitous domestic life without making more than a passing reference to Marx's distinctive economic theories and political activities, or establishing any plausible connection between the first set of facts and the second. It may even make more interesting reading to those unfamiliar with these details than an account from which they are absent but it is hardly likely to be considered a superior biography to one that describes Marx's ideas and personality in such a way as to bring them into relation with the greatest mass movement in the history of civilization. To be sure, it is always open to someone to say: "Who cares about Marx's ideas? I am interested in his carbuncles and the truths about Marx's carbuncles are just as true as the truths about his writing the *Manifesto* and *Capital*, and about his founding of the First International." This approach to Marx would be comparable to a study of the play *Hamlet* which barely mentioned Hamlet and concentrated instead on some of the minor characters and customs of the court. Is there any doubt that if we had to judge between such a study of the play and one that revolved around the character of Hamlet, without neglecting the other characters and their relations to Hamlet, that given the same depth of treatment and fidelity to the facts, the second would be regarded as superior not only by literary critics and scholars but by most readers of the play? Although the analogy falls short in that the play may be taken as defining for us the order of importance of the characters and events worth recording, it still applies to the extent that at any given time the community of historians are more agreed on what facts are worth recording than they are in a particular case on the true relationships among the facts. We would not deem it inappropriate to say of a biography of Marx which gave us more of his medical than intellectual history that it was like a study of *Hamlet* with Hamlet left out.

I find puzzling White's contention that it is possible for a logician of natural science to distinguish between the subject thought to be worth pursuing and the scientific validity of the thought about it, but that the analogous distinction cannot be made by the logician of narration. A scientist's problem, at least in the free cultures of the West, is not imposed upon him even by the state of scientific interest at the time. He may be a lone wolf playing some obscure hunch but he makes good to the extent that his results connect with the knowledge already known, illumines new aspects of it, and bears on the problems others are pursuing. Just as much as the historian, he assumes that certain facts or data are worthier of being colligated than other facts. In one sense there is no one to say him "Nay." In another sense, the existing scientific tradition can and does say, "Nay," if he fails to interest and influence it. He may end up by convincing the community that what *he* regards as worth colligating is worthy of colligation for others too, that it pays off in related discoveries or in ordering power. The very same thing, it seems to me, can be said about the historian who departs from the colligation of customary data to other data that strike him as more interesting. Stated as an abstract problem of choice, there is no problem here at all. Any interest in anything is as valid as any other interest. But once we concretize our illustrations of historical inquiry, make specific the problem or subject or field, we find that differences of judgment concerning what is to be regarded as important or trivial, central or peripheral, typical or aberrant enter themselves into the continuum of historical inquiry. They are not shrugged off with a *de gustibus non disputandum est*. If we dispute about what is worth recording, our activity makes sense only on the assumption that there exist at the time certain judgments about what is worth recording that are not problematic, just as much as an intelligent dispute about the facts in a specific case can only be conducted on the assumption that at least for the time being there is agreement about other facts.

It is possible to subscribe to White's statement: "For given the process of historical investigation, writing, and criticizing as we know it, it is surely true that the historians do judge each other's works not only with an eye to the truth of factual and causal statements but also with an eye to the importance of the facts colligated"—and interpret these words rather differently from the way in which he does. If an historian judges another's account with an eye to the importance the facts colligated has merely for *himself*, if importance is a truth-transcending quality in no way dependent on or controlled or checked by fact or problem, then his judgment is really a piece of impertinence. It is not an historical judgment at all. If we call it a judgment, it can be made by anyone, historian or not, with as much or as little warrant. But when serious debate goes on concerning whether or not certain facts are worthy of being colligated, there is a common acceptance in that particular situation of the importance of some other facts which are taken as controls by serious historians. These controls are challengeable, too, but the challenge in every concrete case can be met in the same way. I do not think it likely that any colleague would be critical of Professor Gershoy's biography of Barère on the ground that he, the critic, was not interested in this comparatively unknown figure. Nor can I imagine that were Professor Gershoy writing a history of the French Revolution he would give Barère pride of place in it over Robespierre. That Barère is an unimportant figure to a particular historian is truth-transcending with respect to the history of the French Revolution; that Barère is an unimportant figure in the French Revolution, compared to Robespierre, Danton and St. Just, is objectively true or false.

Whether there are truth-transcending attitudes in history integral to our attempt to understand the past is not a question which can be settled by logical or linguistic analysis of the concept or language of history in independence of actual historical accounts. Dialectually, one may try to establish that there must be ultimate truth-transcending judgment of importance, unchecked and beyond check, invoked whenever historians try to colligate the data about an event into a true and coherent explanation of what happens. Such judgments would presumably be expressions of an attitude for which no rational grounds whatever can be given. Here as in so many other areas in which appeal is made to ultimates, I have found that the specific judgment, when considered in context, and not as an abstract statement unrelated to a concrete problem of inquiry, turns out to be something short of ultimate, something arguable on the basis of reasons, good or bad, and evidence, adequate or inadequate.

NOTES

1. *The Life and Selected Writings of Thomas Jefferson,* eds. Koch and Peden (New York: London House, 1944), p. 265.
2. *The Early Writings of Frederick Jackson Turner,* ed. Everett E. Edwards (Madison, Wis., 1938), p. 52. Italics in original.
3. *Journal of Philosophy* (1923), 348–49.
4. (London: Macmillan & Co., 1961), p. 105.
5. "Passion and Controversy in Science," *The Lancet* (June 1956), 921–25. My italics. This is certainly not true of Professor Polanyi's expressions of strong difference with other scholars and investigators. If anything, he leans over backward to be gallant to those with whom he disagrees.
6. *Op. cit.,* pp. 73 and 78.

7. *Ibid.*, p. 118.

8. *Ibid.*, p. 120.

9. In personal conversation with the author.

10. *Laws and Explanations in History* (New York: Oxford University Press, 1957), pp. 99–100. This view is developed in an article on "Causal Account of the Civil War" in *Daedalus* (Summer 1962), 578–92, and effectively criticized by Mr. Newton Garver in the same issue, pp. 592–98.

11. *The Origins of the Second World War* (London: Hamish Hamilton, 1961).

12. A careful reading of Taylor reveals case after case in which his judgment is presumably based on "facts" that are violently distorted or misread in order to carry the burden of his conclusions. For example, on pp. 192–93 of the American edition, Taylor quotes Hitler's directive of October 21, 1938, to his generals. "The Wehrmacht must at all times be prepared for the following: (i) securing the frontiers of the German Reich and protection against surprise air attacks. (ii) liquidation of the remainder of the Czech state." One would have imagined that this is a clear indication of plans for post-Munich aggression. Taylor denies this and asserts that these were measures of simple precaution. He justifies his contention by reference to the following sentence in the same directive: "It must be possible to smash the remainder of the Czech state, should it pursue an anti-German policy."

To interpret Hitler's directives to his generals in this way is to assume that Hitler seriously feared that Czechoslovakia, dismembered and weakened after Munich, would attack Germany. To believe that Czechoslovakia, which did not resist German aggression at a time when it had some hope of support from its allies, would attack when it had been deserted by its allies, is to be a political madman. But Taylor emphatically disputes the view that Hitler was a madman.

18

On Rational Explanation in History

BRUCE MAZLISH
Massachusetts Institute of Technology

PHILOSOPHY OF HISTORY runs its course between the Scylla of historians who have no patience with philosophers and the Charybdis of philosophers who have no training or sympathy for history. Much of this dilemma is embodied in the phrase "working historian," unexpectedly accepted with approval by both groups (I need hardly mention that not all historians and philosophers fall into these two camps). For the historians, this phrase carries within it the charge that philosophers are in remote ivory towers, unable to say anything about the practical day-to-day labor which takes place about the Queen Bee, Clio. For philosophers, it bears the implication of a working-class, union-like body, which can hardly be expected to know anything about the theory of their practices. One wonders, too, whether for these historians and philosophers there is the further latent notion that some historians don't work (whatever this would mean).

Even so distinguished a theoretician about history as the medieval historian, Marc Bloch, felt called upon to disclaim being a philosopher of history, acknowledging himself only as a "craftsman." (*The Historian's Craft* [Manchester, 1954], p. 19.) The case of Jacob Burckhardt is even better known.

I believe, and one would have hoped that this hardly needed saying, that the split between the historians and the philosophers and the resultant distrust of philosophy of history is unfortunate. Historians badly need the formal and sophisticated analysis which can be offered them by philosophers on a whole range of problems, and philosophers can only go astray in dealing with history (as a part of philosophy of science) unequipped with a real and intimate knowledge of the discipline.

Having stated my credo on this matter, I should like to consider two problems. The first concerns the question whether the reasons for an historian's choosing a subject affect the way in which we judge the value or validity of his explanation. The second deals with the question of rationality, especially in relation to Professor Dray's paper. My general thesis here will be that Professor Dray has significantly seized on one way in which historians do try to explain historical phenomena, but has overgeneralized it (even if only implicitly) to apply to *all* explanation in history. Professor Hempel, his opposite number so to speak, offers us the correct *general* position on explanation, but his doctrine, unfortunately, is merely formally correct and does not afford the historian much help in practice. In short, as an historian convinced of the value of philosophy of history, I find myself, in this case, reminiscing on Shakespeare's phrase: a pox on both your houses.

1

In his comment on Professor Gershoy's interesting paper, "Some Problems of the Working Historian," Professor Bailyn, a fellow historian, took the position, if I understood him correctly, that the reasons why an historian undertakes a particular investigation affect the grounds on which we judge the validity of his explanation. Indirectly, if not directly, this is a way, I believe, of getting rid of the philosophers and their formal logic. It suggests that not all explanations must conform to a set logic of explanation but that they vary as to the standards by which we judge them, according to the author's purpose. The historian, for example, who seeks to "humanize" his reader, by having him live through various events, cannot be judged on the same grounds as the historian who offers a sociological analysis of the same events. Further, it seems to suggest that the primitive who wishes to offer a mythical, the

Soviet historian who wishes to offer a Marxist, and the American historian who wishes to offer a "liberal" version of the same events cannot really be faulted from any objective point of view. In short, Bailyn's position seems to be that of the sociologists of knowledge.

There is much that is plausible in this point of view. Let me deal, briefly, with two aspects of the problem. First, it is quite true that our basic assumptions color our acceptance of explanations. A primitive who does not accept the modern scientific way of reasoning will hardly admit that the earth circles the sun, or that his plants grow because of fertilizer and not magic; nor would any of our attempts at explanation help until he had come to accept our assumptions. So, too, Marxists and liberals frequently have a basic divergence as to assumptions in the social sciences.

The point is, however, that no form of science can exist unless there is a society which agrees upon certain basic assumptions as to what constitutes acceptable observations, theoretical deductions and inductions, and verifications (for those of Popper's persuasion, this should be "falsification"), what I shall hereafter refer to as scientific methodology. A shared "universe of discourse" is absolutely essential to any public knowledge; and the history of the rise of modern science in the West is as much a history of the rise of a modern scientific society as it is of certain theories, though too few histories are written stressing this fact. So, too, with history; there can be no "scientific" history without a society prepared to acknowledge common rules of procedure and to start from similar methodological assumptions. The following must be said flatly: Marxist history (or any other school of history), for example, when it distorts the evidence, say, by ignoring it, is as unscientific as Nazi physics when it denigrated Einstein's work because he was a member of a particular religious group.

In short, while it is a *fact* that different societies have different assumptions about the natural and historical world, it must simply be affirmed that any discussion about scientific method and proof must be held within the assumptions of present scientific society. We cannot accept, therefore, certainly for the purposes of this discussion, the relativist position.[1]

The second aspect of the problem which makes Bailyn's view plausible is as follows: the type of history an historian chooses to write *does* affect the way in which we judge it. A narrative history will be judged for the felicity of its writing; a monograph, analytic in nature, will not (though we may lament the brambly nature of the work). We judge popular history differently from learned history, and history which seeks to humanize us differently from history which seeks to instruct us "scientifically." But these different judgments pertain to *effectiveness;* we do not, I submit, have different canons of scientific methodology for the explanations offered. The explanation offered by a narrative history must accord with the same standard of scientific methodology as that of an analytic history; the same formal logic holds for both.

Similarly, the reasons why an historian undertook, say, the study of medieval society do not affect the formal grounds on which we judge the worth of his work. A biologist studying the crayfish, a physicist studying atomic structure: we do not judge the product of their work according to the motive which induced them to pursue it. Why, then, in the case of an historian? His desire for advancement, his pure curiosity, his wish to overturn the work of another scholar: what are these to Clio? All such motives are irrelevant to the judgment we pass on him. What Bailyn has recognized is that, in practice, we, the judges of historical work, bring our own motives into the courtroom, and thus equipped sit in judgment on the motives of other historians. This practice, however, ought not to be defended in theory; and, indeed, theory is correct when it insists on formal, objective grounds for judging the validity of a given historical explanation.

2

Professor Dray's paper—and in the light of the strictures which follow I wish to state here categorically my admiration for his path-breaking work—demonstrates the dangers of confusing motives with formal explanation. At the end of his very fine and complete argument, he shows his hand. History, he tells us, is a branch of the humanities as well as of the sciences. "My chief complaint against acceptance of the covering law doctrine in history is not the difficulty of operating it, in either fully deductive or mutilated form. It is rather that it sets up a kind of *conceptual barrier* to a humanistically oriented historiography." To me, this is a shocking admission. Either the covering law doctrine is formally correct in its view of historical explanation, or it is not; and similarly with Dray's doctrine. If neither is formally correct, then, of course, they can both be modified. The question of motive, however, that is, the desire for humanistic history, cannot seriously enter into the logic of historical explanation.

Dray's desire for humanistic history colors his entire theory (and here I might make it clear that I, too, admire humanistic history; my only point is that such admiration has nothing to do with the question of explanation). He begins by identifying the "central" issue in the debate about the nature of historical explanation: "The question of the analysis to be given of characteristic explanations *of the actions of individual historical agents*" (my italics). Hastily backing away from an argument on methodological individualism, however, he adds that this "does not mean that I believe that only individual human actions are subject matter for historical explanations properly so-called; indeed, I should agree with Professor Maurice Mandelbaum that individual actions as such are below the threshold of proper historical interest; they enter history only insofar as they have 'societal significance.'" Then, having made his bow to social history, Dray dismisses it, and, reiterating the importance of individual actions, proceeds to a study of that alone.

The problem of historical explanation is thus, for all intents and purposes, reduced to an explanation of an agent's intentions in undertaking an action called historical. This explanation must be what Dray calls "rational." When we understand "what the agent believed to be the facts of his situation, including the likely results of taking various courses of action considered open to him, and what he wanted to accomplish: his purposes, goals, or motives," we can see the reasonableness of a man's doing what this agent did. Where other philosophers of history have dealt with this understanding in terms of empathy or *Verstehen,* Dray prefers to state that "Explanation which tries to establish a connection between beliefs, motives, and action of the indicated sort I shall call 'rational explanation.' " The latter, it would appear, is simply a new label for what was called "continuous series explanation" in Dray's fundamental book, *Laws and Explanation in History* (Oxford, 1957). We are sustained in this belief by Dray's own admission that his example—Trevelyan's explanation of the invasion of England by William of Orange—is one he has used before for the same purpose.

Now, the meaning of "rationality" for Dray is not always clear. Is the action supposed to be rational to the agent, or to us? Explicitly, Dray states that the action need not be "rational" to the agent:

> What makes an action understandable rationally, is not necessarily a set of propositions which the agent recited to himself. Our understanding of his action may arise out of our perception of a rational connection between an action and the motives and beliefs we ascribe to the agent without any such psychological implications. What is claimed is rather that understanding of what he did is achieved by ordering such ingredients, once made explicit, in the *form* of a practical calculation.

In this form, Dray's historical rationality appears to be a postmortem-type decision-making-study. Implicitly, however, the demands of Dray's humanist history bend him the other way; at the end of his paper he is calling for a view of his agents "as R. G. Collingwood might have put it, *from the inside.*" Dray's rationality obviously hovers between the two definitions. The resultant impression, however, is that basically he is talking about an "irrational" agent (in the sense of one not seeing the action which will result from his motives and beliefs), whom we study "rationally." The flaw here, though, is that Dray immediately drops this latter sort of rationality—which borders dangerously on the social-sciences approach—and goes back to his continuous series explanation.

By his concentration on rationality, as he has defined it, and on the agent, Dray, it seems to me, exposes himself to two charges. The first, I confess, is rather vague. It relates to the tone of his paper. Dray appears to suggest that history is filled with "reasonable" actions rather than with passions; that people operate generally in a sort of Max Weber-type rational pursuit of their goals. (Nevertheless, a scientific ordering of these actions smacks of antihumanism and is to be looked at with distrust.) Opposed to determinism in history, Dray prefers to think of agents as freely and rationally pursuing their own ends.[2] As I have remarked, he does not quite say this explicitly; but his general tone and his neglect of my next point make me suspicious.

The next point is that Dray never really comes to grips with a subject which engages a great deal, perhaps most, of an historian's attention: unintended consequences. And this, of course, is the real meeting place of the actions of all of Dray's various individual agents. On one level, and this is Dray's level, the unintended consequence can be dealt with in terms of narrative: we try to understand what the Algerian nationalists, the French Government, and the OAS (*Organisation de l'armée secrète*) each wanted, and from this concatenation of desires to understand the consequence originally unintended by any of the actors.[3] On another level, where possible, we try to understand such a consequence analytically. So far, our greatest success has been in economic analysis: we understand how the "invisible hand" works, producing business cycles not intended by any single actor. In a simpler example, we understand the operation of Gresham's Law in sixteenth century England.[4] Such *rational* explanations, however, have almost nothing to do with understanding the motives and actions of the individual agents. They relate to the social entities which Dray has dammed with faint praise.

Dray's rationality in history—which in its way is certainly commendable—is simply the common, garden variety of understanding presumably possessed by each of us. For this reason, it has tended to appeal to historians, when they have bothered with philosophy of history at all. Professor Hempel's covering law doctrine has ominously threatened the historian with all sorts of generalizing sciences which he would have to understand. Psychology, sociology, economics loomed over the simple facts of history, implying the need for a "rational" explanation of events and actions instead of the nice commonsense version hitherto obtaining. Dray's genius has been to turn the word "rational" on its head, and make it apply to the ordinary narrative of that good fellow, the working historian.

3

From the above, it must appear as if I embraced the Hempel position. In terms of formal logic, I do. Surely, it is a truism to state that, in theory, every factual statement can be subsumed under some more generalizing statement: a law or an empirical generalization. However, it also appears to me a truism, and here Dray is certainly right, that in practice such laws have to be so greatly expanded as to their boundary conditions or their statistical frequency of prediction as to make them totally useless. (Maurice Mandelbaum's strictures, in his article, "Historical Explanation: the Problem of Covering Laws," in *History and Theory*, I, 3, also strike me as apropos.) In short, like Auguste Comte's view that all phenomena are theoretically under mathematical order but practically not accessible, the Hempel doctrine states a rather useless position—from the historian's viewpoint—as to the nature of historical phenomena.

In sum, the Hempel view is formally correct, but offers

us little in terms of what I should like to call the logic of the discipline. Dray's position, on the other hand, strikes me as formally in error, but as describing *one* of the possible sorts of treatment accorded to events by historians. Let me try to make this clear by two assertions of my own.

The first is simply that, while all explantions must accord with a common scientific methodology, historical explanations are also judged on their *depth*. Professor Gershoy is right in principle when he speaks of a given hypothesis as explaining "the particular event *in greater depth* than the alternate . . . hypothesis" (my italics). In short, there are various levels at which explanation can occur. The level or depth of explanation employed by a particular historian is usually the product of his own sophistication and that of the audience to whom he addresses himself, combined with the purpose for which the explanation is offered.[5] In this sense, Bailyn is right, as we saw earlier, in maintaining that the *reasons* for an historian's work affect his *type* of explanation (though not its validity).

One or two examples will suffice. A narrative history of the decline of Spanish power in the seventeenth century will undoubtedly touch in a general fashion on the economic causes of this decline; if the author has read Hamilton on price movements, as he undoubtedly will have, he will also supply statistical details; if he has in addition studied economic theory he will use his materials in an analytic fashion to offer an explanation in greater depth—what I shall call a more rational explanation—than the mere narrative account. All these explanations must be judged by the same canons of scientific methodology; it is only in the depth of their explanation that they differ. Similarly, an explanation of motives and actions in terms of everyday psychologizing can be compared with one based on psychoanalytic insight and techniques. Both can be perfectly valid; they will differ sharply as to the level of sophistication, as implied in the very term "depth psychology."[6]

My second assertion is even simpler. The historian legitimately uses, and must use, every level of explanation. He employs straight narrative, limited generalizations, and Hempel-type universal laws where he can find them—anything which will serve his purpose—for the very understandable reason that he is trying to explain an individual action or a social event which lends itself only to that particular level of explanation. Sometimes he can appeal to eternal verities or laws—physical laws, for example, which make him doubt miraculous accounts; and sometimes to empirical generalizations of limited scope—in the seventeenth century heretics were persecuted in Spain; and sometimes only to a continuous narrative. Every history, in differing proportions, is a compound of these levels of explanation. All of these levels are "rational" levels of explanation (though some may be accounted more "rational" than others). They are all varying approximations of Hempel's formal logic of explanation, and they are all part, too, of the logic of the discipline.

Perhaps now, it is clear why I have been troubled by both the Hempel and the Dray doctrine, but especially by the latter. My motive for opposing Dray is simply that his description of one level of explanation is generalized into (1) an incorrect formal logic of explanation, and (2) an implied (he would, I am sure, reject the explicit statement) prohibition against more analytic—deeper?—forms of historical explanation. The drawback to Hempel's work is that he tends to distract attention from the pressing problems involved in the logic of the discipline. On the other hand, he at least holds out a formal justification for the historian's asymptotic effort to reach deeper scientific understanding and explanation.

NOTES

1. I am aware that, like Hempel's doctrine, my statement here is only *formally* correct. In practice, while historians have a common methodology in regard to such things as testing the validity of documents, this methodology does not extend to shared ways of handling induction from the documents, or verification of hypotheses. In-

deed, the problem for philosophy of history seems to me to lie precisely in this second area. As an example of such work—but by an historian—see J. H. Hexter, "Storm Over the Gentry," in *Reappraisals in History* (Evanston, Ill.: Northwestern University Press, 1961).

2. Dray's comment is: "Let me confess that I do in fact hold a libertarian position, and that I think the rational model of explanation to be of special interest to anyone who does. It is of interest because it shows a way in which explanation can be given in history which is logically *compatible* with indeterminism regarding human actions."

3. See, for example, Raymond Aron's analysis of the Algerian situation in these terms in "The General and the Tragedy," *Encounter* (August 1962).

4. See, however, F. A. Hayek's communication, "The Uses of 'Gresham's Law' as an Illustration in Historical Theory," *History and Theory,* II, 1, on the need for the historian to understand the law as a theoretical statement and not merely as an empirical generalization.

5. An excellent treatment of explanation in terms of the various purposes for which it is intended is John Passmore, "Explanation in Everyday Life, in Science, and in History," *History and Theory,* II, 2.

6. See, for example, the interesting analysis of Woodrow Wilson's personality and actions in Alexander and Juliette George, *Woodrow Wilson and Colonel House: A Personality Study* (New York, 1956).

19

Comments on White's "Logic of Historical Narration"

GLENN MORROW
University of Pennsylvania

PROFESSOR WHITE is to be commended for insisting that the philosophical problems arising in history are not all concerned with the nature and justification of explanation. "Historical explanation is not the most important problem," he reminded us at the outset of his oral presentation of his paper; "narrative presents problems of similar interest to the philosopher." He might well have stated the matter more strongly. For it is only in narrative that the philosophical problems peculiar to historical inquiry arise. To attempt to explain a past event, considered as a particular occurrence under determinate conditions, involves no problems in principle different from those encountered in attempting to explain a contemporary occurrence, where the evidence is indirect, and the conditions of its occurrence indefinitely complex. It is only when this event is considered as one term of a sequence of events, a sequence that is regarded as having some kind of unity through time, that the logical problems peculiar to history arise. History is narration. Hence we could well say that the logical problems of narration are the fundamental ones underlying all explanations regarded as historical in character or intention.

What these philosophical problems are is made clear in the course of White's paper. They are many in number, although he has adopted the questionable expedient of grouping them all together under one general problem, that of evaluating different true narratives of the same events. "What do historians mean when they say that one history of a given subject is better than any other when all of the competing histories are true . . . ?" In order to attack this problem properly we must first determine the meaning of the qualifying clause. What do we mean when we assert that the competing narratives are all true? For the clarification of this clause, White constructs a model, or schematic form, for narration, which it will repay us to examine carefully.

A model is an ideal schema, ideal in the sense that it is formal, and ideal also in that it presents the norm by which we appraise any example of that activity for which the schema is the model. A model for narration, then, is the ideal which narration "aims at" and by which a narrator should be guided in his construction of the story that he has undertaken to tell—if, that is, he wishes to do his task competently.

White's model is as follows. A narration is a series of statements about a subject (S) at various times (t_1, t_2, t_3 . . .) in its career, each of them true, and all of them connected by true 'because' statements. (The presence of these connecting explanatory statements is what distinguishes, in his terminology, a narrative from a chronicle, the latter consisting only of a series of factual statements about its subject.) If the component statements, both factual and explanatory, are all true, the narration as a whole, being the conjunction of its component statements, is itself true.

This appears to be a correct statement of the schematic form by which we should, and usually do, determine whether something professing to be a narrative really is a narrative, and not merely an assemblage of items such as might be found in a chronicle, a set of memoirs, or a collection of anecdotes. But as a norm for determining whether or not a narrative is a true narrative—and this is the ostensible purpose for which it is constructed—it is patently inadequate. To say that a true narrative is one which consists of true statements brings us no nearer to understanding the point that is essential to the inquiry. White implies in his article, and explicitly asserted in his oral presentation, that his model is neutral as respects the meaning of truth. 'True,' then, becomes another variable in the formal schema and may be replaced by any one of a set of values without the model's losing its validity as a model. This we can readily admit if the purpose of the model is to set forth the structure of a genuine narrative (a 'true' narrative in this sense) as contrasted with other types of literary composition. But if its purpose is to explicate the meaning of the clause "when all the competing narratives are true," taken in the common and unsophisticated sense of the term 'true,' it is obviously unsatisfactory. If one historian should use 'true' in the sense of 'strongly believed by the author,' and another as 'accepted by all competent authorities,' then our comparative evaluation of these competing histories would certainly involve an examination of the adequacy of the respective authors' conceptions of historical truth. The necessity of such an examination would certainly not be lessened, but more probably increased, if we add the requirement that for purposes of fair comparison each of the authors must have used the same value for the variable 'true'; for then other relevant considerations would enter in, such as the relative competence of the two historians, or the adequacy of their judgment as to competent authorities. This shows that White's model is valueless for determining the conditions that must be met before the "central question of the philosophy of narration" can even be considered.

The fact that he has some doubt whether historians are ever in fact faced with the problem of evaluating two or more histories each of which is true, and is forced to state his problem in hypothetical form, should have given him pause. Certainly no philosopher, or student of historical methodology, is likely to take seriously such a problem as White states. To begin by waving aside, or characterizing as irrelevant, all inquiries into the meaning of truth in historical inquiry is to cut the root of all logical or philosophical interest in the procedure of the historians.

There is another feature of White's model which, unless interpreted differently than White has done, limits its usefulness in the solution of the problems that face the historiographer. The model correctly prescribes that a narrative must have a subject, and this presumably means one and only one subject. The "S" that appears in each of the component true statements constituting a narrative must stand for the same subject in all its appearances. This might be interpreted to mean that each component statement must have the same grammatical subject. But such a literal satisfaction of the requirement is obviously not intended, and even if it were realized would not satisfy the philosopher or the historian, who would inevitably interpret the requirement as demanding a unity of subject more fundamental than an identity of terms denoting it. Now it is only when we stray from the literal satisfaction of the requirement, as we must, that the problems of real interest and relevance for the evaluation of different histories arise. What kinds of entities can properly serve as the subjects of historical narration? What is the principle of unity that binds together the successive events described in a history and makes them stages in the career of one subject? What principles are there to guide us in deciding which of the successive events in the career of our chosen subject are to be recorded and which to be omitted as unimportant or irrelevant to our main theme? These are some of the questions which a practicing historian must face and which the philosophical student of historical narration asks in any attempt to appraise the work of historians.

White's model permits, and indeed invites, the raising of such questions; and his subsequent discussion shows that they naturally come up in any attempt to evaluate histories. But the model itself does little or nothing to facilitate their solution. On the contrary, as White employs it, it seems to hinder the free exploration of these problems; for White's adherence to his model makes these problems irrelevant to the logic of narration, and the logic of narration irrelevant to their solution. Of two narratives equally true, if we are required to say which is the better, we can find no answer in terms of our model; and if we are to justify a preference for one of these histories over the other, it must be by relying on some factor outside our model, some "truth-transcending reference," as White puts it, such as interestingness, excitingness, instructiveness, memorableness—all of them (since our model has been left behind) tainted with subjectivism or relativism, and immune to criticism or control by his logic of narration. Surely this is a strange and unhappy result. Specific criteria for unity of theme, for relevance, for importance, for distinguishing between the essential and the nonessential, between the material and the circumstantial, and above all for accuracy and truth, all these would seem to belong in some way to the logic of narration. They certainly belong to the methodology of historical inquiry. Even logicians who restrict logic to principles capable of formulation in symbolic terms should not exclude such questions without a prior and persistent effort to determine how much of and to what extent the procedures of the historian can be formalized. And certainly those who conceive the task of logic more broadly than this will not be content to admit that the logician can be of no help to the historian in these matters.

20

On the Logic of Historical Narration

GEORGE H. NADEL
Harvard University

IT IS IMPOSSIBLE to read Professor White's "The Logic of Historical Narration" without being profoundly impressed with the importance of his enterprise. The very choice of his subject matter, narration, rather than explanation, law, cause, determinism, and the like, must be welcomed by those who ask, and even more so by those who try to answer, questions about the relevance of philosophy of history to the working historian. That makes it all the more important to expose his argument to the kind of critical question which the historians—the consumers of his thesis, so to speak—are likely to ask: are we really faced with the situation he describes?

Professor White himself hints at this kind of criticism. He tells us that historians may in practice never have to face the central question from which his argument takes off: 'What do historians mean when they say that one history of a given subject is better than any other when all of the competing histories are true in the sense of being composed exclusively of true statements?' Perhaps historians are always in the happy position of being able to prefer one history to another in terms of the least number of false statements alone. In that case, Professor White suggests, if the question is to be pursued, we have to put it hypothetically: suppose they were not in that situation, but had to choose among true histories. . . .

I think Professor White would be justified in raising this hypothetical question if the historians' objection to what he asks them to do were based on empirical grounds, like 'histories composed of exclusively true statements have never been seen.' But if logical objections can be raised, the question itself rather than the likelihood of situations in which it is warranted to ask it is at issue—and it is this kind of objection which I wish to raise. My purpose is to throw doubt on the meaningfulness of Professor White's question in terms of the model which he has presented here.

To arrive at a position enabling us to distinguish between judgments of the facts contained in histories and judgments of the grounds for having selected certain facts rather than others, Professor White has set up a model. The concept of a 'chronicle' is defined by means of certain criteria—one of which is that it must be made up of statements of facts ('report things that have been true at different times'); 'history' is defined as a conjunction, in certain specified ways, of the chronicle statements which compose it.

I believe this model would be workable if 'chronicles' (in Professor White's use of the term) were made up of statements of fact only. But chronicles contain not only statements like 'the king died'; they also contain statements like 'the king was the greatest king of Babylon'—in other words, statements ascribing value, or located on a spectrum ranging from factual to evaluative statements, or appearing as factual to some and as evaluative to other observers and vice versa. A model of a chronicle from which such statements are purged would have no place here, because as long as history is defined as a conjunction of chronicle components, exclusion of evaluative statements from chronicles would entail their exclusion from histories and raise the puzzling question in what kinds of historical writings they do occur if not in histories. I do not believe that Professor White proposes to exclude them. He himself gives us an example of a chronicle statement, implied by a history explaining England's declaration of war on Germany, which contains an evaluative element: 'Germany had *invaded* Poland.' (My italics.) Substitution of value-neutral for evaluative terms, while possible, would merely leave us asking once again in what kinds of historical writings evaluative terms occur if not in histories. The answer, that we are engaged in defining 'history' in a strange and narrow way, is of course one which Professor White would rightly reject.

The circumstance that not *all* chronicle components are statements of fact, does not allow us to apply the predicates true and false to chronicles or to say that they can be objectively judged. Hence the notion of judging histories in terms of their implied (or 'associated') chronicle components as true or false and, therefore, the hypothesis that we could be confronted with competing histories all composed of exclusively true statements seem to present logical obstacles, at least until Professor White's model is further clarified.

If the objection I have made is valid, the question arises how it affects Professor White's thesis. He argues that there are two ways in which we judge, or could judge, the merit of competing histories. The objective or factual or true-false judgment which we apply to the chronicle associated with the history, and the evidently less objective judgment which we apply to the selection of particular associated chronicles. These, it will be recalled, move in the 'dimension of truth' and the 'dimension of memorability,' respectively. I have attempted to deny that the former type of judgment can be made in respect of the concept of associated chronicles presented here. (I am denying, of course, neither the presence of statements of facts in these chronicles nor the possibility of objective judgments of such statements.) Since Professor White concludes his paper by observing that we do not break down our judgments of the merit of histories into the categories of truth and memorability in fact, though we may assert the possibility of doing so 'in the abstract,' it is tempting to conclude that the argument which has led to this perverse discrepancy between theory and practice may be at fault. One could argue, perhaps, that this difficulty arises from the difficulty in the model to which I have drawn attention: we do not separate our objective judgments of the facts from the value judgments of our choice of facts, as licensed by the theory, because the chronicled 'facts' contain evaluations, and, it might be added, the process of selection of facts may well partake of at least some objectively assessable procedures. In short, *the distinction between objective and less objective judgments does not apply to the procedures of reporting and selecting the facts, respectively, but in each of these procedures factual and evaluative elements play their part.* Our corresponding refusal (at least more often than not) to make separable judgments of truth and memorability may indicate merely an awareness that this is so. We might go further and claim that it indicates that there is a case prima facie for supposing the factual and evaluative elements in historical narration to be ineradicably intertwined as some philosophers have argued.

But this last claim would deprive us of the two lessons Professor White wants us to learn, lessons which I consider important and relevant to what the historian actually does. Namely, that there are areas of historical narration in which we adopt, and to which we apply, criteria of judgment significantly different from those brought to bear on facts, and that these differences are susceptible of analysis. If it is objected that these propositions are not important, in the sense that they are old familiars that have been around a long time but from which nothing either sufficient or necessary to the writing and judging of histories has yet been deduced, the answer must be that Professor White's task is not to invent philosophical systems but to identify the philosophic problem to which the historian's problem can be reduced before proceeding further. If it is asked in what way Professor White's arguments are relevant to what the historian does, the answer, or rather one of several possible answers, might well be that many disputes that historians are and have been engaged in would be clarified by heeding a distinction which is implied by his propositions. One historical presentation does not get the better of another necessarily by citing more and more supporting facts (and marshaling them in behalf of the presentation for whose support they were collected); historical disputes *may* be immune to this procedure, since conflicting judgments can be maintained in the presence of the same facts—or, conversely, as I understand Professor White to put it, the same judgments are tenable in the presence of different facts, and thus in some sense independent of them.

Whether or not Professor White's delimitation of the 'non-factual' area of historical narration has been successful in all its details, it remains a significant advance over the proposition that fact and value are ineradicably intertwined in historical narration. The latter sounds like a confession of failure of analysis; Professor White's, like a declaration of independence. I merely question the model which he has used to establish the area of independence.

21

Rational Explanations in History

KAI NIELSEN
New York University

PROFESSOR DRAY IS RIGHT when he contends that "rational explanation is a recognizably distinct type of explanation . . ." employing "a criterion of intelligibility which is different from that formulated by a covering law model," and Professors Hempel and Passmore are wrong in arguing that *if* there are rational explanations they must employ a covering law.[1] Dray is also correct in claiming that rational explanations are a distinctive and important type of explanation in history, though—as he rightly stresses—they are by no means the only type of explanation utilized in history and in the "soft-sciences." Here I want to back up these strong and controversial claims.

In sections 1 through 7 I shall develop and elucidate the concept of rational explanation, showing clearly its role in explaining human actions and freeing it from some peripheral confusions. In sections 8 through 10 I shall rebut the criticisms of it made by Professors Hempel and Passmore, and in section 11 I shall try to make clear the motives (motives that are often unwittingly disguised) for adopting so paradoxical a theory as the covering law theory.

1

Certainly a great deal of history is simply a description or an attempt at a description of how things were. That is to say, much of the historian's work consists in simply describing socially significant past events and actions. But he does more than describe; he explains as well. He explains the effect of increased trade and technological improvements on the medieval way of life and he also frequently explains historically relevant human actions. It is the latter that I shall be concerned with here. (This is not to suggest that the former is not of crucial importance in the writing of historical narratives.)

Historians frequently say of some historical personage that he did Y because of Z. The covering law conception of explanation in its naïvest form would claim that to explain that an historical personage A did Y because of Z would involve showing that initial conditions Z hold for A and that there is a law of the form: whenever Z obtains for people of type A, then something that is properly classifiable as an act of type Y will be done. Every explanation or every genuine explanation takes the form of showing how a statement is deducible from a general law, together with a statement of initial conditions. To explain is simply to show how what is to be explained is deducible from certain statements of antecedent or simultaneous conditions, together with certain empirically testable universal laws. Sometimes these laws are not explicitly mentioned, for explanations are often given in a highly elliptical way, but they are at least implicitly contained in all genuine explanations. Without such general laws there can be no satisfactory explanation of anything. Natural scientists are, for the most part, interested in laws; historians, by contrast, are mainly interested in the unique and detailed facts. But explanations in history and in the natural sciences fit into exactly the same formal pattern and are of the same type.

Dray and Scriven have developed some powerful, though *perhaps* not decisive, criticisms of this covering law theory, both in its naïve and more subtle formulations. It will not be my concern here to add more fuel to this fire. I am only concerned to mention this more orthodox view of explanation by way of contrast with the concept of explanation that I shall develop, although what I say here is certainly, in effect, a criticism of the covering law theory since I shall argue that rational explanations need not be covered by laws of the form, 'Whenever Z then Y,' or 'Whenever Z than probably Y,' or by any other law or general dispositional statement.

When we say A did Y because of Z, 'Z' could mark a *cause* or a reason. In 'A fell down because he slipped on the ice,' 'Z' ('he slipped on the ice') marks a cause and we have a causal explanation. By contrast, when a rational explanation is given, 'Z' does not mark a cause but a reason, as in, A avoided B because B bored him. When some Z is the cause of Y, we say that if a condition of type Z occurs then it is physically necessary that something of type Y must occur (e.g., if a chicken's head is cut off, the chicken must die). To say Z is a reason for Y is to say that Z is the rationale of the action—it gives point to, justifies, excuses, or at least partially excuses, the doing of Y (e.g., they picketed the White House because they were against nuclear testing). What made me jump—the cause of my jumping—was that I stepped on a tack. The reason for my disapproving of him—the rationale of my action—was that he is a neo-Nazi. There are explanations in which we give the causes of an event or action, and there are explanations in which we give reasons for an action or set of actions.[2] It is the latter that Dray somewhat misleadingly calls rational explanations.[3] In giving rational explanations or explanations by reasons, we try to see the situation from the agent's point of view and then try to make intelligible his grounds for acting as he did.[4] In short, we attempt to *make sense* of his action. If we can in no way make sense of it, then we must—if we are to explain his action—adopt some other concept of explanation for *this* action; but in explaining an action we typically attempt to render it intelligible by making clear the rationale or the point of the action from the agent's point of view.[5]

While it is certainly a dogma—probably based on some unwitting persuasive definition of 'action'—to assert as a kind of a priori dicta that every action must have a rationale, it seems to me perfectly justified to say, as Dray does, that "in the ordinary course of affairs, rational and non-rational explanations of actions are alternatives—and alternatives sought in a certain order. We give reasons if we can, and turn to empirical laws if we must."[6] Only in history deliberately written to a thesis is the order reversed. The criterion of "rational appropriateness does function for actions not judged to be defective in various ways. . . ." There are situations (paradigms, if you will) in which we do use rational explanations. We can only intelligibly speak of certain alleged rational explanations being pseudo-explanations by way of involving rationalizations, if some acts count as acting in accord with rational principles, for the concept of rationalization is parasitical upon the concept of having a reason for an action.[7]

2

In coming to see the rationale of the use of these rational explanations as explanations of actions, historical or otherwise, it is crucial to get clear about the different contexts in which we can intelligibly ask for an explanation. If I were writing this essay on odd-sized, red-colored paper, it would be in place for you to ask me, 'Why are you writing on *that* paper?' but if the paper were standard and the situation normal (no acute shortage of paper, etc.), it would make no sense at all to ask, 'Why are you writing on *that* paper?' A request for an explanation here is quite out of place. An analogy with what Strawson has said about 'true' can bring out the force of my point. 'True' cannot be correctly used on just any occasion. It is typically used, Strawson points out, when a certain assertion is made that the utterer of 'true' takes to be warranted and wishes to underwrite or endorse. Similarly, explanations can only be given in certain quite definite contexts. We can only properly use 'Why' where there is some definite gap in our knowledge, where there is something odd or unexpected or disturbing about an event or action, or "when from the 'considerations' obvious to the investigator it is impossible to see the point of what was done."[8] In short, we ask for explanations when we are in some perplexity. (In the case of those nonliteral questions that Toulmin has called "limiting questions"—e.g., 'Why did all those children have to die on their *birthdays*?' the perplexity is typically emotional or religious.)[9] It is here that we can appropriately ask for an explanation.

When we get clear about the contexts in which we can appropriately ask for explanations, the function of explanations will not be far to seek. The function or purpose of explanations is, in Dray's words, "to resolve puzzlement of some kind." We are perplexed by the behavior of, say, Henry VIII or Trujillo. To understand their actions—to have a satisfactory explanation of their behavior—is to find out what *reasons* they had for acting in the way they did. When we see the point of their actions, our puzzlement is resolved; we have made sense of their actions. We can see that given *their* beliefs, given *their* grasp of the situation, and given *their* aims, they had *their* reasons for doing what they did. This does not at all mean that we think their reasons are good reasons; we may think their reasons are the abominable or stupid reasons of evil or insane men, but in coming to understand their actions we do come to see that from *their point of view,* their behavior made perfectly good sense. To give a rational explanation of an action is to establish this sort of link between an agent's beliefs and purposes and what he did. To show that his action has a point or rationale is to explain it.

It is worthwhile noting that the above description of the function of an explanation and elucidation of the concept of a rational explanation squares with the way 'explanation' is characterized by the Oxford English Dictionary. 'To explain' is 'to smooth out,' 'to unfold,' 'to give details of,' 'to make plain or intelligible,' 'to clear of obscurity or difficulty.' The last two characterizations, in particular, square well with the elucidation made above and go hand in glove with our concept of the function—or at least one crucial function—of explanations.

3

To appreciate the role of rational explanations in history, it is not only important to come to understand the contexts in which we can properly ask for explanations and the standard function of explanations, it is also important to realize that explanation is a pragmatic concept. Dray makes this claim but he does not stress it sufficiently and he does not see how extensive its consequences are. He particularly fails to note, as Passmore observes, that to speak of *the* explanation of anything is at best a very hazardous venture, if one means by this that a given event or action has one and only one adequate or full explanation.

When I say that the concept of an explanation is a pragmatic one, I mean to say that what will count as a satisfactory explanation depends upon what we already know and what we want to know. What will clear up an obscurity or difficulty, what will make an event plain or intelligible, depends very much on whom one is talking to and for what purposes. There would be a very great difference in what would satisfactorily explain weightlessness to a child, a journalist, or a physiologist. Dray's case of a garage mechanic's explaining why my car conked out on the highway by telling me there was a leak in the oil reservoir is also a good case in point. To someone reasonably knowledgeable about motors it may be a perfectly adequate explanation; to me, it doesn't explain very much at all. We are tempted, in the face of these examples, to say that the more complex explanation is more nearly "the real explanation." But to see that this *need* not be so, consider the following case. Fred goes mad and tries to kill his wife and commit suicide. He is subsequently packed off to an insane asylum. Consider some answers to 'Why did Fred go mad and have to be put away?' To a child who has no notion of what insane asylums are for, and has only just learned a little about insane people, we might say, 'Fred is a very unhappy person and he and his wife have been very unhappy together for a long time. Fred got so he just couldn't stand it any longer and that is what made him do the terrible things he did. When people get like that they put them in an insane asylum and try to help them.' This, in most cases, would be a thoroughly unsatisfactory and evasive explanation, but as an answer to a child's question it might be perfectly all right. To a journalist or a policeman we might say, 'Fred had been drinking a lot and had become increasingly suspicious and distrustful of his wife. They had been having severe financial difficulties and a note was about due at the bank, and Fred didn't know where he was going to get the money to meet it. Fred's wife had secretly drawn out a relatively small amount of money to help her sister—a sister Fred detested. Fred had just discovered that the money had been withdrawn, and that led to a drinking bout and finally to the attempt to strangle his wife and kill himself.' Such an explanation—doing what the OED (Oxford English Dictionary) says an explanation does—gives the details of what is involved in his action and clearly reveals its crazy rationale, thereby making the action intelligible. To a social worker with some psychiatric understanding and only a passing interest in the case, it might be enough to simply say, 'Fred is severely paranoid and he had a real break last night. It's been coming on for some time but when he found that his wife had secretly given her sister some money that Fred desperately needed, that was enough to set him off.' To the clinician or psychiatrist who might work with Fred, a satisfactory explanation of why he went insane and was committed would include even more detailed information of the kind we gave to the journalist, plus information about Fred's early life history, family background, and similar clinical details. To a physiologist interested in making correlations between paranoid breaks and human physiology—a man in search of the physiological causes, if any, of such breaks—a satisfactory explanation of why Fred went insane and was committed would be very different from any given above.

But do we have any good grounds for saying that one of these explanations was *the* explanation?[10] (The temptation to think a physiological explanation would in reality be *the* explanation of Fred's action arises because, as Austin puts it, we have in the background, "a vague and comforting idea . . . that, after all, in the last analysis, doing an action must come down to the making of physical movements with parts of the body; but this is about as true as saying that something must, in the last analysis, come down to making movements of the tongue.") [11] Similarly, to say some historical personage died from a heart attack would normally be good enough for the ordinary historian, unless there were some specific reason to think there might have been something fishy about his death. But to someone interested in medical history, 'coronary thrombosis' would be better, and a physiologist might wish to investigate the cause of his death still further. 'What caused his death?' as 'Why did Fred run amuck?' can take many different explanations, depending on the interests and purposes of the investigator.

I am not trying to suggest that just anything which will relieve perplexity can count as an adequate explanation of an event or action. In certain contexts there are standard purposes and interests involved and certain quite definite expectations that need to be met. But it is also important to avoid the myth of the Last Word. We must not forget that we can in principle always ask further questions about any event or action. We have no criteria for determining some one point where we have reached rock bottom, where we have finally said the last word and where we can stop and say, 'Now here is *the* explanation of the event or action.' Where we stop is dictated by the problem at hand, by the accessibility of relevant data, by our interests and by our practical capabilities and capacities.

4

Keeping in mind the pragmatic nature of explanations and keeping in mind their central function, we are now in a position to give a more adequate elucidation of rational explanations. In explaining a person's actions, we not only need to know the relevant facts about our man and his situation but we must also be able to appreciate the situation from his point of view. We must know what his reasons were and be able to appreciate how they could be decisive for him. That is to say, we can explain an individual's actions when we know the facts relevant to the action and we can show the appropriateness of it from the agent's point of view. (Note we need *not* judge the action to be appropriate or reasonable but only that it is reasonable to believe that it would seem so to the agent. In giving a rational explanation of his action we need only to make sense of it from the agent's point of view, given his particular situation, beliefs, and attitudes; we need not be justifying or excusing the action, though we must be able to appreciate how someone could take it to be an appropriate thing to do.)

To make it perfectly plain how these rational explanations work, we should examine two very different cases in which rational explanations are employed.

A typical use of a rational explanation occurs in the following account in the *New York Times:* The President, the *Times* reports, decided against a tax cut though there was every indication he favored such a cut. This taken by itself is puzzling. It is the kind of act that cries out for explanation. The *Times* begins its explanation by pointing out that President Kennedy did not urge a tax cut because he was convinced that Congressional opposition was too strong. For anyone at all knowledgeable about American politics this is a sufficient explanation. The statement about Congressional opposition explains the President's action, if it makes sense of it, by bringing out a good reason for his acting in the way he did. But to display clearly the rationale of his action, to make us appreciate that the President's reasons were good reasons—from his point of view, at any rate—may, for many at least, require more details. (Remember one of the meanings of 'to explain' in the OED is 'to give details of.') The *Times* follows this cue. Assuming their readers will know that the President cannot cut or raise taxes without the approval of Congress, the *Times* goes on to explain that this Congress is dominated by a conservative coalition of Republicans and Southern Democrats. This conservative coalition has opposed most of the President's policies and they are against a tax cut now. Furthermore, President Kennedy is convinced that if he is to get any of his own legislation enacted he must take a moderate and conciliatory approach. Since he saw clear indications that Congress, and particularly the powerful chairman of the tax-writing committees in Congress, were against a tax cut, Kennedy trimmed his sails. This more detailed explanation makes Kennedy's beliefs and aims still plainer—though it assumes a general knowledge of his liberal (quasi-liberal) policies—and shows how in the light of those beliefs and aims his action was appropriate. Such an explanation will make sense of his action only to someone with an elementary understanding of American political structures and the American political scene, but to someone with that understanding it does exhibit the point of Kennedy's not pushing for a tax cut even though there is every indication that he favored a cut. An anomaly has been straightened out; the *point* of the President's action has been exhibited. To achieve this sort of thing is the aim of rational explanations.

Not all actions have a rational point. Many acts are thoroughly irrational and cannot be said to be appropriate from any sane point of view. But there is often method in madness. Most of Caligula's and Hitler's acts had a crazy rationale; they were appropriate given their crazy beliefs and insane aims and intentions. Rational explanations are used to explain many irrational acts. To show how this works, I shall develop my second case.

We read that four persons committed suicide shortly after Marilyn Monroe did, and that there is independent evidence which shows that their suicides were, in part anyway, a result of hers. Why, we wonder, did Miss Monroe's death trigger these suicides? *United Press International*—clearly going against the more naïve versions of the covering law theory—writes, "Psychiatrists and psychologists could have predicted this sort of thing. It happens just about every time a celebrity dies in this fashion. Why?" Without taking the regularity or alleged regularity noted as an explanation at all, it goes on to try to exhibit the demented rationale of such actions. It tries to make these suicides understandable by first adverting to the common phenomenon of *identification*—giving familiar and obvious examples of identification—and then showing how culture heroes like Miss Monroe are frequently the object of such identification. People who consciously or unconsciously make such identification read of Miss Monroe's death and reason that if such a renowned person was driven to this, "what hope is there for me? I'm just a little person." If they are in a depressed, harassed state and already have a predisposition to suicide, Miss Monroe's death might be enough to bring about their own suicide. By such a "practical calculation," their irrational acts can now be seen to have a rationale.

I do not claim, at least not as something that could be a purely conceptual truth, that all actions can be explained by use of the rational model of explanation and Dray does not claim that, either (a point Krieger forgets in his criticism of Dray). I am inclined to think, however, that as a matter of fact all *actions* can be so explained. But if finally we can make no sense at all of an action, then if we are going to explain it we must give a different sort of explanation. Perhaps in such a situation we should give a causal explanation. Yet not all of our actions are irrational actions; and some—if not all—of our irrational actions can be explained by using rational explanations. Freudian analysis has, in effect, shown how far we can extend this conception of rational explanation.[12]

I need here to leave one cautionary note. I am not, of course, arguing for the content of the above two sample explanations. In terms of their content, they may be quite inadequate rational explanations, but their *form* is that of perfectly proper rational explanations, that for most people would render intelligible the actions of the people in question.

5

To give a rational explanation of an action, then, is to show that from the point of view of the agent (given his understanding of his situation) what he did was the rational thing to do. But there is a further feature of rational explanations that should be characterized, the neglect of which, I should argue, is a major source of Hempel's and Passmore's confusions over these explanations. In *Laws and Explanations in History,* Dray argues that in explaining a person's behavior we sometimes represent it "as the reasonable thing to have done, and when we do, if we appeal 'to general knowledge' at all, it is to *principles* of behavior rather than empirical generalizations; to knowledge of what *to do* rather than of what is usually or always done." [13] In his "The Historical Explanation of Actions Reconsidered," Dray points out that "the aim of such explanations (rational explanations) is not to show that the agent was the sort of man who does in fact always do the sort of thing he did in the sort of circumstances he thought he was in. What it *aims* to show is that the sort of thing he did made perfectly good sense from his own point of view." [14] To accept a rational explanation "does not imply whenever we think we know what an agent's reasons were, we *really do* know." We know, relative to the agent's beliefs and aims, what reasons are *appropriate,* what would count as *good* grounds for action from that point of view. In our highest grade rational explanations, "it is enough that what provides the agent with a reason for acting be a *rationally* necessary condition—that is, that it be shown that without it, he had no reason to do what he did. It is not required that we show that he *could not* have acted in the same way without having that reason." In section 9 I shall argue that if these features of rational explanations are kept in mind and if we do not allow ourselves to forget the general meaning the OED assigns to 'explanation,' we shall see that Hempel-Passmore criticisms of Dray cannot withstand the baptism of fire.

6

It should be noted that there is an implicit generality in the employment of rational explanations, though this generality is quite different from anything the covering law model sanctions. If Z is a good reason for B to do x, then Z would be a good reason for anyone sufficiently like B to do x in relevantly similar circumstances.[15] To see why 'President Wilson sought to elect a Congress more willing to go along with him' it is often enough to elicit the warrant, 'When a man is a President in a democracy, the thing for him to do is to gain a legislative body favorable to his views.' Note that 'the thing *to do*' makes it plain that such a general statement is not an empirical generalization or an empirical law but a *rule* (maxim) or *principle* of action. Often, as in the above case, it is platitudinous or truistic but sometimes the principles involved are anything but truistic. Unlike a law or a generalization, there is no question of confirming or disconfirming such rules or principles, though in a partially parallel manner they can be said to be sound or unsound. When such principles or rules are serving as warrants for some human action, i.e., 'B did x because of Z,' the 'because' derives its explanatory force from the principle or rule of action. In 'Mrs. Finkbine had an abortion because she had good grounds for believing her baby would be deformed,' her warrant for her action might have been 'Don't bear and rear deformed children.'

If we know what a person's principles of action are and if we have reason to believe the person is rational, we can predict with some degree of reliability what this person will do. But when we are explaining the person's action we are attempting to *make sense* of it, to understand why such a person *should* do such a thing, and this is not to predict what he did. Dray puts the matter well when he says, ". . . we sometimes want to explain actions not by representing them as instances of laws, but as the reasonable thing to have done; and when we do, if we appeal to 'general knowledge' at all, it is to principles of behavior rather than empirical generalizations; to knowledge of what to do rather than of what is usually or always done." [16]

7

Some will contend that to stress the role of rational explanations in explaining actions, as I have and as Dray has, will make human behavior appear to be far more rational than it is in actuality. It will not give us a faithful representation of how things have been. To understand Luther's behavior we should think more about his hemorrhoids and less about what, from his point of view, would be the reasonable thing to do.

How a rationalistic distortion can enter into narrative histories relying heavily on rational explanations can be seen from the following considerations. When our historical explanations are at all extended, we attempt to select facts, arrange our materials to form a picture or pattern which will, if possible, make sense of the agent's actions, given his beliefs, motives, intentions, and aims.[17] Gershoy's treatment of Barère in fact beautifully illustrates this procedure. A crucial fact about Barère's behavior that needs to be explained is why he voted for Robespierre's death, though Robespierre was his friend whose ideology he shared. The usual thing that is said is that he acted in the way he did because he was an opportunist. Facts are selected which would naturally be understood as indicating that he was an opportunist. Seeing that he was an opportunist and seeing that he could benefit from Robespierre's death, we now see the point of his action—we have a rational explanation of his voting for the death of Robespierre. Gershoy finds various facts in Barère's life that prima facie do not go well with the contention that he was an opportunist and he seeks another rational explanation which tries, in another way, to dispel the puzzlement about Barère's action again Robespierre. He argues that Barère was a mediator, a man who felt that he must preserve the party. Robespierre's divisive tactics were destroying the party, so Barère reluctantly voted for his death. Again we have a rational explanation. We see the point of what Barère did. In either event, if we are to write narrative history and not propaganda, we must not ignore facts that would conflict with our explanation; but, we must be able to save appearances by so displaying the prima facie conflicting facts that they can be seen to be compatible with the actions of either an opportunist or a mediator—depending on which thesis we are pushing. But it is just such a patterning of the facts into an intelligible whole, it is just this insistence on finding the rationale of the action, that in either case can bring a rationalistic distortion into narrative history. People often are inconsistent, ambivalent, driven by unconscious motives, thoroughly irrational in bits of their behavior. Their behavior frequently does not make sense, does not conform to a pattern. Working with this model we try to arrange the actions of the person(s) in question into a pattern. But this surely indicates that to be committed to placing primary emphasis on rational explanations in explaining historical actions is likely to give a far too rationalistic picture of the human past. We are likely to make a pattern where there is none.

What I have said about irrational actions being explicable on the model of rational explanations and about coming to the situation from the point of view of the agent or agents involved, will only partially meet this criticism. It should be admitted right off that rationalistic distortions can—and do—creep into narrative history written on this model. But there is nothing intrinsic to the model that makes such distortions inevitable or nearly inevitable. There is no reason at all why historical explanations written to this model should be distorted in this way. To explain a man's actions as "dictated" by his ambivalent, unconscious hatred of and homosexual identification with his father is precisely to use a rational explanation. It displays the hidden rationale of his action.

It is also important to remember in this connection that rational explanations, as well as causal explanations, admit of empirical check. There are documents, etc. that cannot be ignored and if there are too many facts which do not square with or do not conveniently square with the proffered rational explanation in question we will have to abandon it. If the facts cannot be plausibly put together so as to make any sense at all of the agent's behavior, we should in this instance abandon the claim to explain the matter by appealing to reasons and explain it in some other way.[18]

Rational explanations like explanations of any other type

can be used stupidly, unimaginatively, or even evasively. They *can* be an instrument of rationalization and no doubt they frequently are. But they need not give rise to rationalizations if the historian is sane and keeps his wits about him. There is nothing at all in the very conception of a rational explanation that need in effect commit the historian to telling a tall tale.

8

There is a related criticism of the use of rational explanations voiced by Krieger, Hempel, and Passmore. After all, they ask, what are the criteria of rationality? Hempel points out that Dray seems to assume that once the situation is clearly spelled out, we can see that there is just one thing that is rationally necessitated—that there is just one thing to do. But is this so? Is there in reality any such rational necessitation? Krieger goes so far as to say that this concept of Dray's is treacherously mystifying—a kind of Pandora's box.

If Dray is arguing that in any situation where the facts are fully and perspicuously displayed we will find a single set of clearly applicable principles of action which will unequivocally tell us what it is reasonable to do, he is indeed creating a rationalist myth. The heart of such rationalism is irrational. It is not at all clear to me that Dray is making any such claim, but at any rate, the parts of his account of rational explanations that I have explicated and no doubt appropriated in my own way are in no way dependent on such a Cartesian dream. The criteria for what is reasonable or rational are surely field-dependent. They vary from subject matter to subject matter and from context to context. It makes no more sense to ask for *the* criteria of rationality than it does to ask for the criteria of a good game. (We need to know what kind of game, played for what purpose, in what context, and by whom.) There are, however, some very general things we can say about what it is to act reasonably. If we are acting reasonably we must be impartial—that is, we must grant that if x is a good reason for B to do Y in Z, it is also a good reason for anyone else relevantly like B and similarly situated; we must also act in accordance with the evidence and not allow our judgments to be distorted by our fears and aversions, and where such considerations are relevant we must conduct our thinking and acting according to principle. Such general considerations give us some guidelines, but by themselves they surely do not enable us to calculate what is the appropriate thing to do in a given situation. 'The reasonable thing to do' typically has an approbative force but its specific criteria are, in Toulmin's phrase, quite field-dependent.[19] Once we give up as absurd the task of asking what in general are the criteria of rationality—beyond the obvious remarks made above—we can readily acknowledge that we need to characterize carefully the actual criteria of rationality for specific activities.[20] Dray has not done this job of philosophical cartography, but to suggest that as a result his talk of rational explanation is treacherously mystifying is itself mystifying. We do not have a proper analysis of 'fact' or of 'seeing' either, but this does not at all mean that we can't recognize a fact or a factual consideration. Surely we should have learned this from G. E. Moore long ago. We know how to use 'that is the reasonable thing to do' in many contexts. If a child cuts in front of my car on his bicycle, if I fall off a stepladder and break my arm, if my account is overdrawn at the bank, if I have an examination to prepare for, or if I am planning to retire, there are a number of things that are quite unequivocally the reasonable thing to do and we all know what they are. Certain complicating factors can and sometimes do arise which make it quite uncertain what course of action should be taken in a given situation. But we should not—in good existentialist fashion—treat this sort of situation as if it were the norm. A rational man will not be so obsessed with reason that he will assume that there must be a reason for everything; he will not be so insecure that he will claim that the use of reason will enable us to solve all our problems of conduct. But he will point out that there are an indefinitely large number of situations in which what is reasonable or appropriate to do is quite clear. To acknowledge this is not to commit oneself to philosophical rationalism or to overrating the powers of reason; it is but to acknowledge a patent and perfectly well-founded bit of common sense. Furthermore, we need actual evidence for the easy claim that such an understanding of what is reasonable is completely or even in large measure relative. Until some good evidence for the claim that such conceptions are relative is actually forthcoming it should not be allowed to count against a reliance on rational explanations. (If the appropriate or reasonable thing to do were completely culturally and historically relative, history as it has been practiced would have been impossible. To be known to be true the thesis must be false.)

9

I have only rebutted one of the Hempel-Passmore criticisms of the use of rational explanations. I have not yet touched, some will say, the main issue—the straw that breaks the camel's back—namely, the claim that if rational explanations really do explain, they only do so in conjunction with a covering law. A *necessary* but not a sufficient condition for being an explanation of any sort is that the statement to be explained be (1) deducible from a statement or set of statements which state a universal law (whenever X then A), together with a statement of boundary conditions, or (2) be inductively inferable from a probability statement (whenever X then the probability of A is such and such), together with a statement of the boundary conditions. If we use (2) in our explanation it only makes it probable that the act will be done or the event will occur, but that it is probable is enough to explain it. But if we cannot deduce the *explanandum* from such an *explanans* or show that what the *explanans* asserts will occur is probable, we have not explained it. If rational explanations really do explain they must fit this form.

But why try to push rational explanations into this rigid

mold, particularly when there seem to be few if any laws of human behavior or even tendency statements relevant to historical explanations which admit of clear statement as probabilistic laws (whenever X then the probability of A is such and such)? We need this form, it has been argued, because otherwise we do not, and cannot, know why a given phenomenon (an event or an action) really did occur. To act in a given way may be ever so reasonable or appropriate and we still might not act in that way. We want to know *why* the agent actually did what he did, we want to know what finally triggered his action, and this we can't know without a universal empirical law (probabilistic or otherwise).

It is not enough, the argument continues, in explaining why x was done to show that doing x was the sensible or reasonable thing to do under the circumstances. In explaining x we want to explain why someone actually did x. If x is a genuine *explanandum* then x is in some way an anomaly or in some way unexpected. We can in some instances *rebut* the charge that a given individual could not possibly have done x by showing how in his circumstances, given his principles of action, it was the sensible or reasonable thing to do, the thing to have done; but this still doesn't explain (show), it will be argued, why he did x, though it does render his action intelligible. It makes plain how he could have possibly done it and would have done it if he were rational and had in this instance acted in character. But it actually explains his action only if we have some general law or at least a tendency statement to the effect that people of his type, in situations like the one described in the "rational explanation," will do (or tend to do in such and such proportion of the times) X. To cite a relevant and even a clearly applicable principle or maxim of action (e.g., 'The thing to do in situations like Z is X') is not by itself to give an explanation of why he did it for people are not always rational—even rational people don't (or at least might not) *always* act rationally. In a given instance, even an accepted and highly prized principle of action might not have the slightest influence on us. As Passmore has well put it: "To take a 'reason' to be the actual explanation of anyone's conduct, when there is no direct evidence that this was the explanation, is to assert, at least, that he is the sort of person who is guided by this particular principle—and this, whatever it means in detail, amounts to asserting the general statement: 'People of type X, in situation Y, act in such a way as to conserve the principle Z', i.e., it is an explanation by reference to a general statement." [21] That a reason which is in accordance with what, in this situation, is a rational principle of action or even *the* rational principle of action (if there is such an animal in our conceptual zoo) need not be *the actual reason* why he did what he did. Unless we know that it is the actual reason why he did what he did, we have not explained his action. We have at best explained why he might have done it or even why it is reasonable to believe that he could have acted in this way, but we have not explained why he in fact did it. To do this we need empirical laws or at least general statements like the ones given above by Passmore; mere principles or rules of action will not do the trick. Thus, if "rational explanations" really are explanations, they must presuppose the truth of covering laws (they must be used in conjunction with covering laws) at least in the form of some tendency or dispositional statements. Such laws or such general statements are a *necessary condition* for the adequacy of any explanation—rational or otherwise. Thus, the basic requirement of the covering law theory remains. Rational explanations are not alternatives to explanations by covering laws; instead, they presuppose the truth of the covering law theory.

There are, in my judgment, grounds within a theory like Dray's for adequately meeting such a criticism, though Dray's specific efforts to meet such a criticism are defective. Dray, himself, tries to rebut such criticisms by arguing that (1) 'He did it because he thought so and so' and 'I did it because I thought so and so' are logically parallel, and (2) that we can know in our own case that we did something because of such and such even though we know no laws from which we can deduce or even inductively infer that we would do it. When I say, 'I went to the Beaverkill yesterday because I thought that the brownies would bite,' I can know, at least in certain favored circumstances, I acted for this reason, even though I know no law or probability statement about what I and others like me will do or probably will do on such occasions. I can, on certain occasions, be perfectly certain of why I acted in a certain way even though I know no laws about my behavior or anyone else's in such circumstances. In such circumstances, I don't explain my actions in conjunction with laws or general empirical statements in the way Hempel and Passmore claim people do. Since I use 'because' without any assumed covering law in my own case when I am explaining my behavior and not just when I am justifying it or excusing it, and since the two types of statement are logically parallel, there is no reason not to believe that 'because' has the same force when we are explaining the actions of others.

Hempel replies that we always use covering laws when we give genuine explanations, for even in our own case we utilize dispositional statements about our character. We know about ourselves in a way that is logically quite on a par with the way we know the dispositions of others. I doubt, for reasons that Anscombe and Hampshire have made current, that this is so, but regardless of whether or not I am justified in doubting this, Dray's reply will not carry us very far. And further, what is really crucial here: it will not carry us to historical explanations. 'He did it because he thought so-and-so' and 'I did it because I thought so-and-so' are not logically parallel. It may be that I know my own intentions or even how I will act or am acting without knowing general laws or even, perhaps, without observation, but that is not the way I know that someone else is doing something or have grounds for believing they will do something or did do something. At the very least, it seems to me the onus is on Dray to show that the first and second person statements are parallel—giving 'because' the same explanatory force in each. At best, Dray has only shown how in my own case I can know 'I did it because I thought so-and-so' without any knowledge of what people, including myself, generally do.

It seems to me, however, that Dray has the resources in his theory to make a far more general and stronger reply to Hempel's and Passmore's objection. It consists of fastening once more on some plain meanings of 'explanation' and on the *aims* of rational explanations. Some of the general meanings of 'explanation' given in the OED (as we have already noted) are 'to smooth out,' 'to make plain or intelligible,' 'to clear of obscurity or difficulty.' When we are explaining an action we are typically trying to make *sense* of the action to ourselves or someone else. We are *not* trying to retrodict the action, or to show the cause or causes of a given phenomenon. Consider again the *aim* of a rational explanation. The aim of such an explanation is not to show that a particular action *had to* or even that it *will* occur but only that a particular action was *appropriate*, given the aims, beliefs, and attitudes of a particular agent at a particular time. Sometimes, as Dray himself puts it, all we are asking "when we ask for an action to be explained, is how it could have seemed rationally possible or 'all right' to do it." To explain an action, it is frequently enough for us to show that "but for this" (and at this point we state the action's rationale) he would have had no *reason* to do what he did. And to proceed in this way is not to confuse justifying or excusing with explaining. It is true that I may, in different contexts and for different purposes, give reasons to justify and/or excuse my and others' behavior; but I also explain my and others' actions—make clear their intent and rationale—by giving reasons for them; and sometimes, I both explain and justify or explain and excuse an action all at the same time. (To understand is sometimes to forgive.) Basically, to explain an action is to make sense of it, to make it intelligible.

People have tried to mediate the dispute between someone like Hempel or Passmore, on the one hand, and Dray and myself, on the other, by arguing that both sides are talking about different but equally legitimate types of explanation bearing different senses of 'explanation.' To this, one defender of Hempel (Paul Edwards, if my memory serves me correctly) argued that there is but one sense of 'explanation' and it is what Hempel says it is. Dray may have shown what it is to make an action intelligible or what it is to understand an action but *not* what it is to explain an action or to explain anything else, for we have only explained something when we have shown why the event (action) did in fact occur.

The mediators *may* be right and it *may* be, as Nowell-Smith has said of this dispute, that "ultimately the dispute may amount to no more than a trivial verbal dispute about the meaning of 'explain'."[22] In certain contexts, it might be argued, one concept of explanation is applicable and in certain concepts another is. But even *if* this is so it is also plain, as the historian Krieger stresses, that we do very frequently use the concept of rational explanation outlined by Dray and we do *not* necessarily use it in conjunction with a covering law. This is enough for Dray's central thesis and mine. Furthermore, while the concept of a rational explanation gains sanction from the OED (as well as Webster) there seems to be little sanction in the dictionary for regarding what Hempel calls "explanations" as explanations. The best face we can put on the kind of argument given by Hempel is to claim *not* that it is the only sense of 'explanation,' but to argue that in sentences like 'B did Y because of Z,' 'Z' is systematically ambiguous. Sometimes it means 'The reason B did Y was Z' and sometimes it means 'What made B do Y was Z.' 'Why did B do Z' could mean either, depending on the context. This would give respite for the mediators of those two positions (though actually Dray's claim is no stronger than this), but it would clearly not at all touch Dray's thesis and mine: that there are rational explanations with or without laws and that they are used in explaining human actions in history and in everyday life.

10

Someone finally might say that, after all, in defending the concept of rational explanations you have repeatedly depended on the ordinary nontechnical meanings of 'explanation' to defend your thesis, but on Hempel's theory 'explanation' is or at least should be a technical notion having nothing to do with the ordinary meanings of 'explanation.' This may be so, but when historians or plain folk—or even not so plain folk—explain actions or try to explain actions, they presumably are using 'explanation' in one of its ordinary ways or at least in a way which is reasonably close to its ordinary employments. For certain purposes it is perfectly permissible to restrict or in some way alter ordinary usage, but if we depart completely from ordinary usage and give the token 'explanation' an entirely new use, we are now patently no longer talking about the same thing that others are when they are trying to explain 'explanation,' and what we say is completely irrelevant to the question: what is an explanation? I have only tried to show that given the ordinary meanings of 'explanation' and given the functions of explanation in history and in everyday life there are rational explanations with or without covering laws.

11

If the covering law theory is so wrong, why have so many admittedly brilliant and sane men so adamantly defended it? What reasons could anyone have for wishing to press all explanations into such a rigid and unrealistic mold? It is often felt that only if the covering law theory is correct can we ever gain an objective, nonculture-bound, genuinely scientific theory of human action. The ideal (if you will, the dream) of a science of man—certainly a worthy ideal—is linked in the minds of many to such a theory of explanation. There remains a persistent fear that if the covering law theory of explanation is not viable, the ideal is indeed a dream of a spirit-seer. More generally, it is often felt that only if we have such laws can we have any clear and distinct knowledge of why it is that various events occur in the way they do. Assuming that at bottom human actions are really a set of physical movements, it is thought that we can in principle—by constantly striving for a more complete filling-in of our "explanation sketches"—work toward what in effect is a Cartesian ideal, an ideal which if realized would enable us to *deduce* how human beings will behave or have behaved, from a set of universal and empirically testable laws. (Certainly this is not true of all covering law theorists. It is not true of Popper, for example, but it is, I suspect, a major motive for adopting and holding on through thick and thin to such a view.) We wish to escape the rub of doubt. In certain moods we profoundly wish to be able to give a completely foolproof explanation which will show beyond a shadow of a doubt why someone acted in the way he did. We do not simply want to know why it would have been reasonable to act in that way. We want to be able to determine what he must do, given certain initial conditions. The Hempelian model holds this out as an ideal. It seems to exhibit what it would be like for this to be possible. It has often been pointed out that in fact we have no laws of the requisite sort; and, insult is added to injury when people like Berlin and Winch give arguments which suggest that we don't even know what such a law of human behavior would look like.[23] But the ideal of such a science of human behavior is so compelling that it is natural for us to try to refute them or to brush off such arguments as "Oxford *apriorism*" (the phrase is Passmore's).[24] Given such a drive for generality and certainty it is natural to be dissatisfied with antinomian approaches to history or to the social and psychological studies.[25] (The other side of the coin is that covering law theories *seem* to entail determinism and determinism *seems* to entail a denial of the freedom of thought and action. If one is convinced that "seems" is in reality "is" here, one will quite naturally, like Berlin, Donagan, and Winch, find such theories deeply repugnant. One will think, as they do, that if we accept such a theory of human action we can no longer, in a sense that ultimately matters, say that there is any freedom of human action.)[26]

This quest for certainty in the form of covering law is natural. In certain moods I share it too. But, as Hempel himself makes perfectly plain, even if we had relevant and strictly universal laws of human behavior which we could use as premises from which (together with statements of antecedent conditions) we could deduce that an historical agent must have acted in a certain way, we still would have laws of universal scope which could only be said to be *confirmed* to a certain degree. We would, even if we could use them in such an explanatory theory, have no certain grounds for asserting that they are true. With the Hempelian model, as with a model like the one I have advocated, we would not get certainty. There would still be room to doubt whether a person actually did what we assert he must have done.

If we wish to avoid being evasive, it seems to me that we must keep firmly before our minds the fact that we are not going to gain any certainty in our explanations of human actions. Explanation is a pragmatic notion. There is no helpful sense in which we can claim we have given *the* explanation of an action. This is as true for rational explanations as it is for causal explanations. Our actions can be subsumed under various principles or maxims of action. Only in the simplest of cases can we justifiably assert that one and only one action was rationally necessary. And, in theory, at least, we can always ask further questions, sometimes from a very different point of view and to a very different end, of any action or event. But this does not at all mean that we end in skepticism. Skepticism and rationalism (to adopt a phrase put to different work by J. L. Austin) live on by taking in each other's laundry. But if we do not go off in search of a falling star but keep our feet firmly planted on the ground, we can hardly help realizing that in many contexts we can and do explain actions fully enough for the purposes at hand. Yet it remains the case, that there always may be some unnoticed and untoward circumstance which makes it unreasonable in *that* circumstance to do what normally would be the thing to do; and, the sanest people might not in a given situation do what is reasonable, or even see what is the reasonable thing to do in that circumstance; and a covering law (no matter how well confirmed) might, after all, be false or demand an important modification. Such contingencies cannot be avoided and this has been well understood for a long time; but even those who understand it very well are prone to forget it when they have in mind some idea of a set of rationally necessary principles of action, or when they dream of a science of man based on universal but still empirically testable laws of human nature. In spite of Peirce, in spite of Dewey, in spite of Wittgenstein, in spite of Austin, such essentially Cartesian ideals die slowly.

NOTES

1. William Dray, *Laws and Explanation in History* (Oxford, 1957), p. 137. Dray's arguments are in the aforementioned book and in his paper, "The Historical Explanation of Actions Reconsidered," given at the Institute and published in this volume. When no specific page reference is given for a quotation from Dray, it is from his paper given at the Institute. Hempel's remarks were made at the Institute meetings and are published in the present volume. Passmore's arguments were made in his "Law and Explanation in History," *Australian Journal of Politics and History*, 4 (1958), 269–75.

2. As G. E. M. Anscombe has stressed, the distinction between causes and reasons is a difficult one to characterize adequately. There are many instances in which it is difficult to tell if one is giving a reason for or a cause of an action. In some situations the words even do the same job but there are, as Anscombe also stresses, clear cases of giving reasons and stating causes, where the words 'reason' and 'cause' do not have the same function. By analyzing these, we can at least indicate the nature of the distinction between causes and reasons. See G. E. M. Anscombe, *Intention* (Oxford, 1957).

3. The label 'rational explanations' is in a way unfortunate for it suggests that to explain a person's actions in this way consists in showing that what he did was the rational or reasonable thing to do in such circumstances. But in giving a rational explanation there is no such endorsement of the person's actions.

4. Dray, *Laws and Explanation in History*, p. 154.

5. 'Rationale' and 'point' can frequently be interchanged. I do not say they always can.

6. Dray, *op. cit.*, p. 138. The reasons for this have been clearly articulated by R. S. Peters, *The Concept of Motivation* (London and New York, 1958), and Peter Winch, *The Idea of a Social Science* (London, 1958).

7. See P. H. Nowell-Smith, "Psychoanalysis and Moral Language," *Rationalist Annual*, 1954, and R. S. Peters, *Authority, Responsibility and Education* (London, 1959; New York, 1960), sec. 2.

8. Dray, *op. cit.*, p. 125.

9. Stephen Toulmin, *An Examination of the Place of Reason in Ethics* (Cambridge, Eng., 1950).

10. It might be thought that in each case the explanations I gave are only partial explanations, given according to the interests and capacity for understanding of the parties toward whom they are directed. They are not different explanations, it might be argued, but fragments, parts, of a fuller explanation. Theoretically, "*the* explanation" is "the complete explanation," that is, the explanation that has taken into consideration and made clear all of the factors that can possibly be known and judged relevant from every possible point of view. This concept of "the explanation" is a myth. There are an indefinitely large number of interests and aims. We have no way of knowing when we have considered all possible points of view or interests; and what will count as 'relevant factors' in an explanation is completely determined by the point of view from which the inquiry is made.

11. J. L. Austin, *Philosophical Papers* (Oxford, 1961), p. 126.

12. See Alasdair MacIntyre, *The Unconscious* (London and New York, 1958), and Peters, *The Concept of Motivation*.

13. Dray, *op. cit.*, p. 135; the italics are mine.

14. The italics are mine.

15. No trick is being played here with 'relevantly similar circumstances.' See John Hospers' discussion of this point in his *Human Conduct* (New York, 1961), pp. 320–22.

16. Dray, *op. cit.*, p. 135.

17. See here D. Gasking, "The Historian's Craft and Scientific History," *Historical Studies: Australia and New Zealand*, 4 (May 1950), 22–24, and P. H. Nowell-Smith, "Are Historical Events Unique?" *Proceedings of the Aristotelian Society*, New Series, LVII (1956–1957), 127–35.

18. Dray's own reasoning on this point has been insufficiently noticed. See Dray, *op. cit.*, pp. 138–39.

19. Stephen Toulmin, *The Uses of Argument* (Cambridge, Eng., 1958).

20. I have discussed these and related points in greater detail in my " 'Appealing to Reason,' " *Inquiry,* V (1962), and in "Wanton Reason," *Philosophical Studies,* XII (1963).

21. John Passmore, "Law and Explanation in History," *op. cit.*, 275.

22. P. H. Nowell-Smith, "Review of *Laws and Explanation in History,*" *Philosophy* (April 1959), 162.

23. Isaiah Berlin, "History and Theory: The Concept of Scientific History," *History and Theory,* I (1960), 1–31, and Peter Winch, *op. cit.*

24. John Passmore, "Critical Notice of G. E. M. Anscombe's *Intention,*" *Indian Journal of Philosophy,* I (August 1959), 57.

25. See Alan Donagan, "Social Science and Historical Antinomianism," *Revue internationale de Philosophie* (1957), 433–49, and John Passmore, "History and Sociology," *Australian Journal of Politics and History,* 3 (May 1958), 218–28.

26. Able attempts to relieve this conceptual malaise have been made by Ernest Nagel, "Determinism in History," *Philosophy and Phenomenological Research,* 20 (1959–1960), 291–317; Francis V. Raab, "History, Freedom, and Responsibility," *Philosophy of Science,* 26 (April 1959), 114–24; Charles Frankel, "Philosophy and History," *Political Science Quarterly,* LXXII, 359–63; and Sidney Hook, *The Quest for Being* (New York, 1961), pp. 26–48.

22

History as Inquiry

SIDNEY RATNER
Rutgers University

UNTIL some twenty years ago a chasm used to yawn between philosophers and historians in America and England. Henry Adams, Charles Beard, and Carl Becker among historians, F. J. E. Woodbridge, M. R. Cohen, and R. C. Collingwood, among philosophers, were among the few pioneers who explored the interrelationship of these two seemingly disparate disciplines.

The Second World War seems to have completed a revolution in the thought-patterns of these two professions, for which the 1929 depression had paved the way. An amazing upsurge of interest in the philosophy of history has occurred that already has enriched and stimulated work in both history and philosophy.[1] Fruitful and illuminating as the main papers delivered at this conference have been, I believe it desirable as a practicing historian to examine critically some of the theses set forth in at least one of these papers.

Professor Morton White's essay, "The Logic of Historical Narrative," is a gallant and important attempt to move beyond the concentration of contemporary philosophers of language on the logic of *single* statements, to a clarification of narrative history as a "unique form of human discourse," with a logic that has been too long neglected by philosophers of history and language.[2] Despite this step forward, I must dissent from many of his positions and formulations.

I. ENTITIES VS. EVENTS

Professor White is free to state that "every history is a history of some entity. . . ." But as an historian I am disturbed by his focusing his attention on "some entity" while most historians center their attention on events and processes. The difference ultimately may seem nonexistent: entities participate in events, and events occur between entities, but I fear that the difference in phrasing involves a difference in philosophical preference by White for entities or things, with possibly timeless or temporarily fixed qualities. Historians, however, in general give philosophical priority to "happenings," "events," "processes."[3]

II. CHRONICLE AND HISTORY

English usage until relatively recently has not distinguished sharply between chronicle and history. The Oxford English Dictionary defines "chronicle" as a "detailed and continuous record of events in order of time." History is characterized in the OED as "a written narrative constituting a continuous methodical record, in order of time, of important or public events, especially those connected with a particular country, people, individual, etc."[4] The Century Dictionary, an excellent authority on usage and philosophic distinctions, improves upon the OED by asserting: "When the order of time is most conspicuous, the history is called a *chronicle,* which is generally divided into sections, with each section covering a separate period of time." "History is sometimes divided into history proper and philosophical history, the former paying attention simply to the events themselves, the latter showing the events in connection with their causes and effects."

Mr. White introduces his own innovation when he calls the Century Dictionary "history proper," a "chronicle," and its philosophical history "history." I have no objections to White exercising his privilege of prescriptive or legislative definition.

Logically the distinctions he draws are permissible. I question, however, how valuable to the working historian will be this division between a set of supposedly pure empirical (descriptive) statements and a set of explanatory hypotheses or assertions. My query arises out of the fact that in any historical inquiry I know of, no *sharp* cleavage exists between the explanatory hypotheses and the purely descriptive statements. Take, for example, the fictitious chronicle related by E. M. Forster and Mr. White: "The King of England died, and then the Queen of England died, and then the Prince of England died, and then the Princess of England died. . . ." These "purely" descriptive statements assume at least five explanatory hypotheses: four which enable one to identify who are respectively the King, Queen, Prince, and Princess of England according to certain criteria of royalty; one, which explains what is meant by the word "died." To anyone coming from a society where no mention of monarchy was ever made, and who had never heard or seen any person dying, all these "descriptive" sentences would require "explanatory" assertions. Conversely, all of Mr. White's explanatory assertions involving "because" contain "descriptive" statements or elements in the assertions about the "causal relations" (e.g., "of grief") between two or more "purely" descriptive statements. This analysis of mine is in harmony with a statement made by Mr. White some years ago, which in this paper he seems to disregard: "I suggest that the effort to draw sharp lines between the analytic and the synthetic, . . . the descriptive and the narrative, will appear silly and futile." [5]

III. THE TRUTH OF A CHRONICLE

Mr. White asserts that the truth of a chronicle is a function of the truth of its component empirical statements. This is trivially true in one sense, but is misleading in many cases. Mr. White assumes that if one tests the truth of each component statement, he may then infer that the truth of all the component statements assures the truth of the chronicle. But this arithmetical additive or summative process only guarantees that the chronicle tells that part or aspect of the whole truth about a complex series of events or situations, for which the author of the chronicle in question may have selected a series of empirical statements, all true, but giving only one side of a story. It is logically possible, and frequently true in fact, for two different chronicles, each consisting of a series of true empirical statements, to be true so far as each states certain selected facts, yet for each chronicle to contradict the other in the implications given about a total situation. Every historian and every judge knows that the most misleading authority or witness is not the man who tells complete falsehoods, but the one who tells the truth and nothing but the truth, but not the *whole* truth about an event. Mr. White undoubtedly is aware of this fact, but his formulation of this point needs correction. His position comes close to being a Logical Atomism for History, as against most historians' tendency to stress the interweaving of different facts in a complex factual synthesis that reveals the place and the relative weight of each empirical statement in the synthesis about the total situation, to which all the singular statements relate.[6]

IV. ESSENTIALISM

Mr. White presents an intriguing doctrine of historical "essentialism": the best history of any subject S would be that history based on statements that give a connected account of the changing essences of subject S within a specific range of time. But he criticizes William James's teleological conception of essence as based upon an unjustified stress on one's *practical* concerns, upon what one wants to do with any concrete thing whose essence one is studying. Surely, he asks, we have no immediate practical interest in doing something overt either to or with the *typical subject* of the historian, the dead and buried individual, or the extinct civilization (e.g., of ancient Greece).

My first comment is that I know of no historian who is

not intensely interested in the contemporary effects of historic facts and interpretations bearing on "dead and buried individuals" whose lives, acts, and ideas still excite controversy: e.g., Stalin, Hitler, F.D.R., Wilson, Darwin, Marx, Lincoln, Jefferson, Napoleon, Cromwell, Luther, Galileo, Julius Caesar, Socrates. This situation holds equally well of historians' attitudes toward extinct civilizations such as those of Renaissance Italy, Periclean Athens, the China of Confucius, or Takugawa Japan, inter alia. Whether we like to admit it or not, historians are human, all too human, and beneath an air of unworldly detachment hide emotions arising from their attachment to their nation, religion, ethnic group, social and economic class, political party. One need only examine past Soviet, Nazi, or Italian Fascist interpretations of ancient, medieval, and modern European history to see how flagrantly class or racial bias can enter into history. But even in the relatively free intellectual atmosphere of western Europe and North America, historians are often consciously or unconsciously affected by their personal positions on politics, economics, and other social matters, and by the attitude of publishers and book buyers in the choice and treatment of the subjects upon which they write. I cite only two examples: Charles Beard's monumental books on American history portrayed only *part* of "history as actuality" and reflected his strongly Progressive, New Deal position on "Welfare capitalism" at home and his equally strong hatred of possible United States' armed intervention in world politics; Arthur Schlesinger, Jr.'s *Age of Jackson,* is now regarded by acute critics as less a contribution to original historical scholarship than as a young humanitarian's politically inspired volume that succeeded in creating a popular image of Jackson as a forerunner of F.D.R.[7]

I admit, however, that many historians often succeed in rising above the prejudices of their nation, race, class, and social group. In fact, I should characterize the best scientific historians I know as scholars with strong commitments to certain views or hypotheses in disputable problems and issues, who feel even more committed to changing their view when the mass of evidence and weight of scientific analysis convinces them that they are wrong. This willingness to follow the "truth" where it leads despite one's own preferences causes the historian often to change his view of what is practical or to oppose doing what is narrowly practical in the short run. Instances of these changes during the last three decades are to be found in the revolutionary change in most American historians' views on the origins of the Constitution, the causes of the Civil War and World War I, the character of the reconstruction period after the Civil War, and the importance of the frontier.[8]

My second comment upon Mr. White's critique of James is that he exaggerates the role of any questioner's practical concern in James's definition of the essence of any one thing or object. In the chapter of the *Principles of Psychology*[9] devoted to reasoning and the teleological conception of essence, James devotes most of his space to an analysis of scientific and artistic reasoning. His key definition of essence is: "The essence of a thing is that one of its properties which is so *important for my interests* that in comparison with it I may neglect the rest." He goes on to say in a footnote: "A substance like oil has as many essences as it has uses to different individuals."[10] These uses may encompass those of pure science, pure history, and pure art, as well as those of business and industry. In fact, James makes the point that perceiving the proper essence (character or trait) for any special objective requires sagacity. He asks "Why does it require the advent of a genius in many cases before the fitting character (essence) is brought to light? Why does it need . . . a Newton . . . a Darwin?"[11] Or we may add, a Thucydides, a Gibbon, a Namier, a Beard, a Rostovtzeff?

My conclusion is that James's pluralistic, teleological conception of essence, when interpreted in the light of the full text of his discussion, withstands Mr. White's attack upon it, precisely because James was not narrowly pragmatic, as Mr. White charged. James's pluralistic view, as against Aristotle's monistic view of essence, permits historians, as well as workers in the natural sciences, to adapt their definitions of objects and the scope of their researches to the varying objectives of their inquiries.

Anything becomes "essential" if it is found indispensable in a given historical inquiry, and anything becomes "accidental" if it proves to be superfluous as an explanatory factor in the inquiry. The varying roles and prestige of economic institutions, geography, race, religion, class war, nationalism, and sex drives in historical writings over just the past century support the need for banishing monistic explanations out of history.[12]

V. ENCYCLOPEDISM

Mr. White propounds, but then rejects the doctrine of encyclopedism on the ground that it is impossible for any historian to give *all* the facts and thereby approximate the whole truth about a central subject. I agree with Mr. White so far as any large-scale historical subject, e.g., the history of modern Germany, is concerned, but I reject the thesis of Mr. White on modified encyclopedism, that the historian aiming at such a history would be limited to selecting and organizing only from the known or given features of his subject. Historians of any distinction who are ambitious to write a panoramic or modified encyclopedia history, e.g., Vernon L. Parrington in *Main Currents in American Thought,* Michael I. Rostovtzeff in *Social and Economic History of the Hellenistic World,* Elie Halévy in *History of the English People in the Nineteenth Century,* usually explore, dig up, and utilize hitherto unknown facts on hitherto *unknown* as well as *known* features of their central subject. In every case of historical synthesis I know of, the author finds that gaps exist on important matters no matter how many special studies have been written. In fact, one may almost lay down the rule that the more encyclopedic or synoptic a scholarly historian aims to be, the more original research he will have to undertake. One major exception is when textbooks or encyclopedia articles are involved. I therefore conclude that the number of features of a given subject with which the modified encyclopedic historian is dealing *may* constitute a class that is either greater than, equal to, or less than the class of *known* features.

VI. VALUE JUDGMENTS

I believe that many historians often connect or colligate facts about *both* previously unknown and known features of a subject on the basis of "a value judgment as to their importance." But I strongly disagree with Mr. White's assertion that judgments as to the importance of facts in human history are of a different kind from similar judgments in natural history or natural science. History, as Mr. White knows, was the original Greek name for all investigations from that of the physical world and cosmology to that of political events. I see no reason for creating a dichotomy between natural history and the natural sciences on the one hand, and human history and the social sciences on the other.[13] There is evidence that mathematicians and natural scientists choose a subject, invent a theory, or colligate the known features of a situation on the basis of a value judgment as to their importance in the ways similar to that of historians. Several great mathematicians, e.g., Henri Poincaré and Jacques Hadamard, have shown that the discovery of important subject and theories in mathematics depends to an amazing extent upon a special aesthetic sensibility, a sense of mathematical beauty, based on the harmony of numbers and forms, and of geometric elegance.[14] Marston Morse, another noted mathematician,[15] confirms this: "Discovery in mathematics is not primarily a matter of logic. The unconscious recognition of beauty must play an important part. In the act of discovery in mathematics a mind, bearing the imprint of many designs, singles out one design for beauty's sake. Afterwards logic sets the pattern right." [16] Often, of course, practical or utilitarian considerations may inspire mathematical research and discovery, especially in the beginning of the science: e.g., geometry and Newton's invention of the calculus for the aid it gave him in theoretical physics.[17]

In the natural sciences—physics, for instance—the criterion of aesthetic value has influenced theory and experimental research, as Erwin Panofsky and Giorgio de Santillana have shown.[18] There are other important criteria besides that of the aesthetic or utilitarian value of a theory in the natural sciences: e.g., (1) the body of experimental evidence; (2) the definitions of key ideas in terms of the operations used to give physical meaning to the ideas; (3) the predictive or explanatory power of the proposed theory. But a variety of possible mathematical theories can be found to fit and embody (1) and (2). *Each scientist has the freedom to choose one of the possible theories.* Most scientists choose that theory which seems the simplest or the most beautiful; and which is also compatible with formulating further crucial experiments.[19] I conclude, therefore, that historians do not differ from scientists when they select facts or theories on the basis of a value judgment as to their importance. History is at one with science in this respect.[20]

VII. RELATIVISM AND MEMORABILITY

Mr. White's abandonment of absolute encyclopedism leads him to accept the idea that history is constructed on a truth-transcending reference to some kind of memorability. I admire his candor in confessing he cannot supply a criterion of *memorability*. I wish however, to suggest first, that the solution to his problem is to consider memorability as a word substitute for some phrase like: "being significant to the social group with which the historian identifies himself on a subject that the group considers important or that he persuades it to regard as important." The more associations a history has with other significant facts and traditions cherished by the group to which a historian addresses himself, the more "memorability" that history will have. What will be memorable for one social group or generation, will not necessarily be memorable for another. Here there is a mutuability and relativity to culture and age that disturbs those who wish to contemplate eternal or long-enduring works of art, history, and science. The realistic or scientific historian, however, cannot guarantee the preservation of the ideal.[21] All he can hope for is a consensus of experts in his own generation. In this situation he is like the scientist who, if he lives long enough, sees as many fluctuations in judgment on key scientific issues as the historian does in his field.

One important phase of the "memorability" definition problem that Mr. White has ignored is this: When a historian says some event or series of events is "memorable," he is not simply making a declarative statement of fact or a purely emotive statement of value. He is engaged in a "performative utterance," as J. L. Austin has defined that phrase: the uttering of a sentence which is, or is a part of the doing of an action, such as engaging in a marriage ceremony, a christening, or a contractual arrangement. For example: "When I say before the registrar or altar, etc., 'I do,' I am not reporting on a marriage: I am indulging in it."[22] Similarly, the historian in ascribing "memorability" to a historic subject is engaged in delivering a verdict on certain facts and values that he hopes will influence his audience into accepting his judgment and transmitting it to others.[23] In short, the historian is acting as a molder of expert and popular opinion. He is successful when the group response *confirms* and *reinforces* his proposal.

But what may be "memorable" for a day, a month, or a year, or a generation may not be memorable for a century or a millennium. In the latter cases it is important for the survival or enhancement of a memorable subject, for its "memorability" that there be sufficiently recurrent occasions when the historic subject or narrative is recalled, repeated, and transmitted to every generation through some vivid or impressive narrative being read, narrated, or seen in some art form such as painting or sculpture. Memorability, in short, requires effective communication and agreement between the historian and his contemporary audience; it also requires a continuity in the transmission of knowledge and values from one generation to another. Memorability of an historic event or subject also involves a *transformation* of the original narrative as new information and new attitudes develop with the passage of time and changes in knowledge and social organization. The result is that memorability of a past subject over long stretches of time depends upon that subject having various aspects or dimensions of appeal or interest. The possible multidimensionality of the subject is an indispensable factor in its enduring or recurrent memorability.[24]

VIII. ERROR, MYTH, AND SUPPRESSION

It is wrong to think of history exclusively as an extension and intensification of memory or as a mere repository of easily available "memorable" events of the past. Every competent historian knows that many of the people he interviews or whose literary remains he studies have often repressed internally certain memories or have suppressed documentary evidence on what they did, thought, and felt. Usually, they believed much evidence to be unfavorable to their reputation; or that of the group with which they identified themselves. Sometimes the subject evoked painful emotions connected with personal humiliation, error, or loss, such as death inside one's family or circle of friends. In any case, a socially conscientious, scientific historian will try to dig up, and write up the evidence on subjects his nation, race, church, economic group, party, friends, or family may disapprove of. Past examples of this tendency toward repression or suppression are to be found in the history of non-Caucasian ethnic groups in the United States, of Jews in Nazi Germany, of groups opposed to collectivization and dictatorship in Soviet Russia, etc.

In all such cases, *scientific* history attempts to discover and to narrate stories that have been suppressed by the dominant power groups. In situations where individuals or groups have repressed memories distasteful to them, biographers and historians may use psychological (and, justly or unjustly, psychoanalytic) techniques to get the individuals to break through their repressions and to tell the truth. But in any event, the historian endeavors to *reconstruct* the events under investigation by obtaining objective evidence in the form of relevant material, remains, and documents. This body of evidence often will be sufficient to reveal a story that has been either suppressed or distorted. History then becomes an extension and a *correction* of honestly believed but incorrect memories, and the deliberately false propaganda that otherwise would mislead or have misled conscientious historians. The information now available on Mussolini, Hitler, and Stalin enable nonparty Western historians to present with irrefutable authority histories of Fascist Italy, Nazi Germany, and Soviet Russia under Stalin that could not be demonstrated *conclusively* before 1945.[25]

NOTES

1. Cf. *Theories of History,* ed. Patrick Gardiner (Glencoe, Ill., and London, 1959); *The Philosophy of History in Our Time,* ed. Hans Meyerhoff (Garden City, N. Y., 1959).

2. See Morton White, *Religion, Politics, and the Higher Learning* (Cambridge, 1959), pp. 61–74.

3. For my own position on historical methodology, and on events as the primary subject of history, see: "Presupposition and Objectivity in History," *Philosophy of Science,* VIII (October 1940) 503 f.; "Dewey's Contribution to Historical Theory," in *John Dewey: Philosopher of Science and Freedom,* ed. Sidney Hook (New York: Dial, 1950), pp. 135–52; and "History as Experiment," *Antioch Review* (Fall 1959), 315–27.

4. A distinction that has come to prevail, according to the OED, is that chronicles and annals are considered as the simpler forms of *history,* with the year or period as the primary division; whereas in a *history,* in the honorific sense of the term, "each movement, action, or chain of events is dealt with as a whole."

5. Morton White, *The Age of Analysis* (New York, 1955), p. 240.

6. For a study of the relation of partial to whole true empirical statements, see my essay, "Was the Supreme Court Packed by President Grant?" *Political Science Quarterly*, 50 (September 1935), 343–58. Confirmation of this position is to be found in Max Wertheimer, "On Truth," *Social Research*, 1 (May 1934), 135–46; and his *Productive Thinking* (New York and London, 1945), pp. 1–13 f; 189–215.

7. See my essay, "The Historian's Approach to Psychology," *op. cit.;* Lee Benson, *The Concept of Jacksonian Democracy* (Princeton, 1961); William M. Rockwell, *Rival Presuppositions in the Writing of Church History* (Chicago, 1935).

8. *The Reconstruction of American History*, ed. John Higham (New York, 1962); *Understanding the American Past*, ed. Edward N. Saveth (Boston, Toronto: Little, Brown & Co., 1959); *Essays in American Historiography*, eds. Donald Sheehan and Harold C. Syrett (New York, 1960).

9. (2 vols., New York, 1890), II, 325–71.

10. *Op. cit.*, II, 335.

11. *Ibid.*, 343.

12. For reinforcement of James's views on essence, see John Dewey, *Logic: The Theory of Inquiry* (New York, 1938), pp. 89–90, 138; Jan Lukasiewicz, *Aristotle's Syllogistic* (2nd ed., Oxford, 1957), pp. 205–208.

13. See my essay, "History as Experiment," *Antioch Review* (Fall 1959), 315–27, for a development of this point of view.

14. Cf. Jacques Hadamard, The *Psychology of Invention in the Mathematical Field* (Princeton, 1945), pp. 30–31, 126–27.

15. "Mathematics, the Arts, and Freedom," *Thought*, XXXIV (Spring 1959), 16–24.

16. *Ibid.*, 21.

17. Cf. John von Neumann, "The Role of Mathematics in the Sciences and Society," address at Fourth Conference of Association of Princeton Graduate Alumni (June 1954), pp. 16–29; and R. Talon, *Reason and Chance in Scientific Discovery* (New York, 1962).

18. Erwin Panofsky, "Galileo as a Critic of the Arts," *Isis*, XLVII (1956), 3–15; and Giorgio de Santillana, "The Role of Art in the Scientific Renaissance," in *Critical Problems in the History of*

Science, ed. Marshall Clagett (Madison, Wis., 1959), pp. 33–65.

19. Cf. Morse, *op. cit.,* p. 22; Alexandre Koyré, *From the Closed World to the Infinite Universe* (New York, 1959); and Stephen Toulmin, *Foresight and Understanding* (Bloomington, Ind., 1961).

20. Cf. my essay, "Facts and Values in History," *Teachers College Record,* 56 (May 1955), 429–34.

21. Cf. Carl L. Becker, *Everyman His Own Historian* (New York, 1935), pp. 242–57; Ian M. Hunter, *Memory* (Baltimore, 1961), pp. 13–38; William James, *op. cit.,* I, 643 ff.

22. J. L. Austin, *How to Do Things with Words* (Cambridge, 1962), p. 6.

23. Cf. F. C. Bartlett, *Remembering* (Cambridge, Eng., 1932), pp. 239–314.

24. Cf. my "Patterns of Culture in History," *Philosophy of Science,* 6 (January 1939), 88–97.

25. On the psychology of forgetting and repression, see Hunter, *op. cit.,* pp. 61–82, and Sigmund Freud, *Psychopathology of Everyday Life* (London, 1914); for a critique of Freud by critics with varying points of view, see *Psychoanalysis, Scientific Method, and Philosophy,* ed. Sidney Hook (New York, 1959).

23

New Issues in the Logic of Explanation

MICHAEL SCRIVEN
Indiana University

INTRODUCTION

Professor Dray has once more made a very useful contribution to the study of historical explanations. I begin by saying that I agree with almost everything he says, that much of it seems to me of great importance, and that I think his overall contribution to our understanding of this topic substantially outweighs that of any other writer: I think here not only of his book and this paper, but also of his very fine paper on causes in history, which has just come out in *Daedalus*. I believe the fruitful path for discussion of this topic now lies chiefly in the direction of improving the alternative to the 'covering law' or 'deductive model' or 'deductive-nomological' account, rather than in criticizing it further. (These are the terms introduced as labels for Hempel's account by Dray, myself, and Hempel.)

I shall therefore make a number of comments, mainly critical but I hope constructively so, on Professor Dray's paper and on his critics, and hope we can pursue them further in the future. (The quotations are from the draft of his paper circulated in advance.)

1. THE FUNCTION OF EXPLANATION

"The function of an explanation is to resolve puzzlement of some kind." No. It is to provide understanding; and only in some cases is understanding preceded by puzzlement. It may be preceded by simple ignorance, as in the audience when a writer or lecturer produces in passing an explanation of the heraldic symbolism in the Black Prince's coat-of-arms. They were not previously puzzled. One might argue that ignorance *is* puzzlement, but the two are normally distinguished in an important way; ignorance is mere absence of knowledge, while puzzlement is *failure* to understand, i.e., assumes a prior recognition of lack of understanding. Thus, *both* ignorance and puzzlement may be remedied by the provision of an explanation, although there are other ways to remedy them.

Sometimes giving information, although it remedies ignorance, is not the same as giving an explanation (e.g., giving the number of one's passport). Such a case would not be a case of remedying puzzlement. Sometimes giving information which is not an explanation *will* remove puzzlement (e.g., giving further evidence for the defendant's story, or cracking the litigant's story removes one's puzzlement as to which account is correct). And sometimes puzzlement is due to the possession of apparently incompatible facts and an explanation can be given which reconciles them. This is Dray's "explaining-how-possibly." But sometimes, to repeat, puzzlement is removed without an explanation, and sometimes explanations are provided which do not remove puzzlement.

2. TAUTOLOGIES IN RATIONAL EXPLANATIONS

Dray says of this kind of explanation of an agent's act: ". . . what it aims to show is that the sort of thing he did made perfectly good sense from his own point of view." This is not enough. It also implicitly claims that it was *because* it made good sense that he did it: otherwise it isn't an explanation. It may have made good sense from his point of view, but he may have done it out of spite (i.e., would have done it whether or not it made sense). So Hempel will, reasonably enough, suggest we need some grounds for supposing the agent was acting on reason at the time. And here we run into some very interesting points.

Suppose we produce as our grounds the facts that the agent seemed to be in possession of his reason, of the facts mentioned, and of the motives ascribed to him at the time. These are all particular claims, not laws. Hempel's model requires that a law be involved. The obvious one is something of the form "A rational man in the conditions specified would act in such-and-such a way." (L) Now this smacks of tautology, as Professor Brandt pointed out at the symposium. If it is a tautology, and still suffices, the Hempelian account is in some trouble since its author requires that the law involved must be empirical. Furthermore, tautology or not, the conjunction of these premises *still* does not show that he acted for the reasons stated. That is, we have sufficient conditions for the action, but not necessarily the explanation. To this important point we shall return later. Let us first investigate the way in which we apparently have to bring in rationality.

At the symposium (*if* my notes are reliable) Professor Hempel argued on this point that the disposition of rationality "included" this performance amongst many others.

If "included" means that this is an *example* of rational behavior, this is true. If it means that performing this specific act in these specific circumstances is part of the *meaning* of rationality, in the sense that we would have to know about this act in order to be said to understand the term "rational," it is certainly false. But, an intermediate and interesting position seems to me to be true, viz., that this is not only an example of, but a *quasi-necessary consequence* of rationality. Suppose we set out the data thus:

(i) X is in circumstances C, at time T, and desires D.
(ii) In C, the act which appears to A to maximize the likelihood of D is A.
(iii) X is rational at T.
(iv) A rational man does what appears to him to maximize the likelihood of his achieving his desires.

X does A at T.

Premises (i)–(iii) are empirical. Premise (iv) looks like a tautology. Actually (iv) is not quite correct; rationality is not an instantaneous disposition, hence may apply despite an occasional minor lapse. We should include "probably" in it: but that would knock us out of the range of the deductive model immediately and into what Hempel calls statistical explanation. (See next section.) Without doing this, we *almost* have an explanation of behavior resting only on facts and a definition—and we can readily modify this example to give it this feature. (We change [iii] to "X acts rationally at T," and change [iv] to begin "The rational act is doing what. . . .")

But suppose we combine (ii) and (iv). We get L. (L) In C, a rational man does A.

We should now be able to see why this is *not* a tautology. The first reason is that rationality only makes its manifestations probable. This is best handled by putting in "should do" instead of "does": but one can alternatively put in "probably" before "does." Secondly, unless C and A are so fully specified that L is automatically provable, L is informative *about* C. For example, "When the oil pressure drops to zero, a rational man turns off the engine immediately" (L_1). The *reason* for this is that zero oil pressure probably means the lubricating system has failed, and if the engine continues to run it will be ruined, which a rational man typically wishes to avoid. But these facts are not included in L_1 (nor are they quite enough to make L_1 a tautology if they were). L_1 requires that such facts exist, and hence is empirical. (L_1 is in this respect like a claim such as "The explanation of ferromagnetism is to be found in the electronic activities in the constituent molecules.") The reason why L *looks* as if it is tautological is, I think, that it is an evaluative rather than an ordinary descriptive proposition. This means, roughly, that given *all* the relevant facts, L is deductible, i.e., that the conditional with all the facts in the antecedent and "the rational man does A" as the consequence, is a tautology. But propositions like L are not, typically, tautologies, since giving these further facts is not merely amplifying the *meaning* of terms in L.

Nor, on the other hand, are they simply descriptive laws of human nature, like "In C, the Urdu say S." They might be regarded as prudential maxims, informative as to what *should* (rationally) be done; or as one kind of rule ("It's a good rule to follow, to stop immediately the oil pressure drops sharply"). This is, of course, a kind of rule that is true or false empirically, just as other kinds of rules may be true or false logically. (There are even *some* kinds of rule-statement which can be construed as neither true nor false [although it is still common to suppose that *all* rules are like this].) Or we might call them, by analogy with a term coined by Hempel, "tautology-sketches," meaning by this that supplementing them with the detailed facts makes them into tautologies. The disposition of rationality has those specific acts as *necessary consequences* which can be correctly described in such a way as to make it a tautology that a rational man will do them. It is in this sense that one may say the disposition "includes" these acts. (I think "covers" or "implies" are better terms because they avoid the suggestion that the disposition involves some direct reference to such acts.)

The chief conclusion of this, then, is that the general propositions which comprise one of the grounds for an explanation may be tautologies *or* evaluations (maxims, rules, tautology-sketches), as well as ordinary descriptive generalizations.

We must now take notice of some loose ends. I have explained the term 'necessary consequence' above; but in fact virtually no *specific* acts are necessary consequences of rationality for the reason previously mentioned, viz., one sin does not make a sinner. Nevertheless, the connection between a disposition such as rationality and its specific manifestations is more than a merely empirical one. For it is logically impossible that someone be rational and exhibit *none* of these manifestations. For this reason, I have called them quasi-necessary in the preceding. I now wish to subsume this type of connection under the term "normic" which Professor Dray asks me to explicate. A normic consequence of being a rational agent is that he will do A in C at T, where A appears to him to maximize his expectations of his desired goals D. This is what he will *normally* do but special circumstances may lead him to do A′ without destroying his claim to be rational. The proposition L ("In C, a rational man does A") is, we shall say, a normic proposition, even when the descriptions of C and A are incomplete.

It should be immediately stressed, however, that the class of normic statements is very much larger than the class of quasi-necessary consequence statements.

3. STATISTICAL ANALYSIS OF RATIONAL EXPLANATIONS

Hempel suggested that "rational explanations" could be regarded as what he calls statistical explanations. For L, we substitute "In C, a rational man *usually* does A." (L′) (In order to produce a valid statistical explanation we would also have to satisfy the 'requirement of total evidence.' (See Hempel's paper in vol. III of *Minnesota Studies in the Philosophy of Science.*)

This certainly meets the complaint that L is too strong. But L′ is too weak to explain and the accessory requirement of total evidence is too strong.

L′ is too weak to explain because subsumption under an empirical regularity is not, as such, explanatory. If one inquires why a child is sprinkling carpet tacks into his soup and is told that everyone (or almost everyone) in his family does it, this would scarcely be said to *explain* it, i.e., to provide any understanding of it. It merely generalizes the problem. Of course, it *might* be the case that the inquirer understands perfectly how *families* come to do this, and just needed to be told this was a family affair, not some hideous idiosyncrasy. But it is not only difficult to imagine such circumstances, it is clear that if we do so, we have imagined the explanatory part, the subsumption under a law is not of itself (in general) explanatory. (This theme is expanded in "Explanations, Predictions and Laws," a paper by the present author in the same volume as Hempel's essay.) The understanding comes from seeing *why* someone might do such an act—and in the case of human actions this often (not always) means giving reasons. Dray's emphasis on these cases calls attention to an essential factor in explanation wholly missing from the deductive model. But Hempel rightly points out one requirement of "tightness" that Dray underestimates (secs. 2 and 5).

As a technical footnote, the 'requirement of total evidence' has the drawback of being virtually unattainable. If *any* action A is described, we automatically have, from an everyday experience, an enormous amount of evidence about it. Most of this is too vague to be put into precise statistical terms, but even vague evidence may be overwhelming—most scientific and legal evidence is vague in this sense. So it is virtually never the case that the premise about rationality either gives all the evidence or that the rest can be stated.

So the statistical analysis of rational explanations seems to fail for at least these two reasons. Is there another way of handling them within the deductive framework? The first reason for failure precludes any such possibility.

4. THE IRREDUCIBILITY OF NORMIC STATEMENTS

We have not so far given a general characterization of normic statements, and will only do so here in rather general terms. They are a class of statements which claim a preferred status for a particular form of behavior or property with respect to a particular subject class, the nature of this preference being that on theoretical or logical grounds, there are good reasons for believing that deviations from this behavior occur only because of the operation of interference factors—or 'disturbing conditions,' or 'special circumstances.' Normic statements may be empirical, necessary, or evaluative: they often involve terms such as 'naturally,' 'normally,' 'properly,' 'typically,' 'tendency,' 'ought,' 'should,' etc.

A normic statement is not statistical, i.e., not equivalent to a "usually" statement, because (a) it does not entail the "usually" statement, and (b) the "usually" statement does not entail it. The reason for (a) is that the normic statement may refer to an idealized norm which rarely or never occurs. A normic statement from physics illustrates this. The natural (normic) motion of a body (in Newtonian physics) is rectilinear; but *no* bodies in the universe have purely natural motion since they are all acted on by external forces. The reason for (b), from the same example, is that what usually happens exhibits the effects of the usual disturbing factors on the norm, and hence is not the norm. Of course, it is *often* true that the normic behavior *is* the most common, as it was in Aristotelian dynamics ("Bodies naturally tend to a state of rest").

For similar reasons, the normic statement is not equivalent to a probability statement. (This does not in any way indicate support for the idea that probability statements are properly analyzed as statistical ones.) There is a more profound reason why normic statements are not in general analyzable as probability (or statistical) statements. Consider the normic quasi-necessary consequence statement, "In C, a rational man should do A," where C and A are only specified in the usual conversational way, i.e., not fully enough to make a tautology out of it as it stands, although if more fully specified they *would* make it analytic. What kind of probability statement or statistical statement could replace this? It contains the normative term "should," and the usual arguments for the facts-value distinction are in this case conclusive.

Another way of looking at the difference between probability or statistical and normic statements is in terms of their refutability. A probability or statistical claim cannot in general be refuted by a single observation; but a normic statement can, provided that the circumstances attending on the observed phenomenon are also known. For the normic claim can be preserved against a putative contrary instance only if the extenuating circumstances are present, whereas the probability or statistical claim is not irrevocably committed about any particular instance. It is this feature of normic statements that makes them more valuable as grounds for explanations of individual actions than statistical statements.

Another suggestion is that normic statements are simply conditional statements. It *is* perfectly true that many normic statements have a conditional version—but there is no general and useful transformation possible. Instead of talking about the natural motion of bodies, we can say, "If there are no impressed forces acting on a body, it will move rectilinearly." And this is very closely related to (certainly implied by) the plain universal "All bodies under no forces move rectilinearly." However, these dynamical examples are atypical in that the 'extenuating circumstances' *can* be simply stated: the natural motion occurs *unless* there is an impressed force. Normic statements in general are characterized by either the complexity or the anonymity of the qualifying phrases. This irritating feature is the source of their utility: they, like causal claims, can be used to describe or—in a very limited way—to predict, even when we lack the detailed knowledge which enables us to formulate a precise conditional or universal proposition correlative to them. I can make, support, and use the normic statements: "Power corrupts" or "The children of wealthy parents tend to (or typically) exhibit low tolerance of frustration" without having to, or even without being able to, say exactly what conditions make for exceptions.

This inability particularly cripples prediction. But (i) people may be very good at *recognizing* exceptional conditions or their descriptions as such even though they do not know exactly what cues they are responding to and hence cannot describe them. Or (ii) they may know *some* of the interfering factors. And (iii) normic statements often imply a usable statistical prediction, though not vice versa. But it does not have a similarly weakening effect on explanation, for reasons which I have elaborated in the Gardiner volume. Nevertheless, the mere fact that a statement is normic does not make it explanatory: see below.

5. THE DISTINCTION BETWEEN GROUNDS AND CONTENT

Although a 'rational' explanation would not *be* the right explanation unless the man to whom it refers acted in terms of the reasons quoted, this does not prove that the explanation contains or should contain any general law about when he acts rationally which proves he did so act on this occasion. Evidence that he did it for these reasons must be *available*, but this fact may well be accepted by the inquirer, who wants to know something else when he asks why the king signed the estate over to Northumberland—he wants to know why the king so acted in the sense of *what* his reasons were, not why he so acted in the sense of *whether* he did so for some reasons as compared to by accident or in a trance, etc. An explanation cannot and should not have to include all the grounds required to defend it against attacks or further inquiries. It should only contain the information needed to provide the understanding required. And even then its grounds do not have to be general laws of the kind Hempel and Nowell-Smith think are necessary: Dray is right to deny their request. But he goes too far, I think. For he also seems to deny the legitimate request that there should be some such connection *available*. And it seems to me that putting forward an explanation in terms of reasons absolutely requires that one be *able* to render plausible the implied claim that this man did act from these reasons. However, trying to do this via what Nowell-Smith calls a 'portentous platitude,' such as that "rational men who have worked out approximate plans tend to act on them unless prevented" is not quite good enough. This truism is an important part of the grounds—but it cannot serve alone. Another important part of the grounds is the judgment that *no other potentially explanatory factors are present*. The peculiar nature of this claim needs further discussion, but not here. Its necessity must be self-evident since several potentially sufficient conditions may precede an event which only one of them actually brings about. But this pinning-down requirement is omitted in *both* Hempel's and Dray's accounts.

6. EXPLAINING MISTAKES AND IRRATIONAL, ILL-JUDGED, OR ILL-THOUGHT-OUT ACTIONS

"It is obvious," says Dray, "that we cannot claim rational understanding of the making of a logical error. . . ." On Dray's analysis the understanding in what he calls rational explanations is due to the *soundness* of the reasoning. But surely the soundness is not crucial; the understanding comes from seeing the *appeal* of the reasons—and of course reasons can look good, and hence appeal, although they are not. Dray legislates that explanations which refer to the appeal of bad reasons are not 'rational explanations.' But I do not think there is any value in using such a restrictive class. "Understanding is achieved," he says, "when the historian can see the reasonableness of a man's doing what this agent did, given the beliefs and purposes referred to. . . ." But if the historian can play the role of judging reasonableness with respect to beliefs he knows to be false, he can equally well do it with respect to inferences which he knows are logically unsound. In both cases it is possible for him to understand the action *only* if he can understand how a man *might well* have such beliefs and make such slips. I think Dray's own example about William of Orange exhibits errors of (inductive) logic.

My suggestion, then, is that we should consider all such explanations in terms of thought processes (possibly good or bad, but necessarily plausible) as essentially similar, and call them reasons-, or motivation-, or purpose-explanations. This will include explanations in terms of unconscious motives, where and if these can be made plausible. Is it really unfair to suggest that this new category is the old bogeyman of teleological explanation in a respectable form?

So we may understand why X did A, namely because he thought it would achieve D, without at all thinking his judgment was defensible. But it is another question to ask exactly why he made this error of judgment. Sometimes we say it was a 'natural error'—a small slip made under great pressure, a confusion of two terms not previously adequately distinguished. Sometimes we invoke the Sage of Sexual Symbolism, and doubtless we shall soon use more neurological and psychoacoustical explanations. But Dray need not fear that allowing teleological explanations of acts where the reasoning is faulty will involve us in the much harder task of explaining the faults, for which—typically—a nonteleological explanation is required. The teleological explanation of an act as based on an error of judgment requires only the *plausibility* of the error—not an *explanation* of it. "Plausibility" here means "comprehensibility of the fact *that* it occurred," not "probability of a particular explanation of *why* it occurred."

". . . one cannot rethink a practical argument one knows to be invalid," says Dray, but rather unsympathetically, I believe. I have no difficulty in rethinking the argument which led me to conclude that determinism is incompatible with responsibility, though I now know very well that and why it is invalid.

7. THE PRIORITY OF RATIONAL EXPLANATIONS

Dray has now sharply qualified his original presumption of rationality. But he still believes that "historians give priority to the search for rational explanations over nonrational ones." I think the only sense of "nonrational" in which this would be a defensible practice by historians is that in which they select, from several types of perfectly sound explanations of a particular act, the one which bears on the type of interest we have; for example, we may pick an explanation in terms of sound reasons over the correlated neurophysiological one (which is "nonrational" for Dray). We could never make this kind of interest-motivated choice of a good-reasons-explanation (Dray's "rational explanation") over an *irrational* one (also "nonrational" for Dray) since only one of these can be true.

In supporting the reasons-explanation we must have grounds for supposing the man did act in terms of what he took to be good reasons, viz., the ones we quote. And these (role-justifying) grounds may well include the truism that intelligent men tend to do this when the matter is of importance and time for deliberation is available; other grounds (mostly particular) will also be required; but no other "presumption of rationality" is required. Now some of Dray's critics are wrong in supposing that any particular form of such a proposition must be in mind, let alone in the explanation, since any version of it will do, with more or less qualifying phrases than the one quoted, provided the correspondingly appropriate antecedent conditions can also be supplied—and other kinds of proposition will also do, e.g., one listing the only significantly likely causes of the action in question plus negative antecedent conditions which rule out all but the effect of reasons. But I think Dray is still overstating the case when he says "Any 'presumption of rationality' is thus logically quite different from what methodologists and logicians would mean by a covering law." Not its nature but its role has been misconceived. It is a ground, not a part of the explanation; and as such may take many forms, provided only that other grounds are also available to make the total effect one of support for the explanation.

8. DISPARITY OF CERTAINTY BETWEEN EXPLANATION AND LAW

The preceding account makes it easier to see how the use of vague truisms as grounds for explanations enables them to meet Sir Isaiah Berlin's complaint (that the deductive model insists that the historian should employ laws when these are obviously less well-supported than the explanations themselves). What have we *got* to be able to establish in order that a reasons-explanation be sound? Only that reasons were operative here and that the operative reasons were the ones quoted. We can do this (if we are challenged) in several ways.

First we may toss down the gauntlet of some normic truism about rational men. Its function is to test the challenger's mettle. He may reject it, or accept it with or without conditions. If he rejects it, we add some more qualifying clauses (from the stock of conditions which we know can be met in this case) until we meet his demands or can show them to be unreasonable by appeal to general principles of evidence, or concede the force of his criticism. If he accepts it conditionally, we proceed to show that it does apply by showing that the antecedent conditions he requires are present. Unconditional acceptance is victory.

Or we may go the elimination route, via the counter-challenge procedure: What else could the explanation be, we ask, relying only on the virtually unassailable truism that the reasons quoted *could*—if the other circumstances are right—make a man do what this man did. The reasons are a possible cause and must be *the* cause if no other candidate is present, whereas they are. And here we implicitly appeal to another truism "Important human actions must have a cause." Both these assumed truisms may be assailed as inconclusive here and will then have to be defended by the first strategy mentioned. But if they are not assailed, we proceed to establish our explanatory claim by elimination of the competition. (I here take as obvious that reasons-explanations are a species of causal explanation: objections to date have been based on confusion as to the nature of causes.)

All this is part of *justifying* an explanation, not part of an explanation. And in the context of justifying an explanation of a normal kind we only have to handle *demonstrably relevant* doubts about it. Hence the dialectic procedure given above is absolutely adequate. But if we had to state our dialectic truisms as precise unconditional laws, i.e., in a form that covers all known behavior, we would be powerless. So it is the deductive model's apparently minor peccadillo, the amalgamation of the grounds with the explanation proper, that has the calamitous effect of requiring what cannot be given—or of giving what cannot be taken seriously—precise general laws about human behavior.

Let us briefly rehearse the application of these remarks to Dray's example from Trevelyan about Louis XIV. Reasons are offered as the factors that led Louis to withdraw pressure from Holland in 1688. There being nothing inherently absurd in the suggestion, the reader will normally accept this as information. No more need be said if the historian is merely seeking to inform us. But he may be challenged by an expert, or he may be writing about a disputed point and wish to meet possible challenges in advance. Let us see what he then does. The explanation might be challenged on the grounds that the considerations mentioned were unknown to Louis. In reply we produce what I have elsewhere called our truth-justifying grounds, our evidence that he *did* know the facts referred to as his reasons. Next, it may be suggested that, although he knew of these facts, perhaps even believed them to be what led him to act, the real explanation might well be something else. It is at this point we begin the truism approach, and the only possible counters to it consist in showing (a) that *in this case* factors are present which constitute exceptions to the (usually normic) truism, or (b) that a *better* explanation is also possible—possibly even another reasons-explanation. (However well we build up one explanation we must still check to see if there is a better one.) The preferred truisms thus do not have to be defended against counterexamples in the *whole field of human behavior,* but only defended for their relevance *here.*

But how could a truism in which one lacks general belief be explanatory in a particular case? It looks as if I am suggesting that one can continue to explain something by appeal to a false law. First, the 'law' is not the explanation. It is a part of the grounds for supposing that a proposed (and non-lawlike) explanation *is* the explanation. In order to make this plausible, against the current challenge, the historian appealing to the truism must in the first place show that the suggested explanation is of a kind that *could* in this case provide an explanation. And the truism, unless proved irrelevant here, does this. In order to show that the suggested explanation actually *does* account for the action, we would have to have grounds for supposing no other significantly likely candidates were present—*and we need those grounds anyway, whether we have a loose truism or a precise general law.*

9. DISPENSABILITY OF LAWS

This is, I think, the key logical point of historical methodology. *The strength that a general law has by comparison with a possibility statement is logically redundant for explanatory purposes.* And hence we can have good historical explanations without having good predictive laws: from (1) "Y is a possible explanation of X, and was present" and (2) "No other plausible explanation of X appears to have been present," it follows that Y is *the* (most plausible) explanation of X, subject to the usual assumption that there is an explanation for everything.

Five comments: (i) We usually get 1 from a relevant normic statement. If causal explanations are being sought, it must be a normic causal statement; in any case it must be one that expresses a comprehensible connection, in order to get 1. (ii) It is much easier to get 2 than it might seem: where studying deliberate actions, as in so much of history, we normally get it from truisms about people tending to act to maximize their expectations of reward (as they see them) plus an inventory of interests—but in criminology and medicine we can often use more precise lists of all known possible causes, where these cover almost all cases. And sometimes we find people develop a capacity to identify possible explanations from an examination of the circumstances surrounding an event although they cannot list them exhaustively. Their judgment that only one such is present may be shown to be very reliable by subsequent events, on many occasions, so that their failure to respond with more than one suggestion becomes good evidence for 2. Many of us can do something very like this about grammatical and spelling peculiarities ("This way just sounds/looks right, and the others do not"), and fishermen, clinicians, auto mechanics, psychoanalysts, and perhaps historians develop such skills in the explanatory field. (iii) Dray says, "There is no assumption in history (as there may be in physical science) that everything is, in principle, explicable." (I believe he means "explicable in historical terms.") Although true (as is the corresponding claim of indeterminism in physics, for different reasons), this is rather misleading. For in the very domain of Dray's main interest, the analysis of reason-controlled behavior, the opposite generalization is almost true; there has to be some reason for a deliberate act. And there are many other subject areas in history where we are rightly confident that there *must* be an (historical) explanation, e.g., of recessions, wars, and periods of great artistic fecundity. In an even wider range of cases we believe there is *probably* an explanation at our level of interest. So historical indeterminism is no handicap to eliminative analysis of the kind mentioned. Notice that believing there is a cause in a particular case is usually justified even if *some* exceptions are known to the generalization *and* we fail to find a cause here; for the likelihood we have missed one that is present is greater than the likelihood that this is one of the truly exceptional cases. Of course, we sometimes discover entirely new causes, for example in medicine, economics, and technology, and for this and sometimes for other reasons we make mistakes about claims like 2 above. But we can make mistakes with equal facility about any general proposition which the deductive model would have us employ. (iv) We are still calling on laws in *backing* or *thinking* of several of these explanations. But even when reasonably precise these are laws of a very special kind, e.g., "All murders are committed from motives of revenge, lust, jealousy, hate, greed, or fear"—they are *lists of possible explanations. They cannot be used to predict the effect they explain.* That someone is jealous of a rival (and not greedy, etc.) does not make it *at all* likely he will kill his rival—

though it makes it *more* likely than if he had none of these feelings. These are not the kind of laws which proponents of the deductive model have had in mind or the famous 'symmetry thesis' about explanations and predictions would never have been proposed. ("Any proper explanation must provide grounds from which one could have predicted the phenomenon explained.) And I believe they also refute Hempel's suggestion at the symposium that any good *statistical* explanation must be such as to show that the explained event "was to be expected." (v) Reasons for thinking that a premise of the form of 2 must be provided *even when we have predictive laws,* whether exceptionless or statistical, will be found on page 229 of "Explanations, Predictions and Laws," in Minnesota Studies, volume III. It follows that (even as grounds) we only need possible-cause claims like 1, and not general-law claims, as Hempel thought; for even the latter requires a type 2 claim, and a type 2 claim is strong enough to enable the deduction of an explanation with the help of a mere type 1 claim, much weaker than a general law. So the answer to Berlin's problem is simple: general laws of the usual kind (i.e., predictively useful) are not needed to enable informative deductions of explanations. And the 'generalizations' that are needed are readily available.

10. ELEMENTS OF AN ALTERNATIVE ANALYSIS OF EXPLANATIONS

On my account, Hempel is right in thinking that some loose generalizations about how reasonable men behave are somehow connected with rational explanations. But Dray is right in thinking they do not and should not have to form part of the explanations: since they may be merely possible grounds for it. But Hempel is also wrong in thinking that statistical regularities are the useful class of such generalizations. If explanation were the same as inference, he would have a case; but since inferability does not of itself provide understanding, we need a narrower class. (Yet since inferability of an explanation is not the same as inferability of the event explained, the class can be wider in another dimension.) The first extra requirement is that any generalization employed in the explanation or in its role-justifying grounds must be *comprehensible,* i.e., it must either be already understood why such a generalization holds, or plausible to claim that it does—i.e., it must at least not contravene other well-understood general principles.

But there is also the problem of exactly *how* we can demonstrate the revelance of an explanatory generalization. The understanding must not be lost in the transition to the individual case. The relation of a simple universal claim to a particular instance seems immediate enough: if we understand how the generalization can be true, surely we also understand how one of its particular cases can be true. But there is something wrong here; for if we understand the generalization it would normally be because we already or simultaneously understand its instances—yet it is about one of these we are inquiring. We need a further requirement; the generalization must either be understood *other* than via its instances, or must be shown to bear on the particular case via another particular or general assertion not previously known, or not previously seen to have this combinatory power; or its relevance may be simple but hitherto overlooked. I shall call this the requirement of *informative relevance,* and I take it to replace inferability.

Now the relevance of universal or normic statements to a particular case is, compared with statistical ones, much more direct. But the statistical statement *plus* the requirement of total evidence justifies an individual probability statement and so gives equally direct relevance to the particular case, and that requirement is part of Hempel's analysis of statistical explanation. However, as previously mentioned, the requirement can scarcely if ever be met. And since true universal statements about behavior can scarcely if ever be found (definitional truths apart), we need to look carefully at the normics. To be revelant to the case in hand, a normic must not be annulled by the presence of abnormal circumstances, extenuating conditions, etc. If these could be exhaustively listed, the normic would simply be shorthand for a complex universal statement with the absence of these conditions as the antecedent. The most important fact about normic statements is that, like causal statements, they can often be known and useful without it being possible to *state* all the special conditions on which their truth depends. Their function is like that of tactical rules in chess or bridge. "Deploy your pawns early," "Second hand plays low," "Don't trump your partner's tricks"; these are all good sound rules—but none are exceptionless generalizations about good play. The experienced player gradually develops his capacity to recognize exceptions. He can, if asked, mention some specific cases which would constitute exceptions. He may even be able to classify these to some extent. But he is nearly always much better at spotting exceptions than anyone who simply read what he could write out about it. The same is true of our normic statements—power corrupts, a rational man tries to maximize expectations of utility, etc. We are better able to spot exceptions than name them; the many cues of the actual situation trigger off unconscious reactions long built in by experience, here as in linguistic contexts where we can easily speak grammatically but hardly state a precise, exceptionless rule of grammar.

Nor are there any grounds for supposing the gap between skill and applicable description of the cues on which the skill depends, to be merely a matter needing a little experimental investigation to take care of it. It is quite certain that the existing vocabulary cannot describe the configural, gestalt cues to which we respond in linguistic or behavioral contexts; and it is very likely that no vocabulary could be devised for the purpose which could be learned any faster than we currently learn the skill of responding. Statability is a fetish in the antimetaphysical phases of philosophy. I think the great truth in the *Verstehen* theories is their implicit and badly conceptualized recognition of the *indispensability* and *efficiency* of the historian's capacity to respond to the cues in a well-described situation, so that he may with justifiable confidence accept or propose a particular reasons-explanation as correct, knowing the truth of the relevant normic truism and knowing that he would have noticed if any annulling conditions were present. (This is like the reaction of a skilled calculator when asked if 811 is a prime number.)

Dray's rational explanations typically include no generalizations, but those produced to *defend* them are normic truisms that are comprehensible because they are either definitional, or are quasi-necessary consequences of either definitions or plausible psychological claims ("Rejected lovers often make bitter enemies"). That is, we *understand* his rational explanations because we, too, can reason (and hence can see them as *possible* explanations); and the grounds produced if we doubt this are usually informatively relevant for obvious reasons. But we should not accept them as actual explanations unless we can show them operative for the man, the place, and the time we are discussing—and to do this we need a further set of grounds both particular and general, or skill in the recognition of exceptional circumstances and alternative possible causes.

11. LIMITED-SCOPE LAWS

When we are talking of historical explanations in general, rather than reasons-explanations of actions, we note they may use many types of generalization. Amongst these are some with limited scope in time of the kind discussed by Rescher, Joynt, and Helmer. Dray's criticism of these is, I think, weak. He suggests they must be derived from unrestricted generalizations and hence are no different from ordinary covering-law explanations. But (a) it is not clear in his example that the subsuming generalization is universal; (b) even if it were, it is *not* part of the explanation, which provides the required understanding via the limited-range generalization alone—it is simply a possible ground; (c) deduction from an unrestricted law is simply *one* way to make a generalization comprehensible (by no means always effective), and it is easy to think of other limited-scope 'laws' which are comprehensible without this having to be done, e.g., "Until Arizona was fully settled and the military unnecessary, the proportion of women settlers was considerably less than half"; (d) It is erroneous to think that particularity, in one or several dimensions, is fatal to explanatory power. Laws expressed as mathematical functions which have *no two instances the same* are a perfectly good basis for explanation, hence generalizations in the usual sense, which ascribe a property to classes with several members, are not the paradigm of the kind of generality needed for underwriting explanations. (See Appendix to "Truisms as the Grounds for Historical Explanations"); (e) *if* we were to accept Dray's argument for rejecting this kind of limited-scope law as explanatory, it is impossible not to reject his own rational explanations; both may require substantiation *as explanations* by appeal to higher level generalizations (although *as an argument* the content of a rational explanation is—by definition—sound); (f) not only does deduction from an unrestricted generalization *not* guarantee comprehensibility, but even the generality of such laws in one simple sense may be less than that of limited-scope laws: the latter may have an infinite number of instances and the former a finite number. Scope, range, number of instances—these are *not* an analysis of comprehensibility but its occasional dull trappings.

CONCLUSION

I should like to go on to discuss several further interesting points in Dray's discussion of more general problems, such as his analyses of the concepts of necessary condition, libertarianism, and history, but I am certain this would considerably prolong an already overlong paper. I conclude by joining with him most heartily in his view that to conceive of historical explanation in terms of subsumption under laws places a serious and unwarranted barrier in the way of a proper understanding of the historically interesting actions of men.

BIBLIOGRAPHICAL REFERENCES

Dray, William. "The Historical Explanation of Actions Reconsidered." This volume.

———. *Laws and Explanation in History*. Oxford, 1957.

Hempel, C. G. "The Function of General Laws in History." Reprinted in Gardiner, P. (ed.). *Theories of History*. Glencoe, Ill., 1959.

———. "Deductive-Nomological vs. Statistical Explanation." Published in *Minnesota Studies in the Philosophy of Science*, vol. III. Minnesota, 1962.

Scriven, M. J. "Explanations, Predictions and Laws." Published in Feigl, H. and G. Maxwell (eds.).

———. "Truisms as the Grounds for Historical Explanations." Reprinted in Gardiner, P. (ed.). *Op. cit.*

24

History as Spirit

STEN H. STENSON
Smith College

THE FACT that metaphysical idealism is now in general disrepute, both in philosophical and theological circles, should not deter us from recognizing the appositeness of some idealist approaches to certain epistemological problems concerning our knowledge of the past. The papers which Professors White and Gershoy read before this symposium, and their off-the-cuff remarks during the discussion afterward, are particularly suggestive of two familiar idealist themes: (1) that all things, including all historical events, are ideas (meanings); and (2) that these meanings are manifestations of human will (freedom).

The fact that historical events *are* meanings, among other things, and that these meanings *are* the results of complex skeins of human choices makes the two theses of metaphysical idealism that I have mentioned extremely relevant: first, to White's philosophical wonder concerning the odd way in which contrary historical interpretations proliferate and compete against each other; second, to Gershoy's candid description of his selective procedure in actually composing history.

White's essay expresses not only a criteriological puzzlement, but an exquisite natural piety. Neither is the result of philosophical confusion, but of a more than common clarity. To any philosopher still capable of enough innocence to see it, nothing is more awesome than that meanings occur as they do. They often seem to bloom by spontaneous generation, revolutionary thoughts springing from hackneyed contexts, as though the mythical act of God's original Creation *ex nihilo* were continuous in man. No mere *theory* of mind sufficiently explains the fantastic common fact that meanings appear on the face of matter. They are the eruption of a cosmos out of chaos. There is *mana* in the enormous, unpredictable exfoliation of ideas, and perceptive men, like primitive men, are aware of it. Nevertheless, the point I wish to make here is philosophical, not religious or even poetic. Keep White's criteriological problem in mind. How are we to understand the fact that there are times when we lack criteria for determining which, if any, of rival descriptions of the past are a true account of the world?

Of course, historical events are matters which we must be able to *think*. We must be able to include them, with all sorts of other things we believe are the case, or which we take for granted, in our overall understanding of our experience. In this sense at least, historical events have a spiritual dimension. They are *signs* which are, or could be, colored by the broader significance of some historian's interpretative vision. Indeed, if an historical event is ever *really* significant—if it becomes a sign which really *is* read—then it cannot escape the valorizing tincture of some historian's spirit. It will reflect his idiosyncratic point of view, and that of his culture refracted through that prism. Matters which are, thus, more than mere possibilities of historical events, are each of them complex phenomena involving the *matter* which is explained, the explanatory *form*, and the *community* of discourse of whose experience that event is an organic part. Both White and Gershoy illuminate the fact that each matter explained—the traditional union of form and matter—is, like Wittgenstein's duck-rabbit,[1] the occasion for a possible eruption of a plurality of meanings, some of which are candidates demanding to be chosen in lieu of others as privileged significations of that sign for the community of discourse to whom those possible interpretations present themselves.

The historian is a member, maybe the sole member, of some community. His special function is to choose among meanings broadly called "historical," and to defend them before the bar of public opinion, as those which shall be valorized as "true." The very *appearance* of a plethora of significant possibilties; his, perhaps, equally spontaneous *selection* of some of them as "true"; and the *elaboration* (or adoption) of the general scheme of things which valorizes them as such, literally constitutes the soul of the historian—the experience, reason, and morality which he hopes to contribute to his community. The historian and his society are one aspect of "the world and the individual." The *content* of truth—i.e., the substance of statements which are destined (but not necessarily determined) to be judged as true—and the *form* (the logic or criteria) of truth are both largely social products.[2]

"Truth" is a word as ambiguous as most words; certainly it has many proper uses. Even the term, "historical truth," has myriad conventional designations depending on how it is used. The criteria of truth and its content are, thus, both *chosen* in the sense that the meanings of all words are chosen by individuals and communities in the presence of brute intrusions of matters which evoke verbalized experience. The existence of the past in the present—history—accordingly involves human freedom; and history writing is, as a consequence, a profoundly moral and cosmically significant activity.

Gershoy's paper nicely illustrates the moral aspect of the historian's trade: the ineluctable necessity to choose among all sorts of inchoate facts and nascent values in a way that must inevitably influence men's lives profoundly, if they listen to historians. That which is, in one sense, the *same* event for two radically differently oriented historians, is, in a deeper sense, only the occasion (the matter) in which two radically dissimilar events start unfolding. In such cases the truth-value of historical statements is still only *ideal* and not yet real. The truth-value that will accrue to these rival explanations of the past has not yet had time to develop, and that which does accrue to them will depend, in large part, on the cultural commitments and passions of the community to whom the historical statements in question are addressed.

Truth has no existence independent of some conventional use of the word "truth," nor does the past exist outside of some narrative account or memory. The past, then, is not finished, and it is philosophically confusing to think of it as though it were. The tricky thing about asking what *truly* happened in the past—as though the subjective element in all answers heretofore were undesirable and could be avoided—is that, by his very asking and answering, an historian becomes a part of the very past he chooses to investigate. He *enters* that past (so to speak) if he can manage it—or (perhaps to speak more properly), it enters him. As Gershoy points out, the historian's situation is analogous, in this respect, to that ascribed to physicists in certain other situations, by the Heisenberg indeterminacy principle. But the historian is *always* in such a predicament: his own spirit is always an integral part of the very matter he investigates. The past *in itself* does not exist. And yet we keep asking questions about the past as though it did.

Rather than comparing history to particular situations within the general experience of modern physics, compare it to a more obviously social activity. Think of prophecy, for instance. No matter how secular an historian's orientation may be, his situation is similar, in certain important respects, to that of the Old Testament prophets. The prophets also were historians, although religious ones, and they were quite aware of the fact that they could not read signs without themselves becoming part of the signs that they read and of the truth that was thereupon established in the Chosen (choosing) People.[3] In general, truth is an eschatological concept, and historical truth, for all its historicity, is no exception. Whether or not he likes what he sees, or approves the way things are going, the most secular historian, like the most God-inspired prophet, is a man who is trying to finish the past in a certain direction. There is an integration of the past and the present with the future, and a fusion of the cosmos with each individual and his society that makes a philosophy of history only an evanescent fad, if it does not recognize the extent to which the human spirit is a continuous part of the world it describes. The world is a *meaning*—a mysterious appearance of signs read with wonderful intelligence. Since, to a large extent, both its form and its content are freely chosen by its interpreters, they will repeatedly experience the kind of criteriological consternation that White's paper expresses, and Gershoy's, in practice, ignores. Historians, after all, must write history, while philosophers wonder how it is possible.

NOTES

1. Ludwig Wittgenstein, *Philosophical Investigations* (New York: Macmillan and Co., 1953), p. 194.

2. Cf. Josiah Royce, *The Problem of Christianity* (New York: Macmillan Co., 1913), II, Lectures XI–XIV. Royce acknowledges his indebtedness to C. S. Peirce's theory of signs. See also, Royce, *The World and the Individual* (New York: Dover, 1959), II, Lectures I and II. The spirit, both of Royce's remarks and my own, is intended to be broadly pragmatic and not essentially in conflict with those expressed, for instance, by John Dewey in *The Quest for Certainty*, chap. V, *passim*.

3. Cf. Martin Buber, *The Prophetic Faith* (New York: Harper & Bros., 1960), pp. 54–59, *passim*.

25

It's About Time

PAUL WEISS
Yale University

THE HISTORIANS and the philosophers in this symposium rarely made contact. Few issues were joined, and as a consequence neither group derived much benefit from the other. This in part was due to the fact, I think, that not enough attention was paid to first principles. Much was blurred because observations were made on the basis of divergent and often unexamined assumptions. It's about time that someone tried to state the first principles on which a satisfactory discussion of the nature of history depend. I offer the following in the hope that it may help bring some of the discussion into better focus.

1. THE FIELD OF HISTORICAL INQUIRY AND THE FIELD OF HISTORIC OCCURRENCES ARE DISTINCT

Relativists—most of whom seem to be practicing historians—tend to overlook this fact. As a consequence they tend to suppose that there is no history other than what historians present, or that there is such a history but that it cannot be known. It's about time that historical inquiry was recognized to be an effective agency for coming to know a realm of happenings which took place before the historian interested himself in it.

2. HISTORICAL NARRATIVES ARE ABOUT HISTORIC OCCURRENCES

Idealists, who seem to make up one of the most influential bodies of philosophers of history, tend to deny this. But then they cannot explain how an historical narrative can be right, wrong, distortive, incomplete. It's about time that we made explicit the conditions which make it possible for a history to be true.

3. THE PAST CAN BE ENCOUNTERED

Historians take this for granted; philosophers ignore the fact. But unless the past can be encountered, there would be no way of determining whether or not what an historian says is true. History would then be indistinguishable from fiction. It's about time we took account of the fact that the past is accumulated and has a role in the present, enabling the historian to check his inferences.

4. HISTORY IS AN AUTONOMOUS ENTERPRISE

Historians take this for granted; philosophers, particularly those in this symposium, tend to deny it. The philosophers were inclined to treat history as though it were a branch of science, logic, or sociology. But a war, a peace treaty, an alliance, though as intelligible as a neutron, as structured as an inference, and as humanly conditioned as a business, have distinctive natures, origins, rhythms, and effects. It's about time that history was recognized to have its own methods, objectives, criteria, and finality.

5. HISTORIC OCCURRENCES HAVE A DISTINCTIVE TEMPORAL SPONSOR

Both historians and philosophers tend to ignore this fact, perhaps because it seems so obvious. An historic occurrence takes place in a present which stretches over a number of the moments appropriate to nonhistoric occurrences. It's about time we asked ourselves how it is possible for there to be presents of different lengths—or what is the same question from another side, how it is possible for the historic and the nonhistoric worlds to be related to one another.

6. AN HISTORIC PRESENT IS INSEPARABLE FROM A PAST AND A FUTURE

All historians and some philosophers—unfortunately not conspicuous at this symposium—know this to be true. They know that the past and the future effectively condition the nature of the historic present, and that any attempt to isolate the present or to subdivide it will involve a loss of something distinctively historic. But this must be reconciled with the fact that a present is precisely that which succeeds a past and precedes a future. It's about time we faced up to the distinctive problems which revolve about the historic present.

7. HISTORIC OCCURRENCES TAKE PLACE IN A DISTINCTIVE HISTORIC SPACE

Historians tend to confound historic space with terrain; philosophers ignore even the terrain. Physical space has room only for physical time, dancing space has room only for dancing time. Historic time moves over no space at all, or over a distinctive historic space. It's about time we took account of the fact that there are many different types of space, and that only one is appropriate to history.

8. HISTORIC OCCURRENCES HAVE A DISTINCTIVE DYNAMISM

Theological and philosophic historians have noted this. But there has been little effort made to understand how it can be. A distinctive historic space and time are traversed in a distinctive historic process. It's about time we attended to the fact that there is a use of energy, and there are changes and causal activity in history which are not to be identified with the kinds of uses, changes, and activities that occur in other domains.

9. ALL HISTORY IS GOVERNED BY AN IDEAL END

This contention seems to lend support to philosophical historians and their teleologies. Their excesses are avoided when account is taken of the fact that the ideal operates through and is affected by the present. Without such operation much that had occurred in history would, because irrelevant to the present, be now without an historic role. The ideal enables these items to be relevant. It's about time that we reexamined the entire question of teleology and its bearing on history.

10. THE PAST HAS AN OBJECTIVE REALITY

Historians take this for granted; the philosophers of the symposium pay no attention to it. A failure of nerve keeps many philosophers from facing hard metaphysical questions. The past is excluded by and excludes the present. But having passed away it has no power to exclude, and has no being which can be excluded. The past has being only because it is sustained by some power, only because it, though it passes away, is endowed with sufficient existence to exclude and be excluded by what is now taking place. It's about time we asked ourselves what history presupposes in order for it and its parts to have reality.

It's about time that contemporary philosophers freed themselves from their positivistic and naturalistic bias and the accompanying attempt to deal with history as though it were some other subject. If they do, they will find that what they say might have some relevance to what historians do and know. The historians in turn will then be able to make use of the distinctions and benefit from the understanding which a large-minded philosophy promotes. It's about time that philosophers and historians contributed to one another's enlightenment.

26

Essentials in History

DONALD C. WILLIAMS
Harvard University

THIS CONFERENCE of historians and philosophers was so remarkably near unanimity that there is little or no philosophically important difference, logical, epistemological, or ontological, between history and the natural sciences, or between either of them and the fact-finding of everyday business. In one respect very heartening, this agreement might have been taken to imply that since the philosophy of science is the more highly developed discipline, the common problems of scientific and historical knowledge should be left to it, while the philosophers of history either disband or turn to the other pursuit sometimes mentioned under their title, what might be called the cosmology of history, large speculative theories of human destiny, which has recently been almost ignored in favor of critical methodology and theory of knowledge. I think indeed that such historical world views may be the medium in which the best of our philosophers of history can best serve the public in this catastrophic age, but the notion that historians and historical philosophers would be no loss to the general inquiry into the forms of scientific knowledge is shown false, I think, by our conference itself, but also could have been corrected by general theoretical considerations. Just because history and natural science do converge by the same logical principles on the same sum of events and objects, the difference of level and angle between the historian's and the scientist's views can valuably compensate the inadequacies of each. The historian's advantage is partly a function, no doubt, of his humane and literate training, partly his lofty habit of looking at things from the topside, through the eyes of the lords of the earth, and partly also his own actual quite humble status—for except for some few advisors and apologists in the ménage of our national administration, historians have no official position to maintain our much occasion to dramatize themselves as keeping the keys of life and death. While they are devoted, professional, and self-conscious knowers, moreover, their concern with objects of middle size and familiar sorts saves them from the distortions and distractions to which the epistemology of the physical sciences is subject by reason of the grotesquerie of its objects, the enormous costs of its research, and the godlike destructiveness of its results, which are easily deemed to be philosophically more significant than they are. Historians and philosophers of history, much less tempted to enlist under the morose and stylized orthodoxies which succeed each other in the sister disciplines, remain in a refreshing state of enterprise and innocence.

Though the questions ventilated by this Institute impinged and interacted in a fairly complicated way, they were principally these two: first, what are the historian's characteristic responsibilities? second, do they make him especially liable to subjectivity and caprice? The replies to the first question, and consequently to the second, were bound to be somewhat arbitrary because both in popular usage and college catalogues "history" covers a wide gamut, and neither of the two principal philosophical speakers, Professor White and Professor Dray, would hold that there is a single authoritative Essence of History laid up in heaven, nor that any particular academic officer should lose his stripes for varying from it. What they did was to try to locate a median procedure among those pursued by persons commonly called "historians," and to make some recommendations about it.

Both Mr. White and Mr. Dray take off from a pair of propositions which seemed to be generally approved, that history is narration of socially significant events, and that it differs from mere chronicle in that it exhibits the links by which the events *explain* their successors. I suspect that the latter of these may already be too stringent, for it seems harsh to deny the title "historian" to a man who produces a fluently coherent chronicle, but I realize that this may be only because our inveterate knowingness would in such a case insist on reading explanatory connections between the lines. Beyond this their main proposals about the nature of the typically historical explanatory nexus were different, not because they conflicted but only because they were addressed to different matters. Again, however, both seem a little rigoristic, Mr. White's in the *amount* of causal consecutiveness he demands and Mr. Dray's in the *kind*.

Mr. White, to be more specific, requires two kinds of connection in the historian's narrative, in traditional terms a unity of substance and also a unity of cause, and these make some difficulty for each other. The first requirement is his prescription that a historical narrative have a single subject, and is so far from being too stringent that it needs a gloss to save it from triviality. This is because, as he would be the first to concede, the world does not afford a complete and aboriginal roster of primary substances or "real" subjects, metaphysically consolidated within and insulated without, and conversely any designable fragment or sum of things, properties, or events is sufficiently a "subject" to meet the fundamental logical and ontological requirements, but not, I surmise, the requirement which Mr. White intends. If a "subject" is just a logically individual entity, then for any event, A, there are an infinity of subjects in whose histories A is an episode, and for every two events, A and B, there are an infinity of subject-histories to which both belong, and also an infinity of subject-histories to which one belongs but not the other. An explosion in New Jersey and an election in California belong to the different historical subjects, New Jersey and California, respectively, and also to the different subjects, American politics and modern industrial accidents; but nonetheless they *both* belong to the history of the United States, both to the history of the Earth, both to the history of the discontinuous object which is the sum of New Jersey and California, and to countless other subjects, continuous and discontinuous, concrete and abstract, including the minimal common subject which is the sum of just that explosion and that election. I think that Mr. White means by "a subject" a continuant like New Jersey *or* California, with more cohesion and saliency than their sum though not necessarily with as much as a man or a boulder, and I think he can rely on our having a sufficient intuitive grasp of this loose but familiar notion, including that trait which I indicate by saying his subjects are "substantial" also in being *concrete*. This contrasts them with any event, which is abstract, with any pair of events, which is both discontinuous and abstract, and with any string of events or what we may call "an abstract continuant." These bits of topical metaphysics are pertinent because they equip us to cope with Mr. White's statement that there may be different true histories of the same subject, and to give their respective rights both to him and to those like Mr. Mandelbaum and Mr. Tomas (if I remember correctly) who demurred at the idea. The latter philosophers surely did not dispute that no one "history," in the sense in which a history is a narration, can ever exhaust *the* total real history of a concretum, in the sense in which its "history" is what actually happens in and to the subject; nor can they intend the mere truism that contrary propositions cannot be true of the same individual. What they had in mind, I believe, was that one might take as the subject, or mean by "the subject," of a history an abstract continuant rather than a concrete one: the adoption of the Constitution, say, or the fluctuations of the stock market. This is the point of their allusions to "aspects" and "facets." Even such subjects are often so complicated as to leave room for supplementary accounts, but it is easy to conceive one so abstract that it does not. The changing population of Middlesex County, for example, that is, the sheer succession of numbers, is a "subject" quite exhausted in one very thin little history. In fact, we need not have gone to even this much trouble, for at the same time that every history ostensibly of an abstract continuant is inevitably a history also of the concretum which embodies it, Middlesex County, e.g., in our foregoing instance, so every history ostensibly of a concretum is also a history of that abstract continuant which its constituent propositions exactly exhaust, and with respect to which it has no true alternative.

The causal connection among the terms of a history which Mr. White requires in addition to the unity of subject would seem at first blush to be readily obtainable: on one hand, most of the fibers which hold together a saliently continuing individual are immanent causal processes; on the other hand, Mr. White is very permissive about the degree and kind of causal relation necessary to bind any pair of events, A and B. He is much more exacting, however, at another juncture, in that he requires a consecution or catenation of pairs, A causing B, B causing C, C D, and so forth, which I think is exorbitant. The causal connections we can divine in human affairs, and generally even among inanimate events, are seldom so tight or traceable as to warrant such a rule for the historian or anyone else, and the problem is magnified by Mr. White's demand, otherwise acceptable enough, that the historian confine himself to one "subject." For no less characteristic of the concrete continuant than its containing immanent causal strands is the incessant incursion upon it of the transeunt causation of other continuants. Within even a single pair of historical items, therefore, the statement that A is "the" cause of B is very elliptical, since B would not have ensued had it not been for a host of auxiliary circumstances, supplied by other, unmentioned, and often unknown, hanks of events, some of them within the same "subject," others outside it altogether. Only a deplorable purism, in most situations, would even pretend that any given narrative is pursuing one isolable causal sequence even long enough to warrant its being called a "chain" at all. To make up for the longitudinal fragmentation which thus is inevitable, the narrator will rather lay out other fragments, in parallel, with temporally overlapping ends, frequent crosslinks, and frequent tributary juttings from outside.

Mr. Dray's contribution to the description of the historical nexus is a new statement and defense of his celebrated thesis that the only proper mode of historical explanation is by reference to the motives or reasons of the actors. If he were not so plainly ingenuous and perceptive we might suspect either mischief or elementary misunderstanding in his reiteration that only what he recommends is "rational explanation" or "the rational way of explaining"; and he is at least inviting confusion between the ordinary sense in which an explanation, in any area, is "rational" in proportion as it satisfies the hearer's reason—by being clear, inclusive, systematic, etc.—and his more special sense in which an explanation of historical action is "rational" in proportion as it treats of the reasons imputable to the agents. Notoriously there has been a considerable negative correlation, by and large, between the two "rationalities" thus designated, though this does not mean that they cannot be positively correlated in the domain of history.

I have submitted that Mr. Dray's demand for "rational explanation" in his sense is too stringent, but this is more because I think that any valid explanation is good enough to make a history a history than because I think I have fathomed just how much Mr. Dray is requiring. Let us suppose we have dodged the equivocation of "rational," as well as the question whether Mr. Dray means that persons called "historians" in fact do conform to his program or only that they ought to. Let us also forgive the wide margin of indefiniteness with respect to how much irrationality and rationalization is compatible with the sort of *rationale* he would accept, agreeing with the proviso that the imputed motive need not be reflective nor even conscious, and refusing to be put off by Mr. Nagel's reminder that there is seldom just one identifiable motive for an act (an objection which might lie against any sort of explanatory factor). Still one wonders whether Mr. Dray's principal commitment, the marrow of his doctrine, is that history proper must explain solely by its agents' reasons, regardless of the eventual metaphysical or semantical structure of this species of explanation, or that the Humean or "covering law" explication of explanation is false; and if he means the latter, does he mean just that it is false to the "rational" sort of explanation or that it is false generally, even of ordinary efficient causation? He seems to have a general suspicion and resentment of the regularity or association theory of causation, as well as a special distrust of it in history, but he did not in so many words declare that it is false in physical science, for example, and did not associate himself with Mr. Scriven's counterexample from the etiology of paresis (a challenge which Mr. Hempel, who appears to be the residuary patentee of the Humean doctrine, unfortunately did not take up).* Indeed, Mr. Dray generally seems to leave open the possibility both that explanation by reasons is a species of a generic explanation by efficient causes, and that explanation by efficient causes conforms to the Humean pattern. He does not argue, for example, that rational explanation entails final causation, a teleological nisus, an ineffable effluxus, nor even the organismic conformation which Whitehead affirmed; and his "antinomianism," even when surest that the explanatory nexus is not engendered by mere regularities, seems content that regularities are engendered by the explanatory nexus—that is, he seems not to disown the common opinion that what is either an effective reason or cause on one occasion will be so on any other occasions exactly like it. He seemed therefore more impressed than I should have expected by Mr. Hempel's sketch of how explanation by reasons can be fitted into the regularity scheme.

Let us imagine, to narrow the issue, that Mr. Dray has granted provisionally that the only way in which reasons can provide historical explanations, of either the *why-necessarily* or the *how-possibly* sort,[1] is by operating as efficient causes,

---

* The reader will note that Mr. Hempel discusses this point in his contribution to this volume.—*Editor's note.*

and that efficient causation can in general, in somewhat more subtle ways than are customarily attempted, be satisfactorily analyzed on the regularity pattern—both of which propositions I believe are correct. Then we can concentrate on the essential claim that causation by reasons, though not incompatible with concurrent strains of nonrational causation, is the one uniquely appropriate form of explanation for the historian. I stick to it that this is too restrictive to suit either usual historical practice or the advice Mr. Dray himself would give on typical occasions. It is true that history is by definition about human beings, and having reasons is a characteristic cause of human action, and is moreover particularly appealing and emphatic to us fellow creatures, and is often also the salient variable among the determinants of the historic course, and sometimes the most instructive for our own future conduct. There is hence no danger that such factors will ever be neglected, but neither are they the only important ones. Though in the course of human events all the occurrences which the historian explains be human actions, not all those by which he explains them can or ought to be. Thus I am sure that Mr. Dray would not recommend that a historian ignore the Lisbon earthquake because it was nobody's fault, nor would he protest, I fancy, at a history which told that General X and General Y both failed to deliver their promised reinforcements, General X because he refused to risk his men in a forlorn effort, but General Y because a sudden flood drowned his contingent en route, and he would be hard put to it to show that the former is in any respectable sense a more explanatory explanation than the latter. Insensate processes of nature, as well as insensate processes in human beings, are the hard skeleton of the historic corpus on which individual decisions are nerved and muscled, and indeed the massed force of even the deliberate acts of all but a very few men are, for the historian's purpose, equally insensate, mere weather, and this "senseless side" of history,[2] Mr. Gershoy's "impersonal forces," are no more saved from Mr. Dray's "model" by his reminder that each human cell in the brute body politic has its own motives than we can in practice explain any one man's behavior by the respective bents of the physiological cells, or the electrons, which make him up. The reasonable historian will cite all such weather indifferently, along with the more or less deliberate choices of salient individuals in proportion to their *de facto* causal importance and explanatory power. Since I believe Mr. Dray would concede as much, and no doubt could and would state it more forcefully than I, all that is needed to do justice all round is that the rest of us pass a resolution of appreciation of the components he has praised.

The question whether and how history is "objective" must take second place chronologically to the question what history is, but it is the more substantial, because in the final accounting the historians can establish by decree that what they do is "history" but no such fiat will make it objective. One happy circumstance of the conference was that the main stem of this question of objectivity was favorably answered almost by default—the question whether the historian can reliably know the actual facts of the past, including both the chronicled events and their explanatory connections. The historians present, being perhaps a little newer to the pleasures of self-doubt, were a little more relativistic than the philosophers, and there was a certain amount of play with such utterances as that historical facts exist only in the historian's mind, or that when a historian says he has proved something he only means that other historians will agree with him; and Mr. Gershoy dutifully toyed with the notion that the historian's hypotheses create his data and the data constitute the object. This genial deprecation, however it transpired under Mr. Nagel's queries, was not so much a return to the old historical relativism as it was an attitude of piety toward a positivistic philosophy of physics and *in situ* it voiced only the wholesome commonplace that the historian cannot be perfectly certain of his conclusions and should be prepared to correct them if they prove to be erroneous. I could not make much of the distinction which some attempted between "subjectivity" and the apparently nicer quality of "relativity," for any epistemic relativity which is not merely a taking note of relations of one known object to another but is a subordination of the known object to its relations with the knowing subject, is what we mean by "subjectivity." It is in this sense, then, that we may characterize Mr. Gershoy's "sane relativism" as saner than it was relativistic. There was a sufficient consensus, at any rate, which would have no truck with either the humility that renounces access to reality or, what comes to the same thing, the arrogance that pretends to manufacture it; and the company seemed agreeable to Mr. Nagel's ticking off the respects in which history is just as objective, and verified in essentially the same way, as any other serious attempt to know and understand, most notably the natural sciences, and, to cap the climax, that this is ample and genuine objectivity and credibility. Mr. Dray's insistence on his variety of rational explanation might have made a rift, implying some extraordinary defect or facility of knowledge, but whether or not anyone thought it required a special clairvoyance, no one contended that attempts to plumb the intentions of other minds long defunct are either more or less reliable than inferences about seismic disturbances or crop failures. This was a needed reassurance, for a reason peculiar to history and absent in natural science—viz., because epistemological relativism in history, as some of the members delicately intimated, can easily be the cause or excuse for renegade historians becoming mouthpieces for ideological propaganda. It may be true, as someone commented, that a man can be a relativist without being a solipsist, and by the same token he may have (let us add) a relativistic opinion about the criteria of valid confirmation, historical or physical, without being impelled to violate the accepted criteria of probability and impartiality in his practice, but this virtue is then maintained only by arbitrary resolve or mere lack of imagination, and has no logical or moral force to counteract contrary solicitations.

Relieved for the time being of carking doubts whether the historian's objects and their causal sequence are real and really accessible, our group could deliberate the better on Mr. White's more specialized question, whether there is any objective or even general warrant for preferring one historian's compilation of true statements about a subject to another's. Mr. White's own principal thesis was that even though the criteria by which we ascertain the particular facts of history are objective enough, those by which we select among these facts to compose a sequence worth narrating are irreducibly evaluative in the subjective sense that the choice devolves ultimately on the historian's preference for one sort of fact over another, which at best can have only that fake objectivity that consists of multiple subjectivity, that is, in this instance, of being shared with other historians. Mr. White does not lament this situation, and prima facie it is not very appalling that the canon by which we can discover the truths we are interested in does not dictate to us what our interests ought to be. We find, however, that the matter is more troublesome than appears.

We may focus the issue a little better by noticing that although Mr. White confines the word "subjective" to just one of his groups of suggested criteria, presumably because their champions call them so, the epithet seems to apply with equal directness to what he calls the "teleological" criteria, and it applies eventually, if we accept his argument, to every criterion which can be intelligibly formulated, including a revised "essentialism" and revised "encyclopedism." Similarly, we may notice, the main objection he brings against his first group of criteria, and only against them, i.e., those which he *calls* "subjective," seems to be equally relevant to all the other criteria that turn out to be no less subjective, and which would indeed be relevant, so far as one can see, to *objective* criteria if there be any. This is the complaint that no such criterion will in general be compatible with the requirement that a history be a connected causal genealogy. The difficulty is that if we adopt edification, for instance, as our standard, we are very unlikely to find that the most edifying episodes in the chronicles of a subject will happen to be successive members of the same causal chain, or conversely. The fact, however, that this sort of objection could be made to any criterion, so that if we accept the rule of perfect genealogy at all it would have to be our only standard of selection, is evidence for my earlier allegation that the rule of perfect genealogy is impracticable—a historian can and does cull his flowers of edification, or what not, without much caring whether they spring from *one* causal stem.

Another complication, much less obvious and more ominous, is Mr. White's concluding, after his main argument that the criteria of selection are bound to be subjective, with a second degree of relativism which threatens to take back his concession that at least the criteria for determining the several truths of history may be supposed objectively valid, namely, his suspicion that it may be in principle impossible to draw a line between the two phases, so that everything in history is infected with the irremediable subjectivism of the second phase. He does not now argue for this, and he thinks it may affect only some historical discourse and not all, but it gives us an additional reason for scrutinizing his arguments that the principles of selection must be subjective. I say "an additional reason" because I believe, in any event, that these arguments were mistaken in a crucial respect, and that what he calls "essentialism" and what he calls "encyclopedism" have always provided, in combination, a principle for strict objectivity of selection which is indeed, though perhaps not for the reasons Mr. White has in mind, inseparable from the objectivity of the scientific logic by which the several facts are ascertained.

The key idea here is that of the "essentialist" criterion, which, in the metaphysical form given it by the Aristotelian tradition, I agree with Mr. White, cannot so much as be intelligibly formulated. The difference between us is that I think it can be adequately revised in terms of empirical realism without collapsing into the relativism he foresees.

The Aristotelian doctrine of real essence, still taught as the overruling principle and almost as sacred revelation by more professors of philosophy, to more students, than any other creed of the Western world, is that every real thing or primary substance is made what it is by one king character or "real essence," its other properties being only "accidental." Essence and accident are supposed to differ absolutely or intrinsically, as qualities differ from relations, or numbers from odors, but far more profoundly, inasmuch as a faithful essentialist would resent our joining them under even so colorless a rubric as "property" or "character." Just what the primacy of the essence ultimately and absolutely *is,* and whether for example it is inherent in the character itself, or pertains primarily to the character's tie with its subject, has been left astoundingly obscure by the traditions to which it is dearest. Mr. White adopts the description which is favored today by persons who come to antiessentialism through logical philosophy when he defines an "essential" character as one which belongs necessarily to its subject. This notion he finds so repugnant that (if I may venture some contemporary history of ideas on my own account) in his general philosophy he repudiates not merely the distinction between necessity and contingency but even the distinction between character and individual, postulating in effect that there are only contingencies and only individuals. I think he exaggerates both the danger that a belief in universals and in necessary truths will implicate a person in the metaphysics of real essences and the role in this metaphysics of the notion of categorical (i.e., singular and unconditional) necessities. I do not think, however, that he exaggerates the error of the metaphysics, and he is rather too generous in his suggestions how, if tenable, it might be revamped to provide the desired historical criterion. Though firm that every genuine individual has a real essence, the tradition does not even pretend to have discovered more than one of them (providentially, the rational animality of human beings). With admirable individualism it expressly denies that political units have real essences, and the real essence it regards as permanent possession of every citizen is the very antithesis of all such episodic characters as the historian must gather for his chronicle. Thus Mr. Dray's emphasis on men's reasons is only apparently in accord with the tradition of rational animality, since his thesis requires that we explain events not by the essential likeness of men and their reasons but by their accidental differences. Adjustment of the Aristotelian theory to the demands of history would virtually expunge it.

Yet there is much more to be said than this quick dismissal. Though the Aristotelian has treated essentiality per se as an irreducible and unarguable prerogative, he has said a good deal about the manifestations which the idea is supposed to explain, and these manifestations constitute the plain fact that some properties do play more important parts in the world economy than others. More specifically, Aristotelianism teaches that the essence of a thing is preeminently the knowable, the effective, and the valuable in it. As the thing's formal cause, it is inherently what is most intelligible about it; as efficient cause, it generates and explains whatever is intelligible among the other characters of the thing and its effects on other things; as final cause, it defines the thing's inherent value, the goal it seeks, and even its worth for other things. There may not be in general any necessary implication among the indicated traits, but surely they do mark out ways of being *important*, and whatever we may think of the antique grounding of them in a single ineffable principle, it remains unmistakable that the fact that Socrates was a man, or rational animal, was and is more important, more essential forsooth, than that he was snub-nosed. Just as the factual pattern which we denote by "cause and effect" is not changed by Hume's doctrine that there is nothing to it *but* that factual pattern, so the scheme of relative efficacies which evoked the Aristotelian doctrine of essence is not discredited but rather enlarged and made generalizable by the abandonment of the doctrine.

Perhaps this question of importance is the most important raised at this Institute. I am suggesting that we can define the importance or essentiality of a character, not by a metaphysical absolute, to be sure, but nevertheless objectively, in terms of sheer number of factual consequences. Since I think that number of consequences was regarded by the Aristotelians as at least one result of essentiality, I must contest Mr. White's proposition that an essential predicate or event would not satisfy the encyclopedist criterion by *explaining more.* There remains, however, his chief contribution, as I see it, his arguing, with chilling moderation, that once we have abandoned the transcendent metaphysics of real essence there is no hope in the idea of essence for an objective and general measure of importance, because even the apparent objectivity of sheer number of consequences is only a temporary illusion: we must always decide what consequences to count by some prior criterion of importance *to us.* This may be questionable as a piece of psychology, but I think Mr. White tacitly backs it up with some such logical thesis as that, independently of our preferences, every kind of event has as many consequences as every other. More can be said for this line of reasoning, unfortunately, than has often been acknowledged, but I submit that there is something seriously wrong with it, including the fact that if it is not wrong, then most of what we thought to be the securest principles of scientific inference are, if not wrong, at any rate not right.

For testimony that some properties have a cosmic and causal preeminence we do not need to return to the Scholastics: the scientists and philosophers of the Renaissance, including da Vinci, Bacon, Kepler, Galileo, Descartes, and even Newton, kept on talking of "essences," in spite of deriding the Scholastic faith, because they transferred the dignity to the characters which Locke taught us to call primary qualities. We have often been told, of course, that their primacy was supposed to consist in their pertaining to things in themselves, independently of the vagaries of perception, but this locus was only incidental. The real intention was to emphasize that they are the "nature-engendering natures" (as Bacon described them), embodying what G. F. Stout more recently has called the "executive order" of the world, i.e., systematic intelligibility, analyzability, causal fecundity, explanatory power. If they happen to be physical properties, or modes of extension, this is because even minds, it turns out, are better, more compendiously and coherently understood by way of their physical correlates than in their own special terms. When Peirce said that Nominalism is "a disgraceful habit of thought" he meant by "Nominalism" not the denial of universals—in which sense he was a Nominalist—but the denial of such real essences or executive kinds. There is a superficial level, no doubt, where James was right that different properties of things are "essential" to our different purposes, but he was fundamentally wrong so far as he dissembled (what in other moods he well knew) that there are executive conditions which are essential to realizing any or all of our purposes, or defeating them, or just making things happen purposelessly—essential, therefore, objectively and *in rerum natura.* Such essentiality, to be sure, would mean little in our daily life if it resided only on the level of submicroscopic physical structure, or even were confined to the Lockean primary qualities, but while the distinction is most striking there, it obtains—for reasons it might be hard to state—in different degrees at all levels. Some characters of things just make more difference than others, more difference to *us,* to be sure, but more to us because they make more in general; the superior difference they make to us is a more or less random sample of the superior differences they make generally. They are in this respect really cardinal—a great deal turns upon them; or, if you prefer, they are what Mr. Frankel called "terminal," because many trains leave from them.

Human beings, to do them justice, have an admirable knack for selecting these essences, though the feat, when we think about it squarely, was by no means difficult. There is a preestablished harmony between the "memorability" of characters or events, in Mr. White's sense that they are most consequential and *ought* to be noticed and remembered, and their "memorability" in the sense that they easily can be and almost inevitably are noticed and remembered. Nor is this only because attention and memory themselves, and the continuing stimuli to them, are among the natural consequences of a consequential event (though this is important enough in all conscience); it permeates the whole logic of inference and understanding. We may be suspicious of the metaphysical principle of Leibniz, that this world was created because it is the one of the possible worlds in which the maximal results follow from the minimal conditions, but something like this is the working assumption of science and not merely an ideal it has for its objects, nor even merely a hypothesis astoundingly borne out by experience, though it is both of these too. The aspiration of every advanced science to a systematic form in which the simplest postulates entail, predict, and explain the richest theorems and most varied observations, is written into the very charter of the knowledge endeavor, and this in two ways, psychological and logical. Psychologically, the only rule by which we can ever know very much, can ever learn it or retain it, to satisfy curiosity, to predict, to control, or to explain, is to tie as much as possible into as few and neat packets as we can; our heads just won't hold enough otherwise. Such problem of memorability is so far from being peculiar to history or even to science that it is the main onus of education and responsible publication. The schools, for example, would not be worth their keep if they taught indiscriminate lists of facts rather than consecrating themselves to inculcating the primary, essential, key, critical, crucial, usable, executive, and explanatory truths. On the logical side, it is a fundamental law of confirmation—the principal if not the only one—that a material proposition is probable or rationally credible only in proportion as it does economically and systematically imply and account for a great deal of very diverse evidence. As facts are memorable because they are rememberable, so the answer to Mr. White's question, what makes facts *worth* colligating, is not some ulterior motive of the colligator, but that the facts are colligable. They make each other important, or, more accurately, the abundance of the colligable subfacts constitutes the explanatory importance of the colligating superfact, while the colligating power of the superfact constitutes the momentousness of the subfacts.

In these respects we must agree with the Scholastics who claim that essentialism, if not the natural metaphysic of the human mind, is at least the philosophical heritage of all minds seriously concerned with truth and reason; and I submit that the historian has in fact applied the essentialist standards, whether he picks over the miscellany of events for essential characters or follows the tried and true method of concentrating on the essential *persons*, the heroes in history who make things move and are the prototypes and exemplars of our ontological elite among characters. The historian who thus observes the essentialist standard, with the same rights and liabilities as any pertinacious knower and understander, is doing the opposite of merely indulging his taste. Unless he is both incompetent and unlucky he is submitting himself to the most objective of authorities—the rules of confirmation which constitute most of what is called "objectivity" in method, and to the chief causal order of nature, which is the backbone of the objectivity of the object. Those topics, moreover, which best serve knowledge per se, and hence everything that knowledge serves, though they may not be "genial" or congenial, will most likely be "essential" for the sundry daily purposes which James would foster, as well as for the more inclusive plans of the statesman. They are, come to think of it, the most likely to preserve even that family eminence through many causal generations which Mr. White prescribed in another connection, and one might be able to work out finally that the human rationales preferred by Mr. Dray have a sort of artificial primacy, just because it is characteristic of intelligent purposes to discount, exploit, and override the insensate variety of events.

Not only may historians, like nearly everyone else, thus seek and find the objectively essential—they in fact do so; and not only do they do so—the historians and philosophers of history at this conference rallied round to testify that such is the case. Mr. Mandelbaum explicitly took up the cudgels for "essentialism" on this account; Mr. Frankel spoke of terminal events and large causal constellations; Mr. Schapiro of the organizing power of concepts; Mr. Bailyn of the new insights which repattern the historical vista. Other historians spoke of fruitfulness and retrodictive potential, and Mr. Gershoy, who spoke of the historian's quest of "deeper and richer understanding" and of a consequent "hierarchy of significance," seemed willing to interpret these in the terms of empirical essentialism. So many respects were paid to the synthesizing power of the right historical concepts that Mr. Hook could, with some ironical justice, affect to feel the freezing breath of monism in the air, for indeed, the absolutism of the last century, for all its religious trappings, was a sort of hypostasis and apotheosis of the scientific ideal of system and convergence.

Now there is an important sense, of course, in which Mr. White is aware of all this. In fact, he wrote most tellingly of the epitomizing power of concepts, of "colligating features," "central in some objective sense," which "most successfully organize" the data, and explain and are confirmed by the latter; and though he did this under the heading of a revised encyclopedism, he probably would not resent our saying it could as well be called a revised essentialism. The rub is that he is steadfast that this notion of colligation, under whatever title, runs out eventually into subjective evaluations. Where then do we stand? He did not prove that it does, but only said some things which made it plausible, and I in turn have not proved that it doesn't, that is, I have not given an analysis or demonstration of a principle or operation which objectively determines comparative amounts of evidence or numbers of effects, nor an explication of exactly how such superiority is a reliable clue to the objectivity of fact. I have only aggregated and emphasized a great number of circumstances, which perhaps Mr. White has never contemplated all at once, so to speak, and whose cumulative impact makes his subjectivism very implausible, and makes highly credible, in any ordinarily careful sense of "credible," the claims of a non-metaphysical but objective essentialism. The latter, which seemed at first a mere luxury for the historian who wants to show that his true history of a subject is really better than another man's true history of it, is thus involved in a rule of explanatory fecundity which in the ordinary affairs of life and science is accepted without cavil, and is so woven into the scientific fabric that its cogency is entailed and required by the objective truth and logical validity of the latter. Since the historian thus has a better justification for the essentialism which he already practices than most of us have for most of the propositions on which we daily wager our lives, I think he can fairly be advised to persist in his confidence.

On a more formal epistemological plane, however, we have not reached the end of the problem. Seeing a revised historical essentialism safely aboard the very flagship of empirical understanding might in a calmer day have made us *completely* confident of it; but in pure logic it is as possible, until the demonstrations I mentioned are forthcoming, that essentialism will sink the ship as that the ship will save essentialism, and we live in a period when philosophers of science rather gloat on anything which impugns the tightness of their vessel's bottom. When they are given that the objectivity of science entails the objectivity of historical importance, therefore, they are at best no more likely to accept the latter because they accept the former than to repudiate the former because they repudiate the latter. We might dismiss this as idle conceptual acrobatics, and one merit of the new philistinism preached in the Wittgensteinian dispensation is that it discourages the pretense that we do not know what we know perfectly well we do know, and we do know that some hypotheses have more credibility than others because they have more evidence and explain more, and correlatively that some causes have more effects than others. If historical essentialism is questionable only in the artificial and precious sense in which scientific method in general is questionable, then nobody need blush to adhere to it. The philosopher who is not a philistine, however, will not rest with so superficial a complacency, but will keep on trying to know how and why, and indeed whether, we know so much. For him, Mr. White's strictures, in spite of a certain slightness and tentativeness, belong to a highly significant and provocative category of negative instruction, which comprises also, for example, Nelson Goodman's professed failure to define a class of entrenched predicates worthy of inductive projection, Russell's complaint of the prevalent definitions of "determinism," that until they have been restricted in a manner hard to formulate they would impute deterministic uniformity to the maddest chaos, Hiram McLendon's criticism of Russell's own doctrine of "isomorphism," that without some similar but hitherto unspecified restriction it makes any two things isomorphic, and Peirce's declarations that any pair of objects must on the whole be as similar as any other pair. Each of these paradoxes is ostensibly fatal to consistent thought about the real world and yet seems also a mere dead snag on which we are hung up by some obscure inadvertence.

I do not know that Mr. White himself is unsympathetic to positive efforts to get us off his particular hook. It is possible that what I have argued is what he meant by his doubt whether the question of the objectivity of particular historic truths can be kept separate from that of the right selection among them, but I do not think so, for he suggested in that connection something more occasional and avoidable than a total inductive agnosticism. It is propitious that he also hedged his scruples against revised encyclopedism, when he wrote "The choice of data to be colligated will *often* rest on a value judgment that will *sometimes* be relative to differing standards of importance," for while the italics in this quotation are mine, it suggests that there are circumstances where we can determine an importance which is not merely relative. Meanwhile, he deliberately sheers off "the difficult problem of characterizing the logical relationship between the colligating feature and the other features of the central subject." Without trying to plot the history of his future any further now, therefore, I shall only register my own belief that examination of the said logical relationship already yields at least partial answers to the difficulties which his rather offhand perspicacity exposed.

NOTES

1. These phrases, which I think are self-explanatory, appear in William Dray, *Laws and Explanation in History* (Oxford, 1957), p. 161.

2. The phrase is from Whitehead, cited in Dray, *op. cit.*, p. 141.

3. On these topics, see Nelson Goodman, *Fact, Fiction, and Forecast* (Cambridge, 1955), pp. 63 to end; C. G. Hempel's discussion of Russell's problem in *Determinism and Freedom in the Age of Modern Science*, ed. Sidney Hook (New York, 1958), p. 160; Hiram J. McLendon, "Uses of Similarity of Structure in Contemporary Philosophy," *Mind*, LXIV (1955), 79–95; C. S. Peirce, *Collected Papers* (Cambridge, 1931), I, 365, etc.

Index

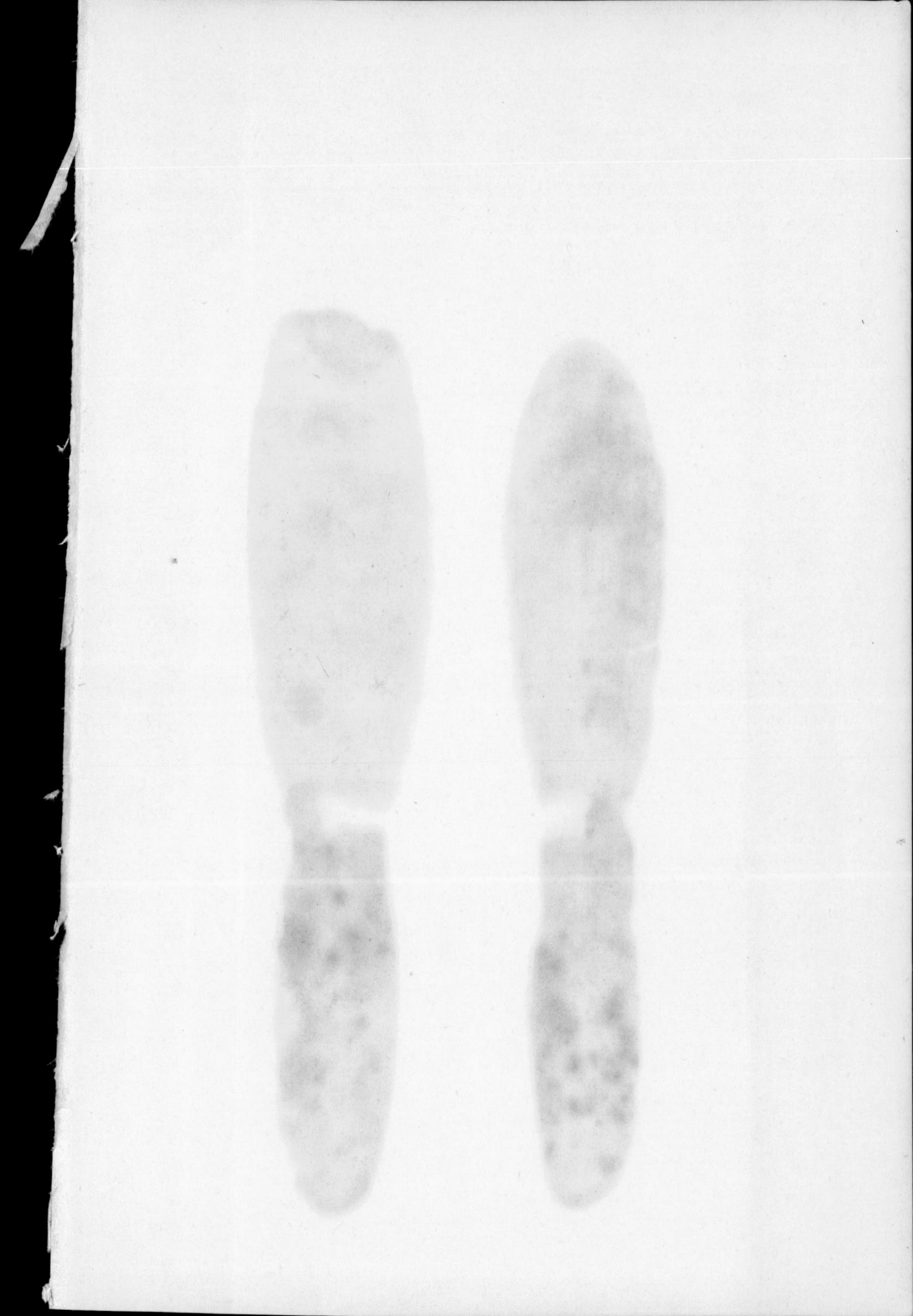